2018
Information and Communications for Development

2018
Information and Communications for Development

Data-Driven Development

Contents

BOXES

FIGURES

MAPS

TABLES

Foreword

It is my pleasure to introduce the 2018 edition in the series Information and Communications for Development, which in this fourth edition focuses on the opportunities and challenges of data-driven development. Since 2006, Information and Communications for Development has been a flagship report of a World Bank team that, this year, was elevated to a department in its own right and changed its name from Information and Communication Technologies to Digital Development. The changes reflect the World Bank's strong push to realize the potential of digital technologies to advance development, particularly in the poorest countries, and mark a shift toward a focus on the applications of technology, rather than technology per se, and from supply to client demand. These principles, introduced by the *2016 World Development Report: Digital Dividends,* guide the World Bank Group's investment and technical assistance in this area.

The theme of data-driven development fits well with this new focus. Data is all around us, and can be invaluable once refined, processed, and analyzed. This report shows how governments in developing countries can enhance their use of data to provide better services to citizens. It also shows how the business sector is starting to capitalize on data for competitive advantage. For citizens, the report argues that new tools can allow them to take more control of personal data and benefit more directly from its value. For the World Bank Group and its development partners, the report contains plentiful examples of how big data and open data can be harnessed for better development outcomes.

But challenges loom. The growth of data platforms is changing the profile of competitive markets and business models, away from subscriber-funded networks to advertising-funded services. This has important implications for how infrastructure is financed. In this evolving context, we must ensure that data is used for inclusion, not exclusion, and for enhanced privacy, not greater threats to security. The final chapter of the report looks at data policies for the digital economy and how conflicting demands can be reconciled. At a time when governments around the world are reviewing existing data policies, and writing new ones, such as the European Union's General Data Protection Regulation, this report seeks to contribute to the debate.

As in previous years, this edition has been researched and drafted jointly with the World Bank's Finance, Competitiveness and Innovation Global Practice. It also benefits from contributions from the International Telecommunication Union and the United Nations Global Pulse, as well as inputs and review from other parts of the World Bank Group. We are likewise grateful for the support of the Digital Development Partnership and its donors, who made the report possible.

Smart use of data holds immense development potential that is already available to governments, businesses, and citizens. I am confident that this report will help these opportunities materialize to boost economic growth, reduce the digital divide, and bring better services and benefits to the people who need them most.

Boutheina Guermazi
Director, Digital Development Department
World Bank

Acknowledgments

This report was prepared by a team from the Digital Development Department (DDD) and the Finance, Competitiveness, and Innovation (FCI) Global Practice of the World Bank Group, supported by the International Telecommunication Union (ITU) and the UN Global Pulse team. The editorial team was led by Tim Kelly, under the guidance of Jane Treadwell (DDD), and comprised Siddhartha Raja and Carlo Rossotto (DDD), Prasanna Lal Das and Elena Gasol Ramos (FCI), Phillippa Biggs (ITU), Felicia Vacarelu (UN Global Pulse), and Andrew Stott and Michael Minges (independent consultants). The team was supported by Christine Howard and Roku Fukui (DDD) and David Hollander (UN Global Pulse). The work was funded by the Digital Development Partnership Trust Fund, whose members include the governments of Denmark, Finland, Japan, and the Republic of Korea as well as Microsoft and the Global System for Mobile Communications Association. Early work on the report also benefited from a contribution from the World Bank Group budget.

The principal authors by chapter are

- **Executive Summary:** Tim Kelly and Roku Fukui

- **Chapter 1, Overview:** Tim Kelly, Andrew Stott, and Michael Minges

- **Chapter 2, Data Supply:** Michael Minges and Tim Kelly

- **Chapter 3, Data for Good:** Phillippa Biggs (ITU) and Felicia Vacarelu, Miguel Luengo-Oroz, Mila Romanoff, and Robert Kirkpatrick (UN Global Pulse)

- **Chapter 4, Data and People:** Siddhartha Raja, Tatiana Nadyseva, Roku Fukui, and Rachel Firestone (DDD) and Michael Minges

- **Chapter 5, Data and Firms:** Carlo Rossotto, Mona Badran, and Tim Kelly (DDD), Elena Gasol Ramos, Eva Clemente Miranda, and Prasanna Lal Das (FCI), and Michael Minges

- **Chapter 6, Data Policies:** Elena Gasol Ramos, Eva Clemente Miranda, and Prasanna Lal Das (FCI)

- **Data Notes:** Michael Minges and Bradley Larson (East Asia and Pacific Global Practice)

Inputs, comments, guidance, and support at various stages of the report's preparation were received, and two formal review meetings were held. At the project concept note review meeting, held November 16, 2016, and chaired by Pierre Guislain (Senior Director, Transport and Digital Development), the peer reviewers were Randeep Sudan (DDD), Holly Krambeck (Transport), and Uwe Deichmann (*World Development Report 2016* Co-Director). Comments were also received from Roku Fukui, Anat Lewin, Siddhartha Raja, and Masatake Yamamichi (DDD) and Prasanna Lal Das and Jill Sawers (FCI). At the decision meeting of April 25, 2018, chaired by José Luis Irigoyen (Senior Director, Transport), the peer reviewers were Charles Hurpy and Casey Torgusson (DDD), Trevor Monroe (Global Themes—Knowledge), and Tariq Khokhar (Development Indicators and Data). Additional comments were received from Mark Dutz, Mary Hallward-Driemeier, and Fredesvinda Montes Herraiz (FCI), as well as from the author team. Inputs were also received from Juan Navas-Sabater, Andrew Stott, and Isabella Hayward (DDD).

Special thanks are owed to Patricia Katayama, of the World Bank's Development Economics unit, and Michael Harrup, of the Bank's Editorial Production team, for oversight of the editorial production, design, printing, and dissemination of the book. The maps, with the exception of Map B3.5.1 from the World Bank's India Lights Platform, were drawn by Bruno Bonansea (Creative Services). The team would also like to thank the many other individuals, firms, and organizations that have contributed through their continuing support and guidance to the work of the World Bank Group, particularly those focused on data for development.

Abbreviations

4G	fourth generation	IoT	Internet of Things
5G	fifth generation	IP	internet protocol
AI	artificial intelligence	ISP	internet service provider
APEC	Asia-Pacific Economic Cooperation	IT	information technology
API	application programming interfaces	ITU	International Telecommunication Union
B2B	business to business	IXP	internet exchange point
DAI	Digital Adoption Index	Mbps	megabits per second
DDD	Digital Development Department	OECD	Organisation for Economic Co-operation and Development
EC	European Commission		
ECLAC	Economic Commission for Latin America and the Caribbean	OTT	over-the-top services
		POS	point of sale
EU	European Union	SDGs	Sustainable Development Goals
FCI	finance, competitiveness, and innovation	SME	small and medium enterprise
FTC	Federal Trade Commission (United States)	UN	United Nations
GDPR	General Data Protection Regulation	UNDP	United Nations Development Programme
IBM	International Business Machines	UNDG	United Nations Development Group
ICT	information and communication technologies	UNICEF	United Nations Children's Fund
		UNCTAD	United Nations Conference on Trade and Development
IOM	International Organization for Migration		

Executive Summary

Data deluge

In a sample *second* in July 2018, it is estimated that some 2.7 million emails were sent and received, 74,860 YouTube videos watched, and 59,879 gigabytes of internet traffic carried.[1] Clearly, we generate huge and growing volumes of data.

The digital economy has become more information intensive, and even traditional industries, such as oil and gas or financial services, are becoming data driven. By 2020, forecasts Cisco (2017), global internet traffic will reach about 200 exabytes per month, or 127 times the volume of 2005, with much of the growth coming from video and smartphones (figure ES.1). And that data may hold huge value. McKinsey Global Institute (2016) estimates that cross-border data flows in 2014 were worth about US$2.8 trillion, up 45-fold in value since 2005.

The vast majority of the data that exists today was created in just the past few years (IBM 2013). The challenge is to extract value from it and to put it to work—for firms, governments, and individuals. Every citizen is producing vast amounts of personal data that, under the right protective frameworks, can be of value for the public and private sectors. Firms are willing to pay ever-increasing amounts for our attention on social media sites and to mine the data we produce. But even data that is produced unintentionally—a byproduct of other processes, known as "data exhaust," such as call data records or GPS coordinates—can have value when effectively analyzed.

Both types of data, their potential uses, and associated risks are all growing exponentially. Figure ES.2 shows common sources of personal data.

Who benefits?

This new report, the fourth in the Information and Communications for Development series (figure ES.3), examines data-driven development, or how better information makes for better policies. The report aims to help firms and governments in developing countries unlock the value in the data they hold to improve service delivery and decision making and empower individuals to take more control of their personal data. The report asks just how we can use this data deluge to generate better development outcomes.

People's lives can benefit greatly when decisions are informed by relevant data that uncover hidden patterns, unexpected relationships, and market trends or reveal preferences. For example, tracking genes associated with certain types of cancer or explaining the potential links of Neanderthal DNA with resistance to the common flu virus or Type II diabetes can help improve treatments. As argued in chapter 3, development partners therefore need to establish strategies to better use data for development, while intervening appropriately in the data ecosystem and respecting data protection and privacy.

The World Bank Group, for instance, has established a Technology and Innovation Lab for improving data use

Figure ES.1 The growing internet

a. Internet users

b. Internet traffic

Internet users (millions)
— Per 100 people

Managed IP (percent, left scale)
Mobile data (percent, left scale)
Fixed internet (percent, left scale)
— Total IP traffic (exabytes per month, right scale)

Sources: ITU (panel a); Cisco (panel b).
Note: An exabyte is one quintillion bytes (1 followed by 18 zeroes). Just five exabytes would be equivalent to all the words ever spoken by human beings (http://highscalability.com/blog/2012/9/11/how-big-is-a-petabyte-exabyte-zettabyte-or-a-yottabyte.html). IP = internet protocol.
* Data for 2017 is an estimate.

Figure ES.2 Types of personal data

Health
• Medical history
• Prescriptions and vaccinations
• Fitness tracking

Government
• Identification number and identity
• Address
• Civil information (birth, marriage, and so on)
• Legal records

Web
• Email
• Browsing and search history
• Content (social profiles, posts, photos, and so on)
• Contacts, followers, friends

Mobile phone
• Number and preferred network
• Call data records
• Location data (GPS)
• Social media contacts
• Purchasing history

Financial
• Accounts
• Transactions
• Debts
• Investments
• Insurance

Other
• Home information
• Travel
• Vehicle information
• Inferred data, created using other data points

in its projects, including using artificial intelligence and blockchain.[2] This is part of a broader work program that aims to leverage data and technology in its work.[3] The International Telecommunication Union has so far hosted two editions of the Artificial Intelligence for Good, Global Summit.[4] And the team from UN Global Pulse, another partner in this report, is working with UN partners to responsibly harness big data and artificial intelligence for development and humanitarian action (see chapter 3).[5]

However, firms and organizations that can make the best use of the data are not necessarily the ones that collect it. An "open data" mind-set is critical to data-driven development. Thus, an open marketplace for data is to be encouraged within limits. It is important therefore to develop appropriate guidelines for data sharing and use, and for anonymizing personal data. Governments are already beginning to release value from the huge quantities of data they hold to enhance service delivery, though they still have far to go to catch up with the commercial giants. To use data intelligently for better development outcomes, national statistical offices will continue to play a core function, including that of objectivity and impartiality, producing data "without fear or favor." But many statistics offices are struggling technically and financially. To remain relevant in an on-demand world, they need to strive for real-time data availability, striking an informed balance between accuracy and timeliness.

Figure ES.3 The Information and Communications for Development series

- 2006: Global Trends and Policies

- 2009: Extending Reach and Increasing Impact

- 2012: Maximizing Mobile

Note: No Information and Communications for Development report was published in 2015, as this coincided with the *World Development Report: Digital Dividends.*

Data-driven business models

Companies are also developing new markets and making profits by analyzing data to better understand their customers. This is transforming conventional business models, as explored in chapter 2. For years, users paying for calls funded telecommunications. Now, advertisers paying for users' data and attention are funding the internet, social media, and other platforms, such as apps, reversing the value flow. The share of the value extracted by the network providers is shrinking, threatening future investment. Good business models for investment in telecommunication networks typically have high up-front sunk costs, but very long-term returns. Twenty to thirty years ago, companies that built networks—such as NTT, China Mobile, AT&T, or Deutsche Telekom—were the champions of their respective national stock markets. Their assets, like the infrastructure that they put in place, represent the backbone services operate on. But their market values have fallen in comparison to the businesses gathering and storing

data—such as Google and Alibaba Global—thanks to these existing infrastructures. Stock markets, in turn, assign huge potential to these data-rich companies, and undervalue the companies that keep the digital plumbing working.

We have seen this pattern before. In the early part of the nineteenth century, the markets of the time afforded optimistic valuations to the companies that built railroads. But as the century drew on, railroad investors went bankrupt or were nationalized because of their huge debts, even as the companies whose products they carried, such as mail-order companies, thrived in the early twentieth century.

Once again, we face an inflection point. For more than a hundred years, infrastructure companies made their money primarily from subscriptions and usage charges paid by users—who paid by the minute, by the mile, and lately by the megabyte. This is changing. The value of telecommunication networks is now not so much in data transport as in data storage. As chapter 2 shows, the companies with the highest market valuations are those that collect then monetize their customers' data through targeted advertising. Services from Facebook, Google, or Tencent are largely "free" at the point of use—yet their bandwidth requirements grow ever larger, as does their customer reach.

Beyond internet business or commercial applications, multiple opportunities also exist for harnessing the value of big data and artificial intelligence to help us achieve shared development objectives, as exemplified in chapter 3. However, global efforts to develop new frameworks for the responsible use of emerging technologies must address their implications for society and the consequences of both using data and algorithms, and of failing to use them.

Data belongs to all of us

People need to exert greater control over the use of their personal data. Their willingness to share data in return for benefits (real or perceived) and free services, such as virtually unrestricted use of social media platforms, varies by country and by age group (figure ES.4). Consumer research from GfK, a German research institute, shows that willingness to share is highest in China and lowest in Japan. Early internet adopters, who grew up with the internet and are now age 30–40, are the most willing to share (GfK 2017). Many countries and regions have taken steps recently to update and reinforce rules on the use of personal data. The European Union's General Data Protection Regulation,

Figure ES.4 Are you willing to share your data?

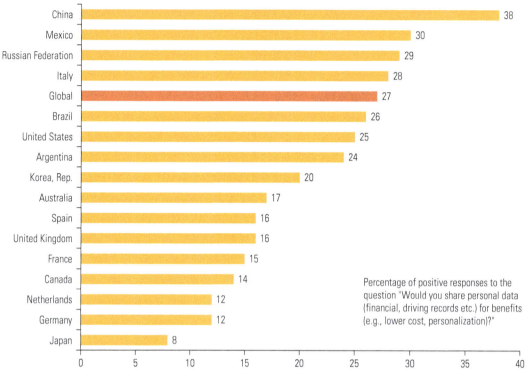

Percentage of positive responses to the question "Would you share personal data (financial, driving records etc.) for benefits (e.g., lower cost, personalization)?"

Source: GfK 2017.

Note: Based on more than 22,000 consumers online in 17 countries with a response of 7 (on a scale from 1 to 7), where 7 represents full agreement.

which went into effect on May 25, 2018, imposes a long list of requirements for companies processing personal data. Violations will result in fines that could total as much as 4 percent of global annual turnover.

Other countries have taken steps to restrict the flow of their citizens' data beyond their borders (data localization). In China, where data localization is strongly championed, restrictions on moving data are severe. Long-established controls over technology transfer and state surveillance of the population are predominant, and such measures form part of the country's "Made in China 2025" industrial strategy. The strategy is designed, in part, to make the country a global leader in tech-intensive sectors such as artificial intelligence and robotics. Chinese technology giants, including Baidu, Alibaba, and Tencent, are among the biggest in the world, and the country is establishing strong positions in new sectors like the Internet of Things (appliances, machines, and other items able to connect with the internet and exchange data). Throughout the world, data is regarded as a new asset class vital for industrial competitiveness.

Other emerging markets, such as India, Indonesia, the Russian Federation, and Vietnam, are also seeking data localization. The Russian Federation has blocked LinkedIn from operating in the country after the site refused to transfer data on Russian users to local servers. Divergent rules on the treatment of data impose significant costs on doing business online. Business organizations, including the International Chamber of Commerce, would like to establish rules to restrain what they call "digital protectionism."[6] However, a serious gap exists in global governance with regard to cross-border trade in data, and a coherent approach is prevented by differing philosophies among the main trading blocs.

The ownership and control of data will continue to be a major question for society. Broadly speaking, there are three possible answers to the question "Who controls our data?": firms, governments, or users. No global consensus yet exists on the extent to which private firms that mine data about individuals should be free to use the data for profit and to improve services. Some governments argue that data from a country's citizens belongs to those citizens and should

Figure ES.5 Toward a new value chain for personal data

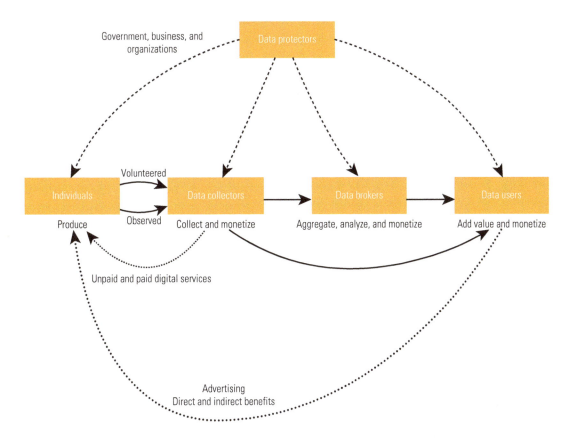

not leave the country without permission. Data dependency leads to new risks of exclusion. The data poor, who leave little or no digital trail because they have limited internet access, are most at risk of exclusion. But, equally, those who live in ways that society deems unconventional may also risk exclusion, for instance, because they lack a digital ID or are considered an insurance risk.

This report espouses the view that citizens should control their own data and should be free to choose how to release it and even to commercialize it (figure ES.5), as explored in chapter 4.

The growth of the data economy therefore requires changes in competition policy and the regulation of privacy. In a traditional, or one-sided, market, dominant firms are bad for overall market development. But when it comes to personal data, splitting the market share too many ways may inconvenience users and complicate matters for the individual if the different platforms do not connect, or if they require different passwords. As data becomes more important in shaping markets, it may reinforce tendencies toward monopoly, and thus

monopoly profits, unless competition rules are modified to deal with new concepts of dominance. The emergence of multisided platforms, explored in chapter 5, poses new challenges for regulators.

Data and the internet have predominantly been regarded by pioneers and campaigners as a decentralized, self-regulating community. Activists have tended to regard government intervention with suspicion, except for its role in protecting personal data, and many are wary of legislation to enable data flows. But that position is under pressure from the increasing centralization of the internet (Economist 2018) and a series of revenue data breaches and media exposés of questionable business practices by social media platforms. The use by political parties in Kenya, the United States, and elsewhere of data harvested from social media profiles does not appear to have broken any rules, but it has led politicians on both sides of the Atlantic to take a closer look at social media giants, such as Facebook and Twitter.[7] The proliferation of "fake news" has also spurred calls for action.[8]

Data collected by governments, and thus paid for by taxpayers, arguably belongs to all of us. But there are limits

Map ES.1 Data protection and privacy legislation worldwide, 2018

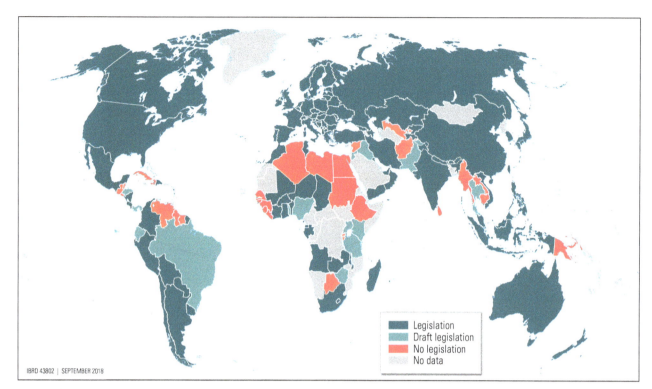

IBRD 43802 | SEPTEMBER 2018

Legend:
- Legislation
- Draft legislation
- No legislation
- No data

Source: UNCTAD (http://unctad.org/en/Pages/DTL/STI_and_ICTs/ICT4D-Legislation/eCom-Data-Protection-Laws.aspx).

to the openness paradigm. Citizens may not want data about themselves to be exposed without protection. And governments often lack the resources to extract value from their data without private partners. Data-driven development needs greater dialogue between the custodians of a country's data and its users. The key to unleashing the power of data-driven development for developing countries lies in intelligent management, use, and supervision of data.

Chapter 6 reviews data-related policy issues relevant to the digital economy. It considers policies geared toward building consumer trust, policies that facilitate or can affect access to data, and the use of data as infrastructure. The chapter also covers mainstreaming policies, such as those that facilitate the use of data for innovation or those that build digital skills. At least 35 economies are currently drafting data protection laws (map ES.1). In addition, a number of economies are considering reforms to their legal frameworks. One factor driving this consideration is the European Union's adoption of the General Data Protection Regulation. While the regulation introduces, or confirms, many important principles for data protection and privacy, it also extends

these principles to firms from other parts of the world that wish to do business in Europe.

Ironically, although data is becoming ever more important, data *about* data is still hard to find. The Data Notes to this report set out some of the indicators that should exist and present data that do exist on an internationally comparable basis for indicators such as the price and affordability of data transmission and the availability of open government data.

This report aims to stimulate wider debate within the development community on the nature of data for development. It is not the first word on this topic and certainly will not be the last. But it is a topic of growing importance that cannot be ignored.

Notes

1. Internet Live Stats (Internetlivestats.com), one second of traffic on July 31, 2018.

2. Blockchain is technology that serves as a decentralized digital ledger that provides immutable record keeping.

Applications are emerging in land registries, money remittances, biometric ID, and so on.

3. See http://blogs.worldbank.org/taxonomy/term/15718 for information.

4. See https://www.itu.int/en/ITU-T/AI/2018/Pages/default.aspx.

5. For information see https://www.unglobalpulse.org/pulse-labs.

6. See https://iccwbo.org/publication/trade-in-the-digital-economy/.

7. See https://www.theguardian.com/news/series/cambridge-analytica-files.

8. See https://www.digitaltrends.com/mobile/google-news-initiative/.

References

Cisco. 2017. Cisco Visual Networking Index: Forecast and Methodology, 2016–2021. https://www.cisco.com/c/en/us/solutions/collateral/service-provider/visual-networking-index-vni/complete-white-paper-c11-481360.pdf.

Economist, The. 2018. "How to Fix What Has Gone Wrong with the Internet." Special report, June 28. https://www.economist.com/special-report/2018/06/28/how-to-fix-what-has-gone-wrong-with-the-internet.

GfK. 2017. "Willingness to Share Personal Data in Exchange for Benefits or Rewards." https://www.gfk.com/fileadmin/user_upload/country_one_pager/NL/images/Global-GfK_onderzoek_-_delen_van_persoonlijke_data.pdf.

International Business Machines Corporation (IBM). 2013. *Harness the Power of Big Data: The IBM Big Data Platform*. New York: McGraw-Hill.

McKinsey Global Institute. 2016. *Digital Globalization: The New Era of Global Flows*. New York. https://www.mckinsey.com/business-functions/digital-mckinsey/our-insights/digital-globalization-the-new-era-of-global-flows.

Chapter 1

Data: The Fuel of the Future

Data, data, everywhere

A self-driving car, one of the most anticipated developments of the next decade, is expected to generate some 4,000 gigabytes of data for each hour of driving, according to chip maker Intel (Nelson 2016). To put it another way, just 3 million autonomous vehicles would generate, or consume, more data than the combined human population of more than 7 billion. Vehicles provide just one example of how data generation and use are growing explosively. Other machines generating an overload of data include satellites, environmental sensors, security cameras, and, of course, the ubiquitous mobile phone.

We are undoubtedly experiencing a data revolution (UN Data Revolution Group 2014) in which our ability to generate, process, and utilize information has been magnified many times over by the machines that we increasingly rely upon. By 2016, according to IBM, some 90 percent of data that exists had been created within the previous 12 months, a rate of 2.5 quintillion bytes per day (IBM 2016). Firms are increasingly finding hidden value in some of that data. Some 7 of the top 10 companies worldwide, by market capitalization, are data driven in that they create value primarily from the data they collect from or sell to their customers. The remaining 3 firms in the top 10—in the more traditional financial services, energy, and health care sectors—also increasingly build data into their products and services or use it to improve them (table 1.1).

With some justification, therefore, data has been called the new gold (EC 2011), the new oil (Toonders 2014), or the world's most valuable resource (The Economist 2017). Like oil, unprocessed data has relatively little value and needs to be mined, refined, stored, and sold on to create value—albeit in data centers rather than in oil rigs. But unlike oil, the quantity of data is ever increasing, not diminishing. Even though data is a nonrivalrous good, in the sense that my consumption of it does not affect yours, it is also excludable, which means it can be sold for profit, many times over. This makes it what economists sometimes call a club good, like privately owned safari parks or pay-per-view television. But because of the ever-increasing quantity of data, extracting value from it requires ever-greater computer power. Thus, the spoils from data-driven markets typically go to the largest players; those with the deepest pockets, the most users, the largest data centers, and most wide-ranging ability to collect and analyze data. Consequently, it is possible for market capitalization in companies like Facebook, Tencent, or Alibaba to exceed their annual revenue by 15 times or more and for the market capitalization of Apple and Amazon to touch the US$1 trillion mark in mid-2018, because investors view them as well positioned to take advantage of future data trends.

How data is changing development

This report is about how the data revolution is changing the behavior of governments, individuals, and firms. Specifically,

Table 1.1 Data hogs: Top 10 private companies globally, by market capitalization, May 2017

Rank	Company	Country	Market capitalization (US$ billions)	2016 revenue (US$ billions)
1	Apple	United States	801	218
2	Google / Alphabet	United States	680	90
3	Microsoft	United States	540	86
4	Amazon	United States	476	136
5	Facebook	United States	441	28
6	Berkshire Hathaway	United States	409	215
7	Exxon Mobil	United States	346	198
8	Johnson & Johnson	United States	342	76
9	Tencent	China	335	22
10	Alibaba	China	314	21
	Top 10 total		4,684	1,090
Data-driven companies as percent of top 10			76.6	55.1

Source: Adapted from Meeker 2017, with market capitalization data from CapIQ and valid for May 26, 2017.
Note: Data-driven companies are shown in red.

the report examines how these changes affect the nature of development—economic, social, and cultural. How can governments extract value from data to improve service delivery in the same way that private companies have learned to do for profit? Is it feasible for individuals to take ownership of their own data and to use it to improve livelihoods and quality of life? Can developing-country firms compete with the internet majors on their own turf and even be more innovative in their use of data to serve local customers better? Several potential audiences could therefore benefit from this report:

- The primary audience is government policy makers, though not in a single line ministry, such as information and communication technology or finance, but rather across government, given that data is a multidisciplinary concern.

- A secondary audience would be individuals concerned about how their personal data is used and those interested in how the data revolution might impact future job prospects.

- Beyond that, private sector firms, particularly in developing countries, looking to expand their markets and improve their competitive edge will find interesting examples of how other firms are doing that.

- Finally, development professionals should find the report relevant as they seek to use data more creatively to tackle long-standing global challenges, such as eliminating extreme poverty, promoting shared prosperity, or mitigating the effects of climate change.

A data typology

Data-driven development is an emerging and rapidly changing field. So it may be useful, at the outset, to define terms recurring across the chapters. These are not fixed or official definitions, but rather working usage for this report:

- *Big data,* a commonly used term, describes data sets so large or so complex that traditional data processing techniques are inadequate. The field of *big data analytics* uses advanced computational techniques to extract meaningful information (such as patterns, trends, repetition) from data. For the moment, big data is largely the domain of large private companies. But as tools to mine it become cheaper and more readily available, smaller companies and governments will also use big data. It can be useful to further distinguish between big data produced intentionally or unintentionally and that produced by humans and by machines, as in table 1.2.

  o *Data exhaust,* which is unintentionally created by humans. This can include metadata (data about data), such as call-data records derived from mobile phones, or the trail of data left by users engaged in other activities, such as keystrokes. Data exhaust generally has low value, but the trail left by millions of users can be mined or combined to extract value or to hack into an otherwise secure system.

Table 1.2 Big data			
	Data generation	Intentional	Unintentional
Data agent	Human	Primary content	Data exhaust
	Machine	Secondary content	Internet of Things data

○ *Internet of Things data*, which is intentionally created, but from sensors and other internet-connected devices, rather than from humans. This mainly has value in the aggregate—and over time—but can also be used to provide alerts for impending events, such as extreme weather conditions.

○ *Primary content* is intentionally created by humans, typically users. An example here might be a social media profile or a browser search history. When thousands or more of these are combined and anonymized they can be used, for instance, for analyzing popular or emerging trends. Humans also create primary content in the form of videos, academic papers, blogs, and the like that can be mined, for instance, for sentiment analysis.

○ *Secondary content* is intentionally created, but through artificial intelligence rather than directly by humans. A benign example would be a chatbot that helps a user fill in a form online by giving suggestions. A malign example would be a fake social media profile that seeks to influence buying habits or political opinion.

• *Personal data* relates to an individual and is generally concerned with private information. Personal data can form large, complex data sets (such as multiple health indicators including weight, blood pressure, or heart rate measured over a lifetime) but more normally constitute *small data*, which can be easily monitored. Personal data may be willingly exchanged in return for convenience (such as a phone number or email address), but it can also be given away unwittingly (such as date of birth provided to enter an online competition) or unwillingly (such as data hacked from a personal email account). The consequences of loss of personal data, explored more in chapter 4, might include loss of privacy and loss of control (over the future use of personal data) and a loss of agency (such as being exposed to a more limited range of news sources or opinions as a result of previously expressed preferences). What is relatively new is how persistence, repurposing, and spillovers from big data increase the risk and uncertainty about how private data can be used in the future (Tucker 2017).

• *Open data* refers to data made freely available and deliberately stored in an easily read data format, particularly by other computers, and thereby repurposed. For instance, data on airline schedules could be easily read by travel companies to generate customized itineraries for travel websites. Governments may use open data to promote transparency and accountability in their operations and allow voters to measure the performance of different government functions. As a philosophy, therefore, open data is intended to encourage the juxtaposition of data from different sources to create value and new applications. It is estimated, for instance, that some 500 different applications use London transport data (World Bank 2014), and the savings to the UK economy from its open data policy amount to some £6.8 billion (about US$9.5 billion) a year (Government of the United Kingdom 2013). Open data tools are particularly useful in the transport sector (see box 1.1).

• *Metadata*, or "data about data," is used to classify, categorize, and retrieve data files. For instance, metadata might include the date on which it was created, the number of pages or data size, and keywords that can be used to search. Data attributes may be added to data according to the way it is typically used, for instance, how popular it is as a function of how frequently it is downloaded. Metadata helps with data analysis and can be applied to data users, such as by giving them attributes, sometimes based on inferred data, that equate to a "reputation."

• *Data platforms* offer a convenient and cost-effective way to link customers and suppliers. Some platforms may connect only peers (such as a dating website) and others might be internal to an organization (such as an intranet). But most of the popular platforms using the internet are multisided platforms. Uber, for instance, connects drivers with riders; AirBnB connects property owners with guests; and Jumia connects sellers with potential buyers. But the biggest platforms are those that connect advertisers with consumers, usually in return for some kind of free service, such as social media or web browsing. As explored in chapter 5, multisided platforms, driven by advertising, are now among the most powerful firms in the world.

Rise in digital data. Digital data has proliferated with the rapid increase in smartphone ownership in advanced and emerging market economies, alongside advances in global positioning systems and digital sensors. This data has the potential to transform transport systems worldwide. The location-tracking data provided by smartphones, for instance, can reveal how and why people travel, information critical for optimizing transport networks. Accordingly, open-source tools and cloud-based platforms have been developed to help collect, manage, and analyze the ever-increasing volume of digital data. These easily accessible tools provide individuals, governments, and private entities with sophisticated analysis capabilities, empowering them to improve all aspects of transport. Such tools will be particularly beneficial in developing countries that have limited resources.

Open-source tools. The World Bank has developed a variety of free-of-charge tools that capitalize on big data to facilitate transport-related development projects across the globe (see Figure B1.1.1). These tools provide numerous capabilities, including transit system analysis, route planning, and road condition and incident reporting. *Open Transit Indicators*[a] allows public transit administrators to assess existing services and identify improvements through the collection and analysis of standardized transit data. This approach has been used to address transit problems in China, Kenya, Mexico, and Vietnam, among others.[b] The *Rural Accessibility Platform* uses freely available *OpenStreetMap* data to evaluate the accessibility of rural population centers to points of interest.[c] Indices of rural accessibility have been used to identify needed transportation improvements in countries including Bangladesh, the Lao People's Democratic Republic, and Zambia.[d] These open-source data and tools make transport analysis accessible for a broad range of users.

Citizen engagement. The increasing ubiquity of smartphones and internet connectivity is allowing individuals to provide valuable data and contribute to development efforts. Citizen engagement is prioritized in many of the World Bank's transport-focused open-source tools. For example, the smartphone application *RoadLab* uses a crowdsourcing approach to obtain route information and roadway infrastructure conditions from users (Wang and Guo 2016).

Figure B1.1.1 How open data tools can assist transport

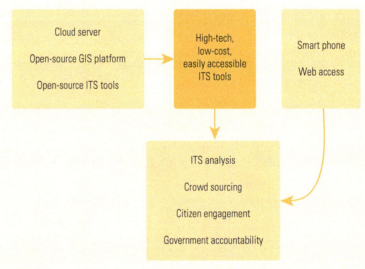

Note: GIS = geographic information system; ITS = intelligent transport systems.

(continued next page)

The related tool *RoadLab Pro* was used to assess the conditions of unclassified road networks in Mozambique (Espinet, Wang, and Mehndiratta 2017), demonstrating the potential of citizen-provided smartphone data in transport planning. These tools provide an easy-to-implement way for traffic engineers to obtain roadway information, particularly when professional pavement testing equipment and base geographic information system maps are not available. Similarly, *DRIVER* capitalizes on crowdsourced data to collect road incident information, which can then be visualized and analyzed to improve enforcement and resource allocation. In the Philippines, *DRIVER* has been applied to identify and prioritize problematic road areas for interventions (World Bank 2016).

Sources: Progress Analytics LLC; Juan Navas-Sabater.

a. For more information, see https://www.transitwiki.org/TransitWiki/index.php/Open_Transit_Indicators.

b. http://www.digitalmatatus.com/about.html; http://www.worldbank.org/en/news/feature/2013/11/05/mexico-city-open
-database-improves-transit-efficiency-helps-commuters; Krambeck and Qu 2015.

c. https://github.com/WorldBank-Transport/ram-backend.

d. https://developmentseed.org/projects/ram/; Iimi et al. 2016.

How governments use data

From e-government to digital government

How governments use data runs throughout this report, although because it is the subject of a separate World Bank Group report (World Bank 2017) it gets no separate chapter here. Chapter 3 nonetheless focuses on big data for social good, by international, nongovernmental, and humanitarian organizations, as well as by governments.

In the first generations of "e-government," much of the emphasis was on *channels*—using web browsers, and more recently, mobile devices, to access government information and services and to perform transactions. In this period, data was often seen as just the payload of the transaction—information supplied by the citizen or the business to support the request for service and the information supplied by the government in return.

However as "e-government" has evolved into "digital government," data is seen increasingly as a strategic asset with value lasting beyond a particular transaction and able to strategically transform the efficiency and effectiveness of government through:

- Making "e-government" transactions more attractive and useful to citizens and businesses by eliminating the need to supply the same information again and again, making transactions more suitable for the mobile channel, and allowing continuity of transactions over time, through different channels, and among different government institutions

- Allowing governments to become more "data driven" at all levels, from policy making through operational management and risk management to individual decision making

- Underpinning the creation of "smart cities" (and "smart nations") whose systems and infrastructure adapt automatically to the needs and behaviors of their inhabitants

- Providing, through "open data" and other programs, authoritative reference, geospatial, and other data to the national economy and society as a whole to improve transparency, to enable economic growth and business innovation, and to increase the engagement of citizens in the co-creation of public services. An example of this would be a National Spatial Data Infrastructure, or Digital Maps.

Viewing government data as a strategic asset leads to requirements for effective and strategic data governance and data management across the entire life cycle of data, including how data is collected, described, and catalogued, as well as secured and controlled (not just to protect confidentiality, but also to ensure availability and integrity). Preparing government data for wider use will require elimination of unnecessary duplication or avoidance of re-collection of data. It will also require a strategic view of how data is shared across government, used within government and other public services, and made available to other economic and societal actors to generate additional economic and social value.

The changing role of national statistical offices

These requirements are in turn leading to demands for new skills and roles, including "data scientists" and "chief data officers," and new functional capabilities such as "data analysis," "big data," and "visualization." Historically, national statistical offices were, appropriately, the central repository of data, along with national archives, as they have the skills and resources to catalogue and manage data. The skills of information scientists and librarians in these offices may not be so readily available to more casual users of data in line ministries. But national statistical offices have had to reinvent themselves in the internet age, in which a simple web search can come up with many more possible sources of information than even the most dedicated librarian can track.

International authorities also need to collaborate on standards for information management. The General Statistical Business Process Model, for example, is a framework for organizing business processes in statistical organizations adopted in more than 60 countries.[1] But as national statistical offices modernize and partner with nongovernmental entities that provide data for official statistics, there is recognition that such frameworks and business models may be too rigid. For instance, Statistics New Zealand's 2020 strategy affirms the organization's role as a producer of official statistics but moves beyond this to acknowledge its place in a broader ecosystem and its renewed purpose of "adding value to New Zealand's most important data" through increased data cooperation, integration, and analysis.

The challenge for national statistical offices, therefore, is to ensure the information they hold is properly catalogued (metadata) and easily searchable, and to offer this expertise throughout government. This requires a changing business model for the offices. They can no longer expect to cover costs primarily through sale of publications, though this may still provide an additional source of income. Instead, they must rely on the central treasury for most of their income, and on payment for services provided to other parts of government. Where the central treasury is already overstretched, as in many developing countries, national statistical offices frequently struggle. Thus, just as the value of data is becoming all the more evident in the private sector, it is too often neglected in government, especially at the regional or local level.

Sharing data across government

Data collected and held by one government agency may be valuable to another agency in its operations. For instance, it may relieve the second agency of responsibility for collecting the data itself. And in countries such as Belgium, Estonia, or the Russian Federation the government is not allowed to ask citizens again for data that it has already collected from them.

Of course, if personal or classified data is shared between ministries, it is important that it is shared securely. In the United Kingdom, two compact discs containing personal details of some 25 million children were lost in transit between two government agencies (Government of the United Kingdom 2016). This led to the mandatory use of encryption when moving confidential data between government agencies.

A number of countries have taken the concept of data sharing further by explicitly recognizing the importance of unified databases accessible to and used across the public sector, rather than each agency keeping its own records. In 2012, Denmark published a strategy for "Good Basic Data for Everyone—A Driver for Growth and Efficiency."[2] Public authorities in Denmark register various core information about individuals, businesses, real properties, buildings, addresses, and more. This information, called basic data, is seen as important for reuse throughout the public sector because it is an important basis for public authorities to perform their tasks properly and efficiently, "not least because an ever-greater number of tasks have to be performed digitally and across units, administrations and sectors." Some of the registers do not contain personal information and are released as open data (for instance, addresses). In the Netherlands. there is a similar initiative for the sharing of 17 "base registers." The United Kingdom, despite past political controversy, is collaboratively developing a data-sharing policy that will allow the use of key databases across the public sector and, in some circumstances, beyond (Government of the United Kingdom, n.d.).

In federated countries those data sets need to be available not just between national agencies, but also regional and municipal agencies. Since changes to master data may first be notified to other agencies, robust processes are essential for the maintenance of the master data using notifications of change as early as possible; this is even more important in federated systems, where important changes, such as of address, may well be notified locally first.

This also exemplifies the increasing extent to which leading governments see databases, not functions, as the key asset of government administration, along with developing strategic plans to introduce interoperability standards and middleware that allow seamless integration of these databases through open application programming interfaces (widely known as APIs).

Structure of the report

Following this overview chapter, with its focus on government use of data and presentation of definitions, Part I of the report looks at the "supply side" of the data sector.

- *Chapter 2 looks at data connectivity and capacity*, considering where data comes from, how it is stored, and where it goes. Specifically, the chapter looks at the technological drivers that make data ever cheaper to collect, store, and transmit, and the relationship between data and economic growth.

- *Chapter 3 examines data technology, specifically big data analytics and artificial intelligence*, and how this is contributing to development, especially in humanitarian interventions. The enthusiasm for the uses of these new tools is tempered by awareness of the ethical issues.

Part II looks at the "demand side" of the data sector:

- *Chapter 4 looks at people's use of data* and asks whether scope exists for a new model for a data market in which individuals may be able to trade access to their personal data. The underlying principle is that the data itself has no value, but the use of it has. The chapter goes on to examine the potential costs of a data market in possible losses of privacy, control, and agency.

- *Chapter 5 examines how firms use digital platforms in the data economy*, and how that contributes to competitiveness, particularly for small and medium enterprises (SMEs). The chapter details several developing-country platforms and emerging business models, and concludes by considering how SMEs in developing countries can make better use of data to improve competitiveness and thereby compete against the dominant international social media companies.

Part III of the report brings together the *policy implications* for developing country stakeholders:

- *Chapter 6 discusses the policy issues surrounding the use of data*, notably over privacy, data localization, and security issues. The chapter also considers the value of digital ID systems, which many countries have adopted in recent years, though some have specifically rejected them. Finally, the chapter returns to the themes of open data and big data and offers recommendations.

The Data Notes appendix to the report looks at statistical indicators associated with the use of data. It also presents the 2018 update of the Digital Adoption Index (DAI), a composite indicator first introduced in the 2016 *World Development Report: Digital Dividends.* The DAI is an analytical tool that compares the relative adoption of digital technologies by governments, people, and firms within a country.

Notes

1. See https://ec.europa.eu/eurostat/cros/content/gsbpm-generic-statistical-business-process-model-theme_en.

2. To see the strategy, go to http://www.digst.dk/Home/Servicemenu/English/Digitisation/Basic%20Data.

References

The Economist. 2017. "The World's Most Valuable Resource Is No Longer Oil, but Data." May 6. https://www.economist.com/news/leaders/21721656-data-economy-demands-new-approach-antitrust-rules-worlds-most-valuable-resource.

Espinet, X., W. Wang, and S. Mehndiratta. 2017. "Low-Budget Techniques for Road Network Mapping and Road Condition Assessment That Are Accessible to Transport Agencies in Developing Countries." *Transportation Research Record: Journal of the Transportation Research Board* no. 2634: 1–7.

European Commission (EC). 2011. "Data Is the New Gold." Opening Remarks, Press Conference on Open Data Strategy, December 12. https://ec.europa.eu/digital-single-market/en/news/data-new-gold.

Government of the United Kingdom. 2013. "Shakespeare Review: An Independent Review of Public-Sector Information." May 15. https://www.gov.uk/government/publications/shakespeare-review-of-public-sector-information.

———. 2016. "Review of Information Security at HM Revenue and Customs." http://webarchive.nationalarchives.gov.uk/20100407163917/http://www.hm-treasury.gov.uk/d/poynter_review250608.pdf.

———. n.d. "Data Sharing in Government." Blog. http://datasharing.org.uk/index.html.

Iimi, Atsushi, A. K. Farhad Ahmed, Edward Charles Anderson, Adam Stone Diehl, Laban Mayo, Tatiana Peralta Quiros, and Kulwinder Singh Rao. 2016. "New Rural Access Index: Main Determinants and Correlation to Poverty." Policy Research Working Paper 7876, World Bank, Washington, DC.

International Business Machines Corporations (IBM). 2016. "IBM10 Key Marketing Trends for 2017 and Ideas for Exceeding Customer Expectations." https://www-01.ibm.com/common /ssi/cgi-bin/ssialias?htmlfid=WRL12345USEN.

Krambeck, H., and L. Qu. 2015. "Toward an Open Transit Service Data Standard in Developing Asian Countries." *Transportation Research Record: Journal of the Transportation Research Board* no. 2538: 30–36.

Meeker, Mary. 2017. *Internet Trends 2017: Code Conference.* Annual Report. Menlo Park: Kleiner, Perkins, Caufield, Byers (KPCB). https://www.kleinerperkins.com/perspectives /internet-trends-report-2017.

Nelson, P. 2016. "Just One Autonomous Car Will Use 4,000 GB of Data/Day." *Networkworld*, December 7. https://www .networkworld.com/article/3147892/internet/one-autonomous -car-will-use-4000-gb-of-dataday.html.

Statistics New Zealand. 2016. "Statistics New Zealand's Strategic Intentions for the Period 2016/17–19/20 Annual Report for the Year Ended 30 June 2016." Wellington. https://www.stats .govt.nz/about-us/corporate-publications/.

Toonders, J. 2014. "Data Is the New Oil of the Digital Economy." *Wired.* https://www.wired.com/insights/2014/07/data-new -oil-digital-economy/.

Tucker, C. 2017. "Privacy, Algorithms and Artificial Intelligence." Working Paper 14011, National Bureau of Economic Research, Cambridge, MA. http://www.nber.org/chapters /c14011.pdf.

UN Data Revolution Group. 2014. "A World That Counts: Mobilising the Data Revolution for Sustainable Development." http:// www.undatarevolution.org/wp-content/uploads/2014/12/A -World-That-Counts2.pdf.

Wang, W., and F. Guo. 2016. "RoadLab: Revamping Road Condition and Road Safety Monitoring by Crowdsourcing with Smartphone App." Paper presented at the 95th Annual Meeting of the Transportation Research Board, Washington, DC, January 10–14.

World Bank. 2014. "Open Data for Economic Growth." Transport and ICT Global Practice, Washington, DC. http://docu ments.worldbank.org/curated/en/131621468154792082 /pdf/896060REVISED000for0Economic0Growth.pdf.

———. 2016. "Philippines: Real-Time Data Can Improve Traffic Management in Major Cities." Press Release, April 5. http:// www.worldbank.org/en/news/press-release/2016/04/05 /philippines-real-time-data-can-improve-traffic-manage ment-in.

———. 2017. "Big Data in Action for Government: Big Data Innovation in Public Services, Policy, and Engagement." Solutions Brief. World Bank, Washington, DC. http:// documents.worldbank.org/curated/en/176511491287380986 /Big-data-in-action-for-government-big-data-innovation-in -public-services-policy-and-engagement.

Chapter 2

Supply: Data Connectivity and Capacity

The ever-expanding data universe

The rapid growth of internet users and faster network speeds is driving an avalanche of electronic data. About 3.5 billion people globally were using the internet in 2017, up 73 percent, or 1.5 billion, since 2010 (figure 2.1, panel a), and penetration has risen to almost half the world (48 percent in 2017). The rapid increase in users is driving demand for more internet content.

End-user internet speeds are also increasing rapidly, in turn driving use of broadband content and applications (figure 2.1, panel b). Global average wired broadband speeds are projected to nearly double from 25 megabits per second (Mbps) in 2015 to 48 Mbps by 2020 as more users move to fiber and higher-speed coaxial cable. As speeds rise, so does demand for video content.[1] Mobile broadband speeds, which are much lower than fixed speeds, averaged just 2 Mbps in 2015. This will more than triple to 6.5 Mbps by 2020 as more users switch to fourth-generation technologies. Mobile speeds vary greatly by device; smartphones are nearly three times faster than the global average, which results in more time spent online. In the United Kingdom, time spent on the internet more than doubled between 2005 and 2015 from 10 hours a week in 2005 to 23 hours in 2015 (Ofcom 2016a).

Data can either be measured as stock (the amount of data stored in a location) or flow (amount of data transmitted from one location to another). One stock indicator is the number of websites providing partial information about content growth on the internet. According to Netcraft, a leading research firm covering the internet, 170 million websites were active in June 2016, up from just 8 million in June 2000 (Netcraft 2017). Worldwidewebsize.com puts the number of indexed web pages at 4.5 billion.[2] Although useful, these numbers still lack the ability to portray the full scale of data accessible over telecommunication networks. They do not include the so-called dark web, ranging from innocuous private sites collecting sensor data to nefarious sites carrying out illegal or semi-legal activities. Furthermore, not all data going over the internet is from websites; it can also arise out of voice over internet protocol, video conferencing, gaming, and machine-to-machine communication.

More is known about data flows over the internet. In the past, separate networks existed for specific content and functions: for instance, telecommunications for voice and, later, text messages; broadcasting for television and radio; and private networks for businesses. The development of the internet and internet protocol (IP) communications has changed all that. Communications networks have generally shifted from circuit-switched to packet-switched IP networks, enabling virtually any type of content, from voice to text to multimedia, to be encoded and distributed digitally. According to information technology (IT) company Cisco, traffic over the internet will grow by more than 20 percent a year between 2015 and 2020. This data deluge has popularized

Figure 2.1 Internet users and broadband speeds

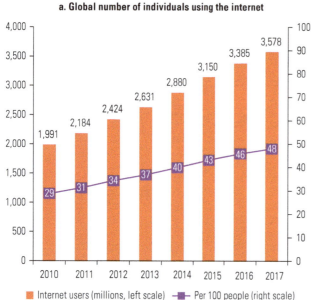

a. Global number of individuals using the internet

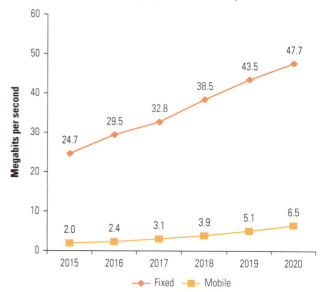

b. Average global broadband speeds

Sources: Cisco; International Telecommunication Union.

Note: 2017 data is an estimate.

a new vocabulary of *petabyte* and *exabyte* that spell checkers have not yet caught up with. Cisco proclaimed that the world entered the *zettabyte* era (an amount equivalent to 250 billion DVDs) in 2016 when annual global internet traffic surpassed 1 zettabyte (Barnett 2016).

It is useful to understand how internet traffic is classified to understand how devices, users, applications, and services are driving this growth. Internet traffic consists of IP and managed IP traffic. The former is exchanged between internet service providers (ISPs), whereas the latter is end to end within the same ISP's network. IP traffic can be further disaggregated by whether it emanates from fixed or mobile networks.[3] The two accounted for three-quarters of internet traffic in 2016, with fixed making up more than 90 percent (figure 2.2, panel a). Managed IP traffic is forecast to decline by 10 percentage points between 2015 and 2020, and the share of mobile data in total traffic is projected to rise from 5 percent in 2015 to 16 percent by 2020.

Businesses and consumers generate traffic, with the latter accounting for more than 80 percent in 2015, a share not projected to change much through 2020. Video dominates consumer IP traffic. It accounted for 38 exabytes a month of traffic in 2016, 71 percent of consumer IP traffic, and 43 percent of total IP traffic. It is forecast to grow

by more than 30 percent a year so that, by the year 2020, it will account for 82 percent of consumer traffic and 57 percent of total IP traffic. Online gaming is projected to be the fastest-growing traffic stream between 2015 and 2020, at 47 percent per year. However, it accounts for a tiny share of total consumer traffic and its contribution will only rise from 0.2 percent to 0.4 percent.

Goodbye data carriers, hello data creators

The rise of the internet has altered communications network value chains. In the past, little value was perceived in the content of traffic carried over communications networks. In the telecommunication world, this traffic was mainly telephone calls. While some of the calls may have triggered wealth, the direct income accrued to telecommunication carriers that transmitted the calls and billed them. In the case of broadcast and private networks, content was more financially significant but intra-industry (such as broadcast transmissions to satellite and cable television companies, banking transactions).

The development of the internet in the 1960s, the World Wide Web in the 1990s, and its iteration in Web 2.0 more recently has modified the way content is obtained and created.

Figure 2.2 Global IP traffic and global consumer IP traffic

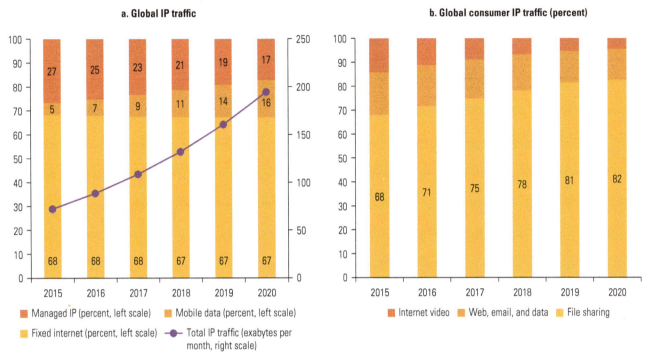

a. Global IP traffic

b. Global consumer IP traffic (percent)

Source: Adapted from Cisco Visual Networking Index Global IP Traffic Forecast.
Note: IP = internet protocol.

Traditional content providers such as the media and audiovisual companies have moved online either with their own websites or by licensing content to streaming platforms. Take the BBC, which has 98 million global internet users viewing 1.5 billion pages a month.[4] Or *O Globo*, one of Brazil's largest newspapers, whose online readers (23 million) outnumber print readers (300,000) by 75 times.[5] A big difference is that not only can anyone access content anywhere on the public internet, they can also create it. Users become creators by sharing their own content with others through blogs, videos, social networking posts, and product and service reviews. Attention has shifted from the carrier of the data to the creator; from "the medium is the message"[6] to the messages delivered over the medium. A company's telephone number is arguably no longer as important as its website, and individuals increasingly exchange their email or social networking links. Similarly, in video entertainment, power is shifting from the company broadcasting the content to the creator. This is reflected in the rise of companies offering internet-delivered video such as Amazon and Netflix and television content creators now embracing the internet (HBO NOW streaming service).

Many of the world's top websites (ranked by a combination of users and page views) are platforms for user-generated content such as social network posts, video sharing, blogs, and collaboration (for example, Wikipedia) (table 2.1). All of the top sites are headquartered in either the United States or China, the two countries with the most internet users (more than 900 million combined, or just over a quarter of all internet users).[7] While the US sites are mostly global, Chinese ones are mainly local. The concentration of so much data on so few sites is concerning, particularly as the giant internet companies behind most of them branch into other domains. Many aspire to be the single window to communications, news, and shopping.

Data centers: Greener and further away, or closer to home?

The growth of internet content is driving the need for places to store it. A data center is a location with networked computers providing remote storage, processing, and distribution of data. They are mainly operated by global IT companies, governments, and enterprises that host other

Table 2.1 Top 10 global websites

	Site	Description	Daily time on site (minutes: seconds)	Daily page views per visitor	Percent of traffic from search	Total sites linking in	Users (millions), 2016
1	Google	Internet portal	8:45	8.63	2.3	3,011,003	~1,000
2	YouTube	Video sharing	9:23	5.40	8.6	2,347,245	~1,000
3	Facebook	Social network	13:56	5.32	4.4	7,278,321	1,860
4	Baidu	Search engine	7:43	6.68	4.5	118,000	657 (2015)
5	Wikipedia	Encyclopedia	4:26	3.31	36.9	1,287,362	374 (2015)
6	Yahoo	Internet portal	4:28	3.90	5.3	529,800	650[a]
7	Qq	Instant messaging	5:05	4.52	3.7	211,248	877
8	Taobao	E-commerce	8:33	4.48	3.8	48,973	407 (2015)[b]
9	Reddit	News links	13:31	9.28	12.3	416,267	234
10	Tmall	E-commerce	5:51	3.45	1.0	8,642	407 (2015)[b]

Source: Adapted from Alexa and Company operating reports.

Note: Extracted March 2017. One month rolling average based on a combination of average daily visitors and page views. Localized Google sites excluded (google.co.in would rank seventh).

a. Monthly mobile users.

b. Owned by Alibaba, which reports a single aggregated figure.

companies' data (that is, colocation). Data centers vary in size, capability, security, and redundancy. A so-called tier 1 data center provides basic nonredundant connections between computer equipment and may be prone to electrical outages, and a tier 4 center has redundant components, multiple connections between computers, continues to operate during maintenance, and is protected against most physical events (Uptime Institute 2012).

Statistics vary widely about the number of data centers in the world. One challenge is that most centers are "small racks in computer rooms in smaller companies" (Gartner 2015). Although the number of data centers has grown rapidly, growth is forecast to slow because of the trend toward larger spaces. More information is available about giant data centers, referred to as "hyperscale" because of their size and ability to add servers and storage as needed. They are operated by about two dozen global IT companies, including heavyweights such as Amazon, Microsoft, and IBM, as well as enterprises providing cloud-computing services. The 259 hyperscale data centers in 2015 are projected to grow to 485 by 2020 (figure 2.3).

Although the majority of hyperscale data centers are in developed nations, data center growth in emerging markets has ticked up. As more users are connected to the internet in lower-income nations, demand for data is rising. IP traffic is forecast to grow fastest in developing regions during 2015–20. Some countries are concerned about data

sovereignty, insisting that government data be stored in the country, driving demand for national data centers. Software parks have also become popular in developing nations as a way to grow their digital economies, and data centers are essential for these facilities. Although the operation of a data center does not create many jobs, they are an essential platform for companies using them to generate revenue and employment (Dutch Data Center Association 2015).

Telecommunications carriers are particularly keen on data centers as a way to offset declining revenue from traditional voice services. Japan's biggest carrier, NTT, is one of the largest data center operators in the world, with more than 140 across the globe.[8] Leading carriers have formed a working group of the Open Compute Project for the adoption of common standards for data centers.[9] Operators in developing nations from Paraguay to the Philippines are busy constructing state-of-the-art data centers. Mobile group Millicom has been launching data centers in African countries (Millicom, n.d.), and its Paraguayan data center won an award in 2016 for its modular design (Millicom 2016). The Philippines Long Distance Telephone Company has constructed eight data centers across the country to be close to IT parks and support its cloud-based service offerings (Verge 2015).

But data centers require significant electricity to power and keep equipment cool. According to a study, data centers in the United States accounted for 2 percent of that country's electricity consumption in 2014 (Shehabi et al. 2016).

Figure 2.3 Hyperscale data centers

Source: Adapted from Cisco Global Cloud Index, 2015–20.

The data center industry is therefore constantly looking for ways to reduce reliance on fossil fuels, particularly given the possibility of data rationing due to shortages of electricity:

> If governments and companies decide to rely upon increased energy generation, they will not be able to keep up with the demands of big data without significantly contributing to environmental pollution levels. In this future, how would the world look? Would governments step in to regulate Facebook usage, only in daylight hours? Would citizens have the right to only 12 Google searches per day? Should we tax companies on their levels of data usage? This might seem laughable now, but data rationing is a likely outcome if we do not tackle data growth and the underlying demands placed on power consumption. (The Green Grid 2016)

This has made geographies with cool climates and abundant hydro or geothermal energy attractive locations for data centers. Google's Finnish data center is built in a restored machine hall designed by renowned architect Alvar Aalto and draws on water from the Bay of Finland for cooling.[10] Its data center in West Dublin does not need air conditioning units because of Ireland's cool climate.[11] Some developing nations have similar environments, making them ideal for data centers. The Data Center Services data center in the Thimpu TechPark draws on mountainous Bhutan's abundant hydropower and year-round cool climate[12] and, in 2017, the government launched its first data center (Moss 2017).

Many developing countries face a challenge competing with hyperscale data centers abroad given that electricity costs tend to be relatively high. In Rwanda, the government is considering subsidizing data center electricity costs to attract more digital companies to the country and for local firms to transition their websites to local hosting enterprises (Internet Society 2017). Small island developing states generally have high electricity costs due to the absence of local energy sources: 8 of the 10 most expensive countries for electricity are such states. However, they are surrounded by a useful resource: cool seawater. As noted, Google uses seawater to cool its Finnish data center and Microsoft is testing underwater data centers (Cutler et al. 2017). Mauritius has also experimented with ocean water to cool data centers (Elahee and Jugoo 2013). Some Pacific small island developing states and other coastal economies have taken advantage of new submarine cable connections to bundle data centers into the landing station, lowering construction costs. Samoa, which has among the highest electricity costs in the world (figure 2.4), installed an energy efficient prefabricated data center in its new cable landing station (Flexenclosure 2017). Many developing nations also have abundant sunshine with great potential for solar energy to lower costs. This is the thinking of mobile group MTN, which deployed Africa's first solar data center at its head office in Johannesburg (van Zyl 2014).

Figure 2.4 Price of electricity (US cents per kilowatt-hour)

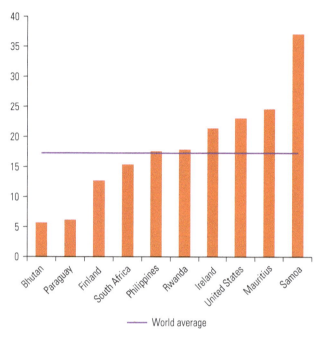

—— World average

Source: Adapted from World Bank 2017.
Note: Figure provides the latest available data.

Reliability is critical for data centers. Developing countries, particularly in Africa, will need to improve the quality of the electricity supply to create the proper environment to attract investment in data centers (box 2.1). This will require electricity sector reform and prioritizing reliability for firms.

IXPs and caches: Closer to the edge

Although trends suggest a move toward larger data centers, the tendency is toward pushing data closer to the user or the "edge" to reduce latency and lower costs (Leavitt 2010). Having data close to end users is critical, particularly in the financial sector, in which a few milliseconds advantage has a huge potential impact (Anthony 2012). This is raising traffic on internet exchange points (IXPs), places where telecom carriers and content providers come together to exchange their traffic (peering). This is cheaper, particularly for developing countries, since internetwork traffic does not need to be sent over costly international links only to return. In addition, ISPs do not need to make peering agreements with each potential partner. IXPs also improve quality since they are situated closer to the user and hence have less latency. "Soft" benefits are also associated with IXPs, such as developing technical skills and fostering a culture of cooperation,

helping to sustain the internet. As the volume of data transmitted over the internet accelerates, IXPs have become even more relevant for ensuring that it is quickly exchanged among different parties.

The largest IXPs (measured by traffic or members) are mainly in Europe, with its long tradition of multistakeholder internet cooperation. The biggest is the German Internet Exchange (DE-CIX) founded in 1995, with locations in Dusseldorf, Frankfurt, Hamburg, and Munich. DE-CIX Frankfurt is the world's leading internet exchange, with peak traffic of 5.6 terabits per second in March 2017. More than 700 networks are connected, and access is available from 20 data centers across the city. The networks connected to DE-CIX are a smorgasbord of giant telecommunication carriers (such as Deutsche Telekom, China Telecom, Verizon, and NTT) and emerging country operators (such as Sri Lanka Telecom, Telkom South Africa, and Telkom Indonesia), big IT firms (such as Apple, Google, and Microsoft), and content and service providers (such as eBay and Facebook). DE-CIX began expanding abroad in 2012 and now operates IXPs in Dallas, Dubai, Istanbul, Madrid, Marseille, New York, and Palermo.

Although IXPs are burgeoning in most developed markets, growth has been uneven in developing nations. According to one source, 78 economies are still without an IXP (map 2.1).

The establishment of an IXP is often hampered by small markets, vested interests, and limited or unbalanced competition. Powerful incumbents with a high level of control over international gateways prefer that ISPs use their overseas links for IP transit. Nevertheless, developing regions, such as Latin America and Africa, have been adding ISPs at relatively high levels (table 2.2). Where no powerful incumbent exists, IXPs can thrive. This is the case of the Rwanda IXP, where the historical operator no longer exists. The IXP has 13 members, including all of the country's infrastructure-based ISPs. Peak traffic load was over 1 gigabit per second in March 2017, up more than 50 percent from the previous year. An IXP is particularly relevant in landlocked countries like Rwanda, which is far from undersea fiber-optic cables.

Cloud computing: Back to the future

The ability to store and process data remotely dates to the early days of computer networks. Back then, end-user devices

Box 2.1 Sub-Saharan Africa: Reliable electricity and the digital economy

Many countries in Sub-Saharan Africa seek to diversify their economies with information and communication technologies (ICT), including expanding ICT as a sector and increasing its use in enterprises. The data center is a core element of ICT infrastructure. These facilities are a vital engine of the digital economy, storing data, hosting websites, and enabling cloud-based applications. Data centers are virtual data factories that make productive use of electricity, with measurable economic impact on gross domestic product, employment, and government tax revenue.

Data centers consume lots of electricity to power computer equipment and keep it cool. In 2011, Google reported that it used 260 megawatts of electric power for its data centers, which is greater than the 2014 installed capacity in 19 Sub-Saharan African countries. Data centers require high reliability to ensure seamless, nonstop data flow. Reliability is defined by industry standards, ranging from 99.670 percent availability with no more than 29 hours of interruption per year for tier 1 data centers, to 99.995 percent reliability with just 0.8 hour of interruption per year for the highest, tier 4 centers. Most Sub-Saharan African nations would find it difficult to meet even tier 1 reliability. The standards also call for a guaranteed source of electrical backup that can power the center for at least half a day.

Lack of enterprise-grade reliability requirements for industry certification generally rules out the feasibility of large data centers in many Sub-Saharan African countries. Although virtually every country in the region has a data center, the centers are small, serving a narrow set of business and government users. Because of the region's challenging environment for reliable and inexpensive electricity, most businesses host their data outside the region. This results in a large volume of data transmitted to overseas data centers, requiring significant amounts of international internet bandwidth. Along with connectivity and storage costs, it takes a longer time to access overseas data centers, raising latency. Security is also an issue, as increasing amounts of government, business, and personal information are transmitted abroad, with vague data protection.

To build up its national data center industry and improve latency, Rwanda launched an initiative to repatriate 1,000 websites hosted abroad (RICTA 2015). An analysis of the program found that quality was improved for domestic users because of faster access to the sites (Internet Society 2017). Visitor engagement was high, with more page views and return visits due to the enhanced performance. The skills of web-hosting employees increased, due to technical requirements to manage additional websites. Although latency improved, it is still difficult to convince local businesses to place their websites in Rwanda because of the lower price of hosting overseas. This is primarily because of the high cost of electricity for data centers in the country. The government is contemplating subsidizing the cost of electricity for local data centers to make local hosting more attractive, improve latency, and strengthen data sovereignty.

Despite concerns about reliability, interest is growing in installing large data centers in the region to achieve better latency and reduce the cost of international bandwidth. In 2017, Microsoft, one of the world's largest owners of data centers, announced it would build two in South Africa to support its cloud-based services. Notably, South Africa's electricity supply is considered the second most reliable in the region after Mauritius. The new data centers will be faster than accessing cloud services in Europe or the United States, international connectivity costs will be lower, and trust higher, as the centers will have to comply with South Africa's data protection law. Electricity reliability is critical for other countries in the region that want to develop their digital economies.

Source: World Bank Group 2018.

Map 2.1 Internet exchange points around the world, 2018

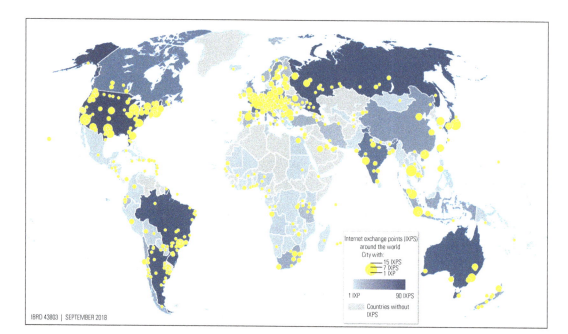

Table 2.2 Internet exchange points by region

Region	Internet exchange points				Domestic bandwidth production			
	February 2016	February 2017	Net change	Percent change	February 2016	February 2017	Net change	Percent change
Europe	136	175	+39	+29	35.9T	41.8T	+5.84T	+16
North America	81	94	+13	+16	3.41T	4.55T	+1.14T	+33
Asia and Pacific	75	92	+17	+23	2.56T	3.51T	+953G	+37
Latin America	45	72	+27	+60	2.22T	2.75T	+524G	+24
Africa	30	42	+12	+40	325G	417G	+92.6G	+29

Source: Packet Clearing House, internet exchange point directory reports, http://wwww.pch.net/ixpdir/summary.

Note: G = gigabytes; T = terabytes.

were "dumb" terminals hooked up to large mainframe computers that did all the work. The invention of the personal computer was revolutionary in providing users with their own device that could run applications and store data. The process is again reverting to centralized control, where data is increasingly stored and processed over the "cloud" on anonymous data servers. Three main reasons explain this:

- *Faster networks.* Rising internet speeds are making the transfer of data between device and cloud increasingly transparent. According to Cisco (2017), average global fixed broadband speeds were 25 Mbps in 2015, up from

7 Mbps in 2010. Average mobile speeds were considerably slower at 2.0 Mbps in 2015, but with large device differences; smartphones averaged 7.5 Mbps around the world in 2015 and are forecast to rise to 12.5 Mbps by 2020.

- *Greater storage.* Storage available over the cloud is vastly superior to what can be saved on a desktop, laptop, or tablet computer or smartphone.

- *Proliferation of smart devices.* As the number of devices a person owns increases, the cloud provides a useful way of keeping them all synced. There were 2.2 devices per person worldwide in 2015, projected to rise to 3.4 by 2020.

Several acronyms are used to identify different cloud services. *Infrastructure as a service (IaaS)* offers computing power and storage. *Platform as a service (PaaS)* offers computer programs and other tools for users to develop their own applications. *Software as a service (SaaS)* offers complete applications and supporting upgrades and maintenance.

There are a number of benefits for cloud users, including reduced need for IT expertise, flexibility for scaling, and consistent application rollout and maintenance for large organizations. Free cloud services also exist that provide office-like application tools useful for small and medium enterprises (SMEs), as well as social network pages and blogs. This is particularly relevant for developing countries where the cost of licensed software can be an obstacle to creating applications and services.

Though cloud computing offers a number of benefits, it comes with costs and risks. Users will utilize more of their data allowance accessing cloud services, and businesses face migration costs either converting to the cloud or changing cloud providers. Risks include security and privacy breaches as well as potential loss of service due to communications or electrical failures. These risks have been well publicized through headline stories detailing cyberattacks, such as against IT giant Yahoo, affecting some 1.5 billion accounts (McGoogan 2017).

Internet of Things: Data is all around

According to Swedish IT equipment manufacturer Ericsson, "things" connected to the internet will overtake devices used by humans in 2018 (Ericsson 2015). Cisco reckons some 12 billion devices will be connected to the internet by 2020 that talk to other devices or computers, up 20 percent a year from 2015 (figure 2.5, panel a). These so-called machine-to-machine connections form the heart of what is referred to as the Internet of Things (IoT), an interconnected ecosystem of sensors, meters, radio frequency identification chips, and other gadgets. Traffic from these things will grow at twice the rate they are being connected, or 40 percent a year from 2015 to 2020, from 1 exabyte per month to 6.3 (figure 2.5, panel b).

Machines have talked to each other for years over communication networks using electronic data interchange and other formats, largely to exchange financial information such as transactions from bank automated teller machines or companies ordering products or services from each other. The IoT expands scope, as the things doing the

Figure 2.5 Global machine-to-machine connections and traffic

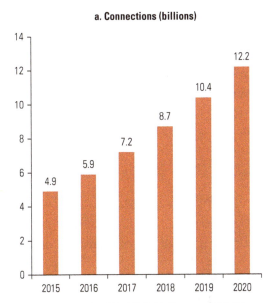

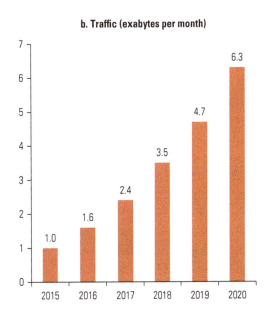

Source: Cisco Visual Networking Index Global IP Traffic Forecast, 2015–20.

Figure 2.6 Machine-to-machine connections per 100 people, OECD member countries, June 2016

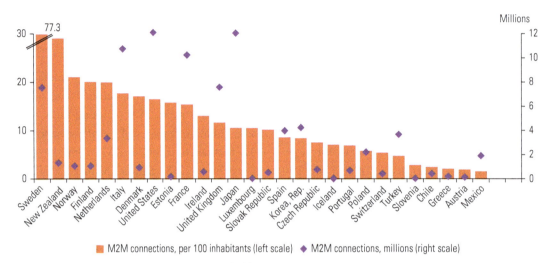

Source: Organisation for Economic Co-operation and Development (OECD).
Note: M2M = machine-to-machine.

communicating are generally small devices and sensors tracking everything from utility use to automobile movements.

A report from the International Telecommunication Union (ITU) and Cisco argues that the IoT could be beneficial for developing countries,[13] since it lowers the cost of service monitoring and delivery, allowing countries to gain in areas such as health and energy over a shorter timeframe than ever before. The ITU has formed a study group to enhance global standardization and collaboration on the IoT.[14] One example is Ghana, where sensors are helping improve the vaccine supply by indicating whether refrigeration was affected during transport.

The gap in IoT adoption is wide, according to statistics. For example, adoption of machine-to-machine communications, a subset of the IoT, varies tremendously in Organisation for Economic Co-operation and Development (OECD) countries, with Sweden and New Zealand ahead by some margin in respect to machine-to-machine connections per 100 people (figure 2.6). Sweden's telecommunication companies are striving to be leaders in Internet-of-Things services, and the country also has a sizable Internet-of-Things startup ecosystem (Luleå University of Technology 2014). And a major reason for New Zealand's high penetration is that the main gas and electricity company has installed more than a million smart meters in homes and businesses across the country (Vector 2017).

Many analysts see fifth-generation (5G) wireless technology as critical for the IoT because of its expanded data handling. According to one report, 5G networks can process about a thousand times more data than today's systems (Hellemans 2015). Of particular relevance for the IoT is 5G's ability to connect many more devices (such as sensors and smart devices) than previous generations of wireless. A major milestone was reached in December 2017 when the first 5G specification was approved by the 3rd Generation Partnership Project and endorsed by many of the world's leading telecommunication equipment manufacturers and operators (3GPP 2017). The ITU's World Radiocommunication Conference 2019 aims to establish standards for spectrum management and harmonization for 5G.[15] Some countries cannot wait, such as the United Kingdom, which earmarked some 3.4 GHz for 5G and auctioned it in March 2018 (Ofcom 2018). Operators in several countries have announced commercial deployments of 5G before the end of 2018.

Data-driven business models

This section looks at how access to the internet and its content is priced and which parties earn the revenue. It examines the different ways for earning revenues from network access and content, including subscriptions (postpaid and prepaid), advertising, and transaction fees. It looks at the consequences of data-driven business models for the traditional pricing approach used by telecommunication operators, with potential impacts on network investment, market concentration, and net neutrality.

In reviewing alternative pricing structures, the difference between access to the internet and to its content varies in their financial significance. Users typically pay for access to the internet based on the volume of data they use, whereas content is not generally priced by volume. While a user may view free video streaming services that generate large amounts of traffic, an online shopping transaction generates little data traffic but, in aggregate, creates significant value for the seller. This contradiction poses a significant challenge for measuring the economics of data:

> The great challenge for economic measurement stems from the fact that the consumption of digital products often does not involve a monetary transaction that corresponds to its value to consumers. Digital products delivered at a zero price, for instance, are entirely excluded from GDP (gross domestic product), in accordance with the internationally-agreed statistical standards. . . . The gap between what is measured and what is valued grows every time access is gained to a completely new good or service or when existing goods or services are offered free as is often the case after digitalisation. The question is how these new forms of consumption should be accounted for in economic statistics such as GDP. (Bean 2016, 74)

Consumer pricing at telecom network operators has evolved with technological change, from price per minute, to price per speed, to price per data consumed. Before the internet, voice was king and operators generally charged for it on a per-minute, metered basis. Before broadband, consumers mainly accessed the internet using dial-up connections with pricing as if it was a voice call (that is, minutes of use). The emergence of fixed broadband led to pricing by speed. With mobile broadband, it is harder to guarantee speeds because of different coverage ranges and a variety of handsets. Three main models exist for pricing data for mobile networks. One is *flat rate*, in which data usage is not metered but there is a fine-print data cap that, if surpassed, results in the speed being lowered. The second is *postpaid*, in which a certain amount of data is included with a monthly subscription.

The third, and most predominant, particularly in developing countries, is *prepaid*, in which the price is tied to a fixed amount of data. Prepaid must generally be used within a specific time, but does allow for flexibility in that a small amount of data can be purchased for a day or a week.

To justify investment in higher-bandwidth infrastructure, a number of telecom operators around the world have diversified into providing video services, enabling them to provide so-called triple-play offers (such as voice, data, and video). This has led to bundled offers in which all three services are offered together at a price higher than that for buying any single service alone, but at a discount compared with purchasing each service separately. Ironically, although traditional broadcast operators moved to protect their markets through legal challenges, neither they nor the telecom operators foresaw the greater threat looming from streaming video services.

The challenge today is that data traffic is exploding while the traditional revenue earner for telecom operators, voice and text, is declining as users shift to over-the-top (OTT) services delivered over the internet. Data traffic from smartphones surpassed voice traffic in 2011 and since then has grown at a tremendous rate, accounting for 96 percent of mobile traffic (figure 2.7, panel a). However, operator revenues have not kept pace. In 2015, voice still accounted for almost half (46 percent) of telecom operator revenue (figure 2.7, panel b), down sharply from two-thirds of operator revenue in 2010. Total telecom revenue has only been growing at 2 percent a year.

How to pay: Advertising-funded versus subscriber-funded networks

The internet has largely been characterized by "free" content. Although some sites, mainly news and streaming audio and video, charge subscriptions, the most popular websites are free. Most of these sites earn revenues from advertising through a two-sided market strategy of providing users with incentives to join their platform (Dallas 2014). As the internet audience has grown, firms are increasingly flocking to place ads on the web and smartphone apps.

The growth of digital advertising is astonishing. Global internet advertising accounted for more than a third of advertising expenditure in 2016, slightly behind television (figure 2.8, panel a).[16]

Figure 2.7 Global network traffic and retail telecom revenue, selected countries

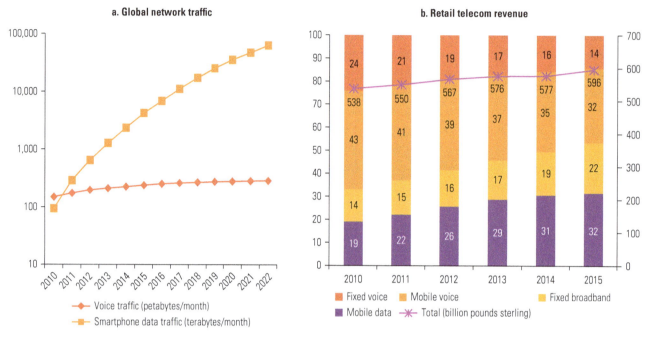

a. Global network traffic

b. Retail telecom revenue

Legend:
- Fixed voice
- Mobile voice
- Fixed broadband
- Mobile data
- Total (billion pounds sterling)
- Voice traffic (petabytes/month)
- Smartphone data traffic (terabytes/month)

Sources: Adapted from Ericsson 2016 and Ofcom 2016a.

Note: Panel a has a logarithmic scale. Panel b is based on 18 major economies: Australia, Brazil, China, France, Germany, India, Italy, Japan, the Netherlands, Nigeria, Poland, the Republic of Korea, the Russian Federation, Singapore, Spain, Sweden, the United Kingdom, and the United States.

Digital advertising spending is highly concentrated, with the vast majority going to two companies: Google and Facebook, who between them received US$106 billion in internet ad revenue in 2016, 64 percent of the global total (figure 2.8, panel b). Their share is growing, up 20 percentage points since 2010. They both have huge user bases, with each reporting more than a billion users of their services, which is attractive to advertisers. But reasons for placing ads on them differ, partly explaining why advertisers often put ads on both. According to one digital ad analyst, "Facebook believes the most important thing is identity in ensuring ad effectiveness … they know who you are and so much about you" whereas "Google believes identity is secondary to intent. What's important is what you want right now because advertising products and services fulfils a want or need" (Garrahan 2016).

Digital advertising is causing a huge transfer of wealth from traditional advertising outlets (such as newspapers and radio) to internet companies. Telecom network operators have also not largely benefited from the value advertisers place on internet content. However, in a highly contested

decision, the U.S. government decided in 2017 that ISPs can sell browsing histories to advertisers without the user's consent (Kelly and McLean 2017).

The concentration of advertising spending reinforces the large properties at the expense of the millions of smaller ones. It also threatens infrastructure investment, since the large websites sit on top of telecommunication networks, yet the networks do not necessarily receive advertising revenues. Although there are payments from content businesses to carriers for bandwidth, it is not clear that they make up for the huge amount of traffic generated. At the same time, if not transparent, the payments between content providers and telecommunication carriers pose net neutrality concerns, since a payment may imply an enhanced traffic service, to the detriment of other content providers.

Another concern is that as a few global sites thrive they are branching into areas they have no expertise in and for which their automated content controls pose challenges. One area is news, with traditional news outlets hit hard by a rapid decline in advertising. The rise of news on IT content sites is of particular concern, with

Figure 2.8 Global advertising revenue

a. Distribution of global advertising spending (percent)

b. Percentage of internet advertising revenue

Legend (panel a): Cinema, Outdoor, Radio, Magazines, Internet, Newspapers, Television, Total (US$ billion; right scale)

Legend (panel b): Others, Facebook, Google

Source: Adapted from Zenith Media, various years.

objectivity and facts increasingly called into doubt given the explosion of sources (Garret 2016). At the same time, legitimate news and information is sometimes blocked, illustrating the weaknesses of robotic software agents trying to determine what is appropriate. For example, Facebook blocked a 1972 Pulitzer Prize winning photo of a Vietnamese girl over concerns about nudity (Scott and Isaacs 2016). The company was accused of abusing its power and the photo was later reinstated (Wong 2016). Google has been under fire for placing ads next to extremist content on its YouTube video-sharing site (BBC 2017). These examples have led to a growing argument that IT firms posting news stories should be subject to regulations similar to those that media firms face (Ingram 2017).

Advertising does support free services for users, which is particularly attractive for developing countries. These services include email, office applications, storage, and maps delivered over the cloud (Greengard 2010). The availability of free and legal cloud-based applications and services is putting a dent in software piracy, which has been dropping, and the focus has shifted from loss of revenues to the cybersecurity dangers of unlicensed software (BSA The Software Alliance 2016).

Besides advertising, some internet companies charge subscription fees, particularly those involved in content. One example is Netflix, which offers streaming television and film delivered over the internet. E-commerce sites such as Amazon, eBay, Rakuten, and Alibaba earn revenue in two ways. One is as a normal retailer, charging a *markup* over price. The second is when the platform is provided to third-party sellers, in which case the platform owner earns *transaction* fees.

Table 2.3 contrasts average revenue per user per month for the various internet payment models and for large internet-based companies. Prices have also been converted to purchasing power parity to adjust for differences in the cost of living. Subscription-based video viewing has the highest average revenue per user, and advertising on social media the lowest (but more subscribers). The telecom carrier in the list has the second highest average revenue per user (purchasing power parity).

Some content companies are becoming involved in developing networks, feeling that infrastructure development is not keeping up with the vast growth in data traffic. A desire to capture more users from developing countries by making it easier for them to get online is also driving this effort.

Table 2.3 Average revenue per user from internet data, 2016

Company (Country)	Revenue model	Average revenue per user (month) US dollars	Average revenue per user (month) At purchasing power parity	Users (millions)	Note
Facebook (United States)	Advertising	2.63	2.63	1,860	World's largest social network platform
Alibaba (China)	Retail margin/ transaction fees	2.37	4.47	423	World's largest business-to-consumer retailer (gross merchandise value)
China Mobile (China)	Subscription and usage	4.31	8.14	849	World's largest mobile operator
Netflix (United States)	Subscription	8.61	8.61	94	World's largest paid video streaming service

Source: Adapted from operating reports of companies shown in table.

Facebook and Google are investing in a variety of communication ventures.

At Google, this includes providing fiber internet access in several U.S. cities,[17] offering fiber backbones and Wi-Fi in Ghana and Uganda,[18] using hot air balloons to extend internet connectivity,[19] and supporting the use of white spaces for making more spectrum available.[20] It also controls Android, the leading mobile phone operating system.[21]

Facebook has been looking at satellites, drones, and solar-powered airplanes for extending internet access (O'Brien 2016), and is getting involved in networking gear (Bort 2016). The growing involvement in data transmission by large content firms raises questions about the separation of carriage and content, with the possibility of a few companies dominating both internet content and access.

The rise of "over-the-top" service providers

OTT refers to data services provided over telecommunication networks. The impact of OTT on telecommunication operators comes from either competing with traditional revenue sources, such as voice calls and messaging, or depositing a lot of traffic on their networks. A lack of clear metrics makes understanding the OTT market a challenge. Some of the most popular OTT services have been purchased by larger companies that do not provide disaggregated financial or operating indicators. Nevertheless, considerable circumstantial evidence suggests the impact is significant.

Notable OTT providers include the following:

- WhatsApp, purchased by Facebook in 2014, offers messaging and calling services and claims to have about a billion users in more than 180 countries.[22]

- Viber offers calling, video, and messaging services to more than 800 million people and is owned by Japanese e-commerce company Rakuten.[23]

- Skype, owned by Microsoft, offers calling, video, and messaging services.

- Netflix provides paid video to 94 million subscribers (as of the end of 2016) around the world. It competes with telecommunication service providers that also offer video (such as IPTV). However, the bigger impact on the telecoms is the volume of traffic Netflix generates.

The impact of OTT has been particularly strong in what has long been a traditional profit center for telecommunication carriers: international voice telephone calls. By 2012, Skype was already handling a third of international telephone traffic (Goldstein 2013). By 2016, OTT traffic using voice over internet protocol exceeded international traffic provided by telecommunication operators (figure 2.9).

Similarly, telecom carriers have seen a sharp fall in conventional messaging services (such as SMS) used on their networks. In 2015, an analysis of 17 countries found that the number of messages declined in 14 of them (figure 2.10).

The danger is that if carriers cannot offset the loss of revenues, less money may be available for future infrastructure investments to handle the rapid increases in data traffic. The ITU has created a study group to examine this issue.[24] The West African telecommunication operator Sonatel paints a dire picture, estimating that between 2016 and 2020, its losses from OTT in the international segment will be CFA francs 256 billion (US$432 million) in Senegal, CFAF 164 billion (US$277 million) in Mali, CFAF 79 billion

Figure 2.9 International carrier and over-the-top traffic (billions of minutes)

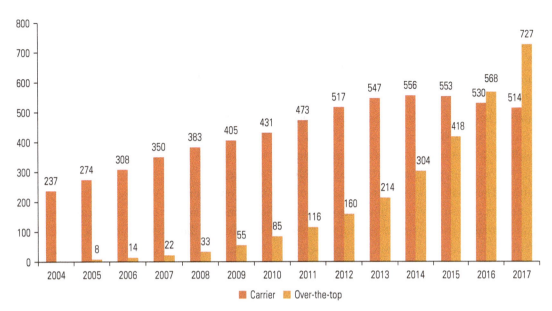

Source: Telegeography.

Figure 2.10 Mobile messages, year-over-year change (percent), 2014–15

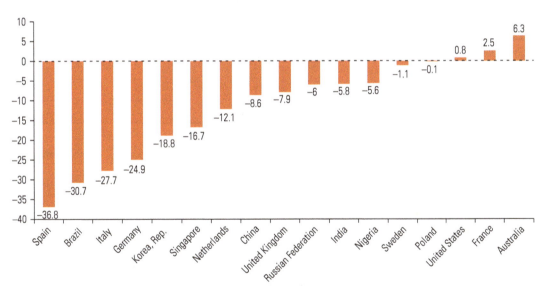

Source: Adapted from Ofcom 2016b.

(US$132 million) in Guinea, and CFAF 12 billion (US$20 million) in Guinea Bissau.[25] It also estimates that taxes paid to the government and dividends for its shareholders will fall CFAF 243 billion (US$410 million).

Telecom operators have developed several responses to OTT. They have argued for regulating OTT providers that provide voice and text services in the same way that telecom operators are regulated. Some operators

are developing their own OTT products. Others are including large bundles of their own offerings, such as free calls or text in packages. Many are diversifying into opportunities in areas such as cloud computing, IoT, and mobile money. Some operators are trying to do all of the above. Also relevant is taxation for OTT firms without a physical presence in the country in which they are providing service. Though they may offer the service for "free," digital advertising revenues often subsidize this. The lack of OTT taxation in most developing countries gives them a cost-structure advantage over domestic telecommunication operators.

Some OTT services compete with traditional telecommunication services such as voice and text. However, others provide a different challenge, particularly OTT video providers. These include those that provide television and films through subscription services such as Netflix as well as free services such as YouTube and Facebook, in which video posts are increasing rapidly (Peterson 2015). They not only compete with telecom operators that provide video services, but are also responsible for a substantial portion of traffic going over the networks. Netflix, YouTube, and Facebook are among the top traffic applications in most regions, comprising 42 percent of fixed-access and 34 percent of mobile-access, peak-period traffic (table 2.4). When all of the properties of Facebook (that is, Instagram, WhatsApp, and so on) and of Google (YouTube, Google Cloud, Google Market, and so on) are considered, they account for an even larger share. The two account for more than 60 percent of total traffic on Latin American mobile networks, for instance (Sandvine 2015).

The promise and perils of zero-rated services

Many internet applications are based on the so-called freemium model, in which consumers get basic features at no cost and can access premium functionality for a subscription fee. However, users must still pay for the data consumed using these applications. Zero-rated services provide access to certain content without it applying to a user's data cap. Some firms with desirable content, such as Facebook, have worked with operators, mainly in developing countries, to provide access to their services without its affecting a user's data allowance. At the same time, some operators are striking agreements to provide access to some services free to their customers. For example, T-Mobile in the United States does not charge data usage for customers on certain subscription bundles when they stream music.[26] Other operators provide discounted access to a bundle of social networking services, but this is technically not zero rated, since users still pay for data access but at a discounted rate.

It is argued that zero-rated services provide a taste of a slimmed-down version of a service and users will eventually pay for access to the full internet (Facebook: Internet.org 2015). Text-only versions may also be relevant for users who do not have access to high-speed mobile internet and rely

Table 2.4 Percentage of aggregate peak period traffic by region, 2015–16

	Africa	Asia and Pacific	Europe	Latin America	Middle East	North America	Simple average
Fixed access							
YouTube	16	27	21	30	NA	15	22
Netflix			4	6		34	15
Facebook	9	3	7	6	NA	3	6
Other (top 10)	44	45	38	41	NA	22	38
Other	31	24	29	17	NA	27	26
Top 10	69	76	71	83	NA	73	74
Mobile access							
YouTube	10	17	20	20	21	19	18
Netflix				2		4	3
Facebook	6	8	16	26	10	16	14
Other (top 10)	49	36	38	34	43	35	39
Other	35	39	26	19	26	26	29
Top 10	65	61	74	81	74	74	71

Source: Sandvine **2015.**

Note: NA = data not available; blank cells indicate that the service in question is not offered in a particular area.

on slow 2G connections. One example is Facebook Zero, launched in 2010, providing access to a text-only version of the service. It has now been renamed the *Free Basics* service, available in more than 60 economies (Facebook: Internet.org, n.d.), with about 40 million users (Constine 2016). In addition to Facebook, access is provided to other websites, such as Wikipedia, Accuweather, and Bing, as well as to local social impact sites for health and employment.

A variation on zero-rated services is sponsored data, in which companies pay for data usage if a user agrees to receive ads. Sponsored data is also used for companies to pay for their employees' mobile data usage for work. AT&T, a U.S. mobile operator, offers sponsored data in which users are not charged for usage if they access a sponsor's site.[27] Syntonic, one of the AT&T sponsors, notes: "Millions of prepaid consumers ration their data, impeding discovery and exploration of mobile apps and content" and is expanding its product reach outside the United States to southeast Asia, India, and Mexico (Syntonic 2017).

While providing free content seems commendable, only making certain content available runs contrary to the net neutrality principle of the internet. In February 2016, the Telecom Regulatory Authority of India issued a regulation prohibiting the use of what it called discriminatory tariffs for data services. The authority formed its decision based on "the principles of Net Neutrality seeking to ensure that consumers get unhindered and nondiscriminatory access to the internet. These Regulations intend to make data tariffs for access to the internet to be content agnostic" (Telecom Regulatory Authority of India 2016). Several other countries have also banned zero-rated services. On the other hand, the United States Federal Communications Commission struck down net neutrality provisions in December 2017. The 3–2 vote by commissioners was along political lines in an allegedly "contentious and messy" public comment process (Kastrenakes 2017). ISPs in that country are now allowed to block, throttle, and prioritize content. About 20 states have filed lawsuits against the ruling, and the United States Congress is considering overturning the ruling if it can muster the votes (Fiegerman 2018).

At the same time, it is argued that zero-rated services give an advantage to large companies to the detriment of new startups. As one report notes: "Ironically, if zero-rated services were available when large internet companies were startups, it is unlikely they would have scaled to the size they are now."[28]

Importantly, cost is not the only or even, in many countries, the main barrier to internet access. Users often cite reasons such as no need or lack of skills as the reason they do not use the internet. In Thailand, 97 percent of those who do not use the internet said the main reason was because they did not know how to use it or it was unnecessary or a waste of time (National Statistical Office, Thailand 2016). In Brazil, 70 percent of those not using the internet cited a lack of interest as a reason.[29] So it is not clear to what extent zero-rated services get new users online. As one report puts it: "Even with a zero-rated service, the user must still have a device and an active account with the operator that offers the zero-rated service. This raises the question of whether zero-rated services can bring people online who had not previously used the internet" (Alliance for Affordable Internet 2016). The report looked at the impact of mobile data apps across eight developing countries, finding that 88 percent of users had already accessed the internet before using a zero-rated plan. This suggests that digital literacy challenges are arguably more important than affordability to get more people online.

Data holes: Filling the gaps

This section explains why data location, language, and limits are becoming more important than plain access. It also explores links between data and economic development.

From access to usage

Significant attention has been devoted to the uneven distribution of access to information and communication technology (ICT). As mobile phone penetration rises and access to the internet increases, the access gap is shrinking. Nine in ten people around the world were covered by a 2G cellphone signal in 2016 and 65 percent by 3G; by 2020 these figures are forecast to rise to 95 percent and more than 90 percent, respectively. The unconnected are increasingly those who are not interested in using or do not know how to use the internet rather than those who have no access or cannot afford to pay. Investment in digital literacy training is becoming as important as infrastructure.

The geography of data creation, distribution, and use is lopsided, resulting in a new global *data divide*. One manifestation of this gap is content concentration. More than half of the world's websites are in English (figure 2.11, panel b), yet only 984 million people speak English as a first

Figure 2.11 Global internet protocol traffic and websites by language

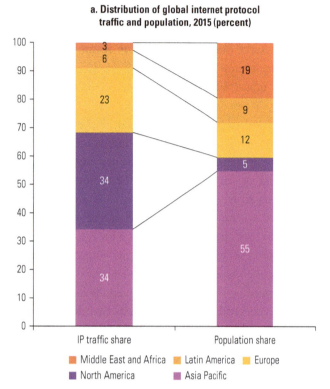

a. Distribution of global internet protocol
traffic and population, 2015 (percent)

Legend:
- Middle East and Africa
- North America
- Latin America
- Asia Pacific
- Europe

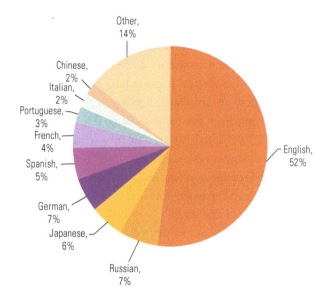

b. Percentage of websites by language, March 2017

- Other, 14%
- Chinese, 2%
- Italian, 2%
- Portuguese, 3%
- French, 4%
- Spanish, 5%
- German, 7%
- Japanese, 6%
- Russian, 7%
- English, 52%

Sources: Cisco; W3Techs; and World Bank.

or second language (Simons and Fenning 2018), 13 percent of the Earth's population. Another manifestation of the data divide is from where it flows. Just over one-third of IP traffic is generated by North America, with only 5 percent of the world's population (figure 2.11, panel a). On the other hand, the Middle East and Africa, home to 19 percent of the world's population, only generate 3 percent of global IP traffic.

New metrics of the data age

Data holes are reflected by uneven data consumption across communities, regions, and nations. The amount of data used per smartphone—measured as gigabytes of data per month or GB/user—varies tremendously. Smartphone users in North America consumed almost four times more data than those in the Middle East and Africa (figure 2.12, panel a). Average global use is forecast to grow more than fivefold between 2016 and 2022, from 1.9 GB per month to 11. Within North America, U.S. mobile broadband subscribers use more than 1.8 times as much data as their neighbor to the north, Canada, and 3.6 times more than their neighbor to the south, Mexico (figure 2.12, panel b).

Data usage is driven by factors such as coverage and device, with pricing a major influence. Data pricing varies significantly throughout the world, measured by the metric of price per GB per month or for comparability, US$/GB (figure 2.13, panel a). In absolute terms, average price ranges from US$5 per GB per month in South Asia to US$28 in high-income OECD nations. However, in relative terms, high-income OECD nations have the cheapest prices (0.9 percent of GDP per capita) compared with 12 percent in Sub-Saharan Africa. Prices vary significantly in Sub-Saharan Africa, with relative data prices ranging from a little over 1 percent of gross national income per capita in Mauritius to 45 percent in Zimbabwe (figure 2.13, panel b).

Being data starved is a constraint when it comes to rich multimedia educational, health, and livelihood content. However, many useful activities require just narrowband: a quick e-commerce transaction, a text message to check produce prices, or a phone call in an emergency. Hourly, daily, and weekly prepaid options can enhance affordability in these circumstances.

Figure 2.12 Mobile data usage

a. Data traffic per smartphone
(gigabytes per user per month)

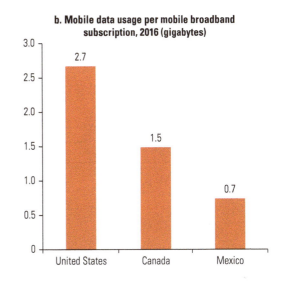

b. Mobile data usage per mobile broadband
subscription, 2016 (gigabytes)

■ 2022 ■ 2016

Sources: Adapted from Ericsson 2016 and OECD 2017.

Data and economic development

Could the data divide be affecting economic growth in developing nations? Various studies have looked at the impact of ICTs on economic growth. As businesses and consumers obtain more high-speed connectivity, they have realized important benefits in terms of efficiency, new businesses models, market information, and so on. Some research has focused on the impact of data on the economy. Four studies looking at public sector open data found impacts ranging from 0.4 percent to 4.1 percent of GDP (ODIHQ 2015). A European Parliament report states that big data and the data-driven economy will bring 1.9 percent in additional GDP growth by 2020 (European Parliament 2016).

A Deloitte study suggests that data usage affects economic growth (Williams et al. 2016). Based on mobile data usage for 14 countries between 2005 and 2010, the study found that a doubling of mobile data consumption added 0.5 percentage point to GDP growth a year.

While the study suggests an econometric link between data consumption and economic growth, the exact reasons seem fuzzy. It is puzzling, given that most internet traffic is video entertainment, which is not likely to have a tremendous economic effect. Other studies suggest that it may not be the quantity of data that is important, but rather the value of the data. In many developing countries, economic impacts have been noted from basic cell phone voice calls and narrowband 2G applications such as text messaging or mobile money, which do not use much data. For example, a study of grain markets in Niger found that prices dropped 3 percent after the introduction of mobile phones because of better access to market information (Aker 2010). A study analyzing the economic impact of mobile money in Kenya found its use decreases prices of competing money transfer services and increases levels of financial inclusion (Mbiti and Weil 2011). An econometric analysis on the impact of telecommunications in Senegal found no statistically significant effect from broadband; on the other hand, plain mobile communications had a significant contribution, with each percentage point increase in mobile penetration contributing 0.05 percent to GDP (Katz and Koutroumpis 2012). These findings suggest that the data nuggets are small, often lost in the sea of video and social media traffic, and sometimes not even transmitted over the internet.

Conclusions: Toward sustainable national data ecosystems

As the universe heads inexorably into the data era, there are winners and losers. Consumers have access to "free" content and services in exchange for their personal information and time spent posting information (Thornhill 2018). It has also

Figure 2.13 Mobile data pricing

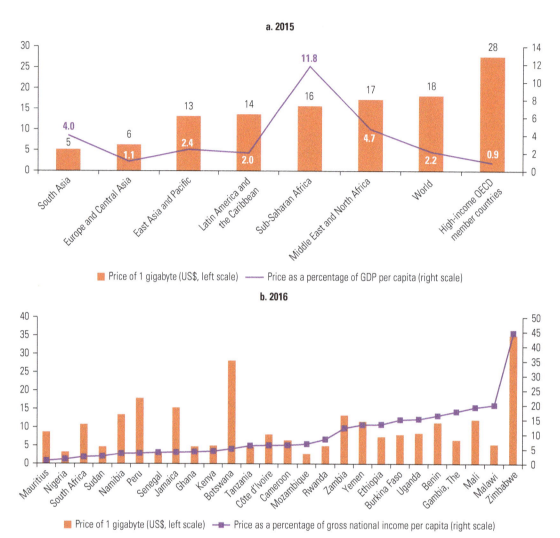

a. 2015

Price of 1 gigabyte (US$, left scale)   —— Price as a percentage of GDP per capita (right scale)

b. 2016

Price of 1 gigabyte (US$, left scale)   ——■—— Price as a percentage of gross national income per capita (right scale)

Sources: Alliance for Affordable Internet; and International Telecommunication Union.

Note: OECD = Organisation for Economic Co-operation and Development.

been great for content platforms that get free user-generated content and even more valuable, their personal information that is sold to digital advertisers and data analytics firms. On the other hand, the emerging data economy is requiring adjustments for telecommunication carriers who are finding it difficult to fund investment needed for rising data use. The money they are making from data access has not offset falling revenue from traditional sources due to OTT. Governments are finding it increasingly challenging to deal with concerns such as net neutrality, privacy, computer crime, and false or incendiary information on the internet, as well as automated platform censorship.

The globalized nature of the internet is its beauty, but also its peril. Users can access content from Argentina to Zambia using free platforms to store data and run applications. SMEs in developing countries have benefited from free online tools and global platforms to increase their visibility. This "free lunch" has resulted in just two U.S. companies—Google and Facebook—dominating the platforms by which many of the world's internet users interact, earning the majority of online ad revenue, controlling vast amounts of personal data, and generating much of the traffic. They are also extending their operations horizontally and vertically, from online shopping to the provision of telecommunication services. This has made some governments anxious about the power a few U.S. companies wield over the internet:

> Several recent attempts have been proposed by other countries such as Brazil, Germany, China, and Russia to better regulate their data sovereignty requirements against the domination of the US communications infrastructure and services. These technical proposals are national email, localised routing of internet traffic, undersea fiber optic cable and localised data centre (Nugraha, Kautsarina, and Sastrosubroto 2015).

The rise of dominant internet platforms affects the development of national data ecosystems. Developing country telecom operators not only pay for a physical link abroad, they also need to pay for data traffic to be exchanged for transmission to an overseas hyperscale data center. Local digital businesses struggle to develop new applications and services already dominated by a few free platforms that have achieved giant scale because of network effects. The development of local internet infrastructure facilities such as IXPs and data centers suffers, since so much content resides abroad.

The challenge for many lower-income countries is how to develop a relevant and sustainable data ecosystem in the current environment. Much of the data consumed around the world is entertainment oriented. Yet governments need development-oriented data to enhance social and economic growth.

A starting point is boosting linguistically and contextually relevant local content. This needs to be accompanied by investment in infrastructure such as fiber-optic backbones and data centers to bring data closer to users. Applications and services that can enhance health and education, such as telemedicine and online learning, need to be implemented rather than talked about. National infrastructure deployment and the take-up of local content and services can be encouraged by taking a page from mobile tariff structures. Access to locally hosted sites and services such as e-government can be stimulated with a low "on-net" internet access price, particularly since access to locally stored content is cheaper than content stored overseas. Furthermore, digital literacy has to be boosted so that taxi drivers can use GPS and not just play smartphone games, and SMEs need to move from streaming music in their shops to using e-commerce. Digital scientist skills are needed, so instead of being overwhelmed by data,

developing countries can analyze it and put it to good use. And rather than digital advertisers using personal data to sell something, developing country digital scientists can use data to pinpoint the locations of those living in poverty to better target assistance (Bohannon 2016).

In short, developing nations need to leverage data to drive development through locally relevant content and a thriving employment-generating digital ecosystem. This will require better understanding of data's potential, investment in core infrastructure such as data centers and IXPs, and development of data-driven development applications and services.

Notes

1. According to Cisco, "There is a strong correlation between experienced speeds and number of video minutes viewed per viewer. As speeds increase … the number of video minutes per viewer also increases." For more, see http://www.cisco.com/c/en/us/solutions/collateral/service-provider/visual-networking-index-vni/vni-hyperconnectivity-wp.html.

2. See World Wide Web Size at http://www.worldwidewebsize.com.

3. Note that fixed and mobile traffic can also go over managed IP networks in the case of business or government closed networks.

4. British Broadcasting Corporation, BBC at a Glance. https://advertising.bbcworldwide.com/brands/bbccom/.

5. See the Metro Network "O Globo – Brazil" at TMN Worldwide. http://www.tmnww.com/premium-network-global-reach/premium-latam/premium-brazil-rio.

6. From the Estate of Corinne & Marshall McLuhan, "Commonly Asked Questions (and Answers)," viewable at http://www.marshallmcluhan.com/common-questions/.

7. According to the China Internet Network Information Center, there were 710 million internet users age 6 and older in June 2016 (see CNNIC 2016). According to the United States National Telecommunications and Information Administration, there were 227 million internet users age 3 and older in July 2015 (See "Digital Nation Explorer" at https://www.ntia.doc.gov/data/digital-nation-data-explorer).

8. See http://www.ntt.com/en/services/data-center/nexcenter.html.

9. For more information, see http://www.opencompute.org/projects/telco/.

10. For more information, see https://www.google.com/about/datacenters/inside/locations/hamina/.

11. See https://www.google.com/about/datacenters/inside/locations/dublin/.

12. For more information, see http://www.dcs.bt/index.html.

13. See http://www.itu.int/net/pressoffice/press_releases/2016/02.aspx#.WNVwdBjMzYI.

14. See http://www.itu.int/net/pressoffice/press_releases/2015/22.aspx#.WNVxbjMzYI.

15. See https://www.itu.int/en/mediacentre/Pages/2017-PR66.aspx.

16. For more on the shift and drying up of print advertising revenues and move to digital advertising, see WAN-IFRA, 2016, *World Press Trends*. http://anp.cl/wp-content/uploads/2017/02/WAN-IFRA_WPT_2016_3.pdf.

17. See https://fiber.google.com/about/.

18. See https://www.google.com/get/projectlink/.

19. See https://x.company/loon/.

20. See https://www.google.com/get/spectrumdatabase/.

21. See https://www.android.com.

22. See https://www.whatsapp.com/about/.

23. See https://www.viber.com/en/about.

24. See http://www.itu.int/en/ITU-T/studygroups/2013–2016/03/Pages/ott.aspx.

25. See http://wholesalesolutions.orange.com/content/download/47961/1369504/version/1/file/OTT+in+Senegal_Birago+Beye.pdf.

26. See https://www.t-mobile.com/offer/free-music-streaming.html.

27. See https://www.att.com/att/sponsoreddata/en/index.html.

28. See http://www.itu.int/en/mediacentre/Pages/2016-PR48.aspx.

29. See CETIC, "C15—Proporção de Indivíduos Que Nunca Utilizaram Internet, por Motivos Para Nunca Ter Utilizado a Internet," at http://www.cetic.br/tics/usuarios/2015/total-brasil/C15/.

References

Aker, Jenny C. 2010. "Information from Markets Near and Far: Mobile Phones and Agricultural Markets in Niger." *American Economic Journal: Applied Economics* 2 (3): 46–59. https://www.aeaweb.org/articles?id=10.1257/app.2.3.46.

Alliance for Affordable Internet. 2016. "The Impacts of Emerging Mobile Data Services in Developing Countries." Research Brief No. 2. http://1e8q3q16vyc81g8l3h3md6q5f5e.wpengine.netdna-cdn.com/wp-content/uploads/2016/05/Measuring ImpactsofMobileDataServices_ResearchBrief2.pdf.

Anthony, Sebastian. 2012. "$1.5 Billion: The Cost of Cutting London-Tokyo Latency by 60ms." *ExtremeTech*, March 20. https://www.extremetech.com/extreme/122989-1-5-billion -the-cost-of-cutting-london-toyko-latency-by-60ms.

Barnett Jr., Thomas. 2016. "The Zettabyte Era Officially Begins (How Much Is That?)." SP360: Service Provider, September 9. https://blogs.cisco.com/sp/the-zettabyte-era-officially-begins -how-much-is-that.

BBC (British Broadcasting Corporation). 2017. "Google Apologises after Ads Appear Next to Extremist Content." March 20. https://www.bbc.com/news/business-39325916.

Bean, Charles. 2016. "Independent Review of UK Economic Statistics." Final Report of the Independent Review of UK Economic Statistics (to the Government of the United Kingdom), led by Professor Sir Charles Bean of the London School of Economics. https://www.gov.uk/government/publications/independent-review-of-uk-economic-statis-tics-final-report.

Bohannon, John. 2016. "Satellite Images Can Map Poverty." *Science*, August 18. http://www.sciencemag.org/news/2016/08/satellite -images-can-map-poverty.

Bort, Julie. 2016. "Now Facebook Plans to Eat the $500 Billion Telecom Equipment Market." *Business Insider*, November 1. http://www.businessinsider.com/facebook-voyager-optical -switch-telecom-infra-project-2016-11.

BSA The Software Alliance. 2016. "Seizing Opportunity through License Compliance." http://globalstudy.bsa.org/2016/index.html.

Cisco. 2017. "Cisco Visual Networking Index: Forecast and Methodology, 2016–2021." https://www.cisco.com/c/en/us/solutions/collateral/service-provider/visual-networking -index-vni/complete-white-paper-c11-481360.pdf.

CNNIC (China Internet Network Information Center). 2016. "Statistical Report on Internet Development in China." https://cnnic.com.cn/IDR/ReportDownloads/.

Constine, Josh. 2016. "Facebook Has Connected 40m People with Internet.org." *Tech Crunch*, November 2. https://techcrunch.com/2016/11/02/omnipresent/.

Cutler, Ben, Spencer Fowers, Jeffrey Kramer, and Eric Peterson. 2017. "Want an Energy-Efficient Data Center? Build It Underwater." *IEEE Spectrum: Technology, Engineering, and Science News*, February 21. http://spectrum.ieee.org/computing/hardware/want-an-energyefficient-data-center-build-it -underwater.

Dallas, George. 2014. "Making Sense of Internet Platforms: Network Effects and Two Sided Markets." https://georgemdallas.wordpress.com/2014/06/05/making-sense-of-internet-platforms-network -effects-and-two-sided-markets/.

Dutch Data Center Association. 2017. "The Economic Impact of Multi-tenant Data Centers in the Netherlands." https://www.vijfhart.nl/wp-content/uploads/2017/02/report_-_2017_-_economic_impact_dutch_data_centers.pdf.

Elahee, K., and S. Jugoo. 2013. "Ocean Thermal Energy for Air-Conditioning: Case Study of a Green Data Center." *Energy Sources, Part A: Recovery, Utilization, and Environmental Effects* 35 (7): 679–84. doi:10.1080/15567036.2010.504941.

Ericsson. 2016. "Internet of Things to Overtake Mobile Phones by 2018: Ericsson Mobility Report." Press release, June 1.

https://www.ericsson.com/en/press-releases/2016/6/internet-of-things-to-overtake-mobile-phones-by-2018-ericsson-mobility-report.

European Parliament. 2016. "Towards a Thriving Data-Driven Economy." http://www.europarl.europa.eu/sides/getDoc.do?pubRef=-//EP//TEXT+TA+P8-TA-2016-0089+0+DOC+XML+V0//EN.

Facebook: Internet.org. 2015. "One Year In: Internet.org Free Basic Services." Blog, July 27. https://info.internet.org/en/blog/2015/07/27/one-year-in-internet-org-free-basic-services/.

———. n.d. "Where We've Launched." https://info.internet.org/en/story/where-weve-launched/.

Fiegerman, Seth. 2018. "More than 20 States Sue to Stop FCC's Net Neutrality Repeal." CNN, January 16. http://money.cnn.com/2018/01/16/technology/net-neutrality-lawsuit/index.html.

Flexenclosure. 2017. "Flexenclosure to Deploy Two eCentre Cable Landing Stations for SSCC in Samoa." Press release, February 27. http://www.flexenclosure.com/flexenclosure-deploys-two-ecentre-cable-landing-stations-for-sscc-in-samoa/.

Garrahan, Matthew. 2016. "Advertising: Facebook and Google Build a Duopoly." *Financial Times*, June 23. https://www.ft.com/content/6c6b74a4-3920-11e6-9a05-82a9b15a8ee7.

Garret, R. Kelly. 2016. "Facebook's Problem Is More Complicated Than Fake News." *Scientific American*, November 17. https://www.scientificamerican.com/article/facebook-s-problem-is-more-complicated-than-fake-news/.

Gartner. 2015. "Gartner Says Australian Organizations to Spend A$2.5 Billion on Data Center Systems in 2015." Press release, May 17. http://www.gartner.com/newsroom/id/3054918.

Goldstein, Phil. 2013. "Report: Skype Makes Up One-Third of All International Phone Traffic." *FierceWireless*, February 15. https://www.fiercewireless.com/wireless/report-skype-makes-up-one-third-all-international-phone-traffic.

The Green Grid. 2016. "The 'Big Bad Data Police' Will Call If We Don't Get More Efficient." News release, September 5. https://www.thegreengrid.org/en/newsroom/news-releases/green-grid-big-bad-data-police-will-call.

Greengard, Samuel. 2010. "Cloud Computing and Developing Nations." *Communications of the ACM* 53 (5): 18–20. https://cacm.acm.org/magazines/2010/5/87255-cloud-computing-and-developing-nations/fulltext.

Hellemans, Alexander. 2015. "Why IoT Needs 5G." *IEEE Spectrum*, May 20. http://spectrum.ieee.org/tech-talk/computing/networks/5g-taking-stock.

Ingram, Matthew. 2017. "Facebook and Google Need to Be Regulated, Says British News Industry." *Fortune*, March 9. http://fortune.com/2017/03/09/facebook-google-regulated/.

Internet Society. 2017. "A Case Study in Local Content Hosting: Speed, Visits, and Cost of Access." https://www.internetsociety.org/doc/case-study-local-content-rwanda.

Kastrenakes, Jacob. 2017. "The FCC Just Killed Net Neutrality." *The Verge*, December 14. https://www.theverge.com/2017/12/14/16776154/fcc-net-neutrality-vote-results-rules-repealed.

Katz, Raul, and P. Koutroumpis. 2012. "The Economic Impact of Telecommunications in Senegal." *Communications & Strategies* 2 (86): 21–42. https://www8.gsb.columbia.edu/citi/sites/citi/files/files/Senegal_Telecoms_Report_version%20finale%5B1%5D.pdf.

Kelly, Heather, and Scott McLean 2017. "Your Browser History Is for Sale, Here's What You Need to Know." *CNNMoney*, April 6. http://money.cnn.com/2017/04/05/technology/online-privacy-faq/.

Leavitt, Neal. 2010. "Network-Usage Changes Push Internet Traffic to the Edge." *Computer* [IEEE] 43 (10): 13–15. http://ieeexplore.ieee.org/document/5604156.

Luleå University of Technology. 2014. "National Agenda for the Internet of Things: Summary of the Project IoT Sweden." https://iotsverige.se/wp-content/uploads/2014/12/Agendan-eng-29-sep-2014-korr4.pdf.

Mbiti, Isaac M., and David N. Weil. 2011. "Mobile Banking: The Impact of M-Pesa in Kenya." Working Paper 17129, National Bureau of Economic Research, Cambridge, MA. https://ssrn.com/abstract=1866089.

McGoogan, Cara. 2017. "Yahoo Hack Warning: What Happened and Should You Be Worried?" *The Telegraph*, February 16. https://www.telegraph.co.uk/technology/2017/02/16/yahoo-hack-warning-happened-should-worried/.

Millicom. 2016. "Tigo Business Paraguay's Data Center Awarded 'Best Modular Implementation' by Prestigious International Sector Magazine." Press release, September 28. http://www.millicom.com/media/6762386/Data-Center-Award_-Eng.pdf.

———. n.d. "Investing in State-of-the-Art Data Centers." News feature. http://www.millicom.com/media/millicom-news-features/data-centers.

Moss, Sebastian. 2017. "The Kingdom of Bhutan Opens First Government Data Center." *Data Centre Dynamics,* March 27. http://www.datacenterdynamics.com/content-tracks/colo-cloud/the-kingdom-of-bhutan-opens-first-government-data-center/98052.fullarticle.

Nugraha, Y., Kautsarina, and A. S. Sastrosubroto. 2015. "Towards Data Sovereignty in Cyberspace." Working paper presented at the Third International Conference on Information and Communication Technology. https://www.cs.ox.ac.uk/files/7463/Towards%20Data%20Sovereignity%20in%20Cyberspace_Nugraha.pdf.

National Statistical Office, Thailand. 2016. "The 2016 Household Survey on the Use of Information and Communication Technology." Ministry of Information and Communication Technology. http://web.nso.go.th/en/survey/ict/ict_house16.htm.

Netcraft. 2017. "February 2017 Web Server Survey." https://news .netcraft.com/archives/2017/02/27/february-2017-web-server -survey.html.

O'Brien, Sarah Ashley. 2016. "Why Facebook Was Launching a Satellite into Space." CNN.com, September 1. http://money.cnn .com/2016/09/01/technology/facebook-satellite-explosion/.

ODIHQ (Open Data Institute). 2015. "The Economic Impact of Open Data: What Do We Already Know?" Medium, November 2. https://medium.com/@ODIHQ/the-economic-impact-of-open -data-what-do-we-already-know-1a119c1958a0.

OECD (Organisation for Economic Co-operation and Development). 2017. "Mobile Data Usage per Mobile Broadband Subscription, 2016: Gigabytes per Month." Figure 3.27 in *OECD Digital Economy Outlook 2017*, 146. Paris: OECD Publishing. https://doi .org/10.1787/9789264276284-graph53-en.

Ofcom. 2016a. "Adults' Media Use and Attitudes." https://www .ofcom.org.uk/__data/assets/pdf_file/0026/80828/2016 -adults-media-use-and-attitudes.pdf.

———. 2016b. *The Communications Market Report.* https:// www.ofcom.org.uk/__data/assets/pdf_file/0026/95642 /ICMR-Full.pdf.

———. 2018. "Ofcom Kicks Off Auction to Improve Mobile Broadband and Prepare for 5G." https://www.ofcom.org .uk/about-ofcom/latest/media/media-releases/2018/start -spectrum-auction.

Peterson, Tim. 2015. "Facebook Users Are Posting 75% More Videos Than Last Year." *AdAge*, January 7. http://adage .com/article/digital/facebook-users-posting-75-videos -year/296482/.

RICTA. 2015. "Growing the Rwandan Internet Content Hosted in Rwanda." https://ricta.org.rw/sites/default/files/resources /1kwebsites_project_finalversion_0.pdf.

Sandvine. 2015. "Global Internet Phenomena: Latin America & North America." https://www.sandvine.com/hubfs/downloads /archive/2015-global-internet-phenomena-report-latin-america -and-north-america.pdf.

Scott, Mark, and Mike Isaacs. 2016. "Facebook Restores Iconic Vietnam War Photo It Censored for Nudity." *New York Times*, September 9. https://www.nytimes.com/2016/09/10 /technology/facebook-vietnam-war-photo-nudity.html ?_r=0.

Shehabi, A., S. J. Smith, N. Horner, I. Azevedo, R. Brown, J. Koomey, E. Masanet, D. Sartor, M. Herrlin, and W. Lintner. 2016. "United States Data Center Energy Usage Report." Lawrence Berkeley National Laboratory, Berkeley, California. https://pubarchive.lbl.gov/islandora/object/ir%3A1005775 /datastream/PDF/view.

Simons, Gary F., and Charles D. Fenning, eds. 2018. "English." *Ethnologue: Languages of the World.* 21st ed. English.

Dallas, TX: SIL International. https://www.ethnologue.com /language/eng.

Syntonic. 2017. "Syntonic Expands to Latin America and Lending Mobile Carriers." January 21. https://syntonic.com/2017/01 /syntonic-expands-to-latin-america-with-leading-mobile -carriers/.

Telecom Regulatory Authority of India. 2016. "TRAI Releases the Prohibition of Discriminatory Tariffs for Data Servi- ces Regulations." http://www.trai.gov.in/notifications /press-release/trai-releases-prohibition-discriminatory -tariffs-data-services.

Thornhill, John. 2018. "Social Media Users of the World Unite." *Financial Times*, February 5. https://www.ft.com/content /ea6c3a0c-0843-11e8-9650-9c0ad2d7c5b5.

3GPP. 2017. "Industry Support for 3GPP NR Announce- ment." Press release, December 21. http://www.3gpp.org /news-events/3gpp-news/1931-industry_pr_5g.

Uptime Institute. 2012. "Data Center Site Infrastructure Tier Standard: Topology." http://www.gpxglobal.net/wp-content /uploads/2012/10/TIERSTANDARD_Topology_120801.pdf.

van Zyl, Gareth. 2014. "MTN Unveils Africa's First Solar Data Centre Cooling System." *ITWeb Africa*, July 10. http://www .itwebafrica.com/cloud/517-south-africa/233194-mtn -unveils-africas-first-solar-data-centre-cooling-system.

Vector. 2017. "Operational Performance for the 9 Months Ended 31 March 2017." Market release, April 26. https://www.vector.co.nz /news/operational-performance-for-the-9-months-ended-31.

Verge, Jason. 2015. "PLDT Building Eighth Philippines Data Center for $29m." Data Center Knowledge, April 28. http:// www.datacenterknowledge.com/archives/2015/04/28/pldt -building-eighth-philippines-data-center-29m.

Williams, Chris, Davide Strusani, David Vincent, and David Kovo. 2016. "The Economic Impact of Next-Generation Mobile Servi- ces: How 3G Connections and the Use of Mobile Data Impact GDP Growth." Chapter 1.6 in *The Global Information Tech- nology Report*. Geneva: World Economic Forum. http://www3 .weforum.org/docs/GITR/2013/GITR_Chapter1.6_2013.pdf.

Wong, Julia Carrie. 2016. "Mark Zuckerberg Accused of Abus- ing Power after Facebook Deletes 'Napalm Girl' Post." *The Guardian*, September 9. https://www.theguardian .com/technology/2016/sep/08/facebook-mark-zuckerberg -napalm-girl-photo-vietnam-war.

World Bank. 2017. *Doing Business 2017: Equal Opportunity for All.* Washington, DC: World Bank. http://www.doingbusiness.org /reports/global-reports/doing-business-2017.

World Bank Group. 2018. *Africa's Pulse*, no. 17 (April). https:// www.openknowledge.worldbank.org/handle/10986/29667.

Zenith Media. Various years. *Advertising Expenditure Forecasts.* London: Zenith Media.

Chapter 3

Better Data for Doing Good: Responsible Use of Big Data and Artificial Intelligence

Introduction

The data universe is ever expanding, as chapter 2 illustrates. In fact, it is estimated to double in size every two years (EMC Corporation 2014) with some 2.5 quintillion bytes of information being generated daily (Kapoor 2017). Because we increasingly use digital devices to communicate, buy and sell goods, transfer money, search for information on the internet, and share our lives on social networks, we leave digital trails or "digital exhaust." A growing amount of digital data is thus being generated as a by-product of our daily lives, but also through the increasing digitization of content and the spread of the Internet of Things. This growing volume of data is driving the development of big data analytics and artificial intelligence (AI), the subjects of this chapter.

The chapter describes opportunities for harnessing the value of big data and AI for social good, and how new families of AI algorithms now make it possible to obtain actionable insights automatically and at scale. Beyond internet business or commercial applications, multiple examples already exist of how big data and AI can help us achieve our shared development objectives, such as the 2030 Agenda for Sustainable Development[1] and the Sustainable Development Goals (SDGs).[2] But ethical frameworks need to be developed in line with increased uptake of these new technologies—any discussion of ethics is not limited to the privacy of the data, but also relates to the impact and consequences of using data and algorithms—or failing to use them.

Public recognition is growing that AI simultaneously creates unprecedented opportunities for societal benefit and grave risks to human rights—we are thus at a critical juncture in the evolution of these technologies. We must seize the opportunity to shape future use as a force for good, ensuring that the technologies are leveraged in ways that address inequalities and avoid widening the digital divide.

The big data revolution

As chapter 1 notes, the concept of big data typically describes data sets so large, or so complex, that traditional data-processing techniques often prove inadequate. The term "big data" thus captures not only the large volumes of data now available, but also the accompanying processes and technologies for collecting, storing, and analyzing it. In other words, "big data" is not just about data—"no matter how big or different it is considered to be"—it is primarily about "the analytics, the tools and methods that are used to yield insights," including the frameworks, standards, and stakeholders involved in the field and ultimately the knowledge generated (Maaroof 2015).

Although businesses increasingly are mining the digital trails we leave behind to predict consumer behavior, track emerging trends in the market, and monitor operations in real time to improve sales and profit margins, big data analytics also holds enormous potential to help understand and address pressing socioeconomic and environmental issues.

Big data can help inform policy and interventions that set us on a more sustainable development path and improve responses to humanitarian emergencies.

Innovation labs across academia, government, the international development community, civil society, and the private sector have been using big data and AI to develop a wide range of applications, from mapping discrimination against refugees in Europe (UN Global Pulse 2017a) to facilitating the rescue of migrants at sea based on shipping data (IOM 2017), detecting fires in the Indonesian rainforest (UN Global Pulse 2016), predicting food insecurity due to changing food prices via Twitter (UN Global Pulse 2014), or fighting the effects of climate change.[3] Box 3.1 describes how big data is also being used to predict and respond to disease outbreaks.

The evolution of artificial intelligence

Historically, the term "artificial intelligence" has been applied where computer systems imitate thinking or behavior that people associate with human intelligence, such as learning, problem solving, and decision-making. Modern AI comprises a rich set of subdisciplines and methods that leverage technologies such as visual, speech, and text recognition, as well as robotics.

Machine learning is one such subdiscipline. Whereas hand-coded software programs typically contain specific instructions on how to complete a task, machine learning allows a computer system to recognize patterns and make predictions. Deep learning, a subset of machine learning, goes one step further—with deep artificial neural networks, based on complex algorithms, computers can learn from large volumes of data while reaching new levels of accuracy (Touger 2018).

In sum, AI is enabling computer systems to collect, analyze, and process large amounts of data in real time to recognize patterns, make decisions, and, more significantly, to learn from said data and from their own experiences.

Meanwhile, recent advances in sensors and imaging technologies and data storage, processing, and transfer technologies, as well as complex and self-improving algorithms, to name but a few, are the range of expanding AI applications available today. AI is already incorporated in several online products, including Google search, Google Translate, and Facebook's automatic photo-tagging and translation applications. Financial companies rely on AI to produce the financial modeling that underpins their insurance, banking,

---

Box 3.1 Using big data to predict dengue fever outbreaks in Pakistan

Dengue fever is the most rapidly spreading mosquito-borne viral disease in the world. It is endemic in Pakistan, where human mobility and hospitable conditions for mosquitoes have helped it spread. Those infected typically suffer from severe illness, and mortality rates are high.

A partnership involving Telenor Research, the Harvard T.H. Chan School of Public Health, Oxford University, the U.S. Centers for Disease Control and Prevention, and the University of Peshawar used big data to anticipate and track the spread of dengue in Pakistan. The partnership leveraged anonymized call data records from 40 million Telenor Pakistan mobile subscribers during the 2013 outbreak to map the geographic spread and the epidemiological timeline of the disease. The analysis combined transmission suitability maps with estimates of seasonal dengue virus importation to generate detailed and dynamic risk maps, helping to inform national containment and epidemic preparedness in Pakistan and beyond.

More broadly, the project illustrates the potential of mobile data to reveal mobility patterns that can help accurately predict the spread of disease. The insights it generated helped predict the spread days or even weeks earlier than traditional means.

Source: Adapted from Wesolowski et al. 2015.

---

and asset management products. Moreover, leading research hospitals have started using AI tools to help medical professionals diagnose and choose the best course of treatment for their patients.

Although the current application of AI is mostly limited to internet business, digital marketing, gaming, and self-driving cars, a wealth of opportunities exist for AI methods to perform different tasks that can accelerate achievement of the SDGs and inform humanitarian practice. Box 3.2 describes how AI can help transform traditional sectors, such as transport.

Using big data and AI as a force for social good

AI and big data are generating new tools and applications creating actionable insights, real-time awareness, and predictive analysis on numerous topics for sustainable development and humanitarian action. More and more compelling examples illustrate the value of this technology to improve early warning systems and inform policy and programmatic response. These individual use cases

represent a small but significant innovation in learning about the world around us. Taken together, they provide new ways to detect and respond to world events, influence policy debates, and drive development, in a way that is both safe and fair (figure 3.1, table 3.1).

The following sections examine the benefits and applications of big data and AI—including for (a) speech and audio processing, (b) image recognition and geospatial analysis, and (c) text analysis. They also describe how AI is being leveraged to support the SDGs and address the emerging challenges and risks that accompany the uptake of these technologies.

Speech and audio processing

Arguably, one major achievement of big data and AI has been to facilitate real-time translation of a growing number of the world's languages. Although language translation is not an SDG *per se*, greater language and cultural understanding could help increase the efficiency and effectiveness of development efforts across all SDGs—for example, by helping to map public opinion (see box 3.3). Google and Microsoft systems, for example,

---

Box 3.2 Artificial intelligence and the transport sector

The proliferation of big data is helping to transform the transport sector. Fueled by data and connectivity, a variety of intelligent transport systems have been introduced as the sector rapidly evolves.

Alongside other disruptive technologies, such as connected vehicles and automated driving, these intelligent systems are soon expected to completely change the way people and goods are moved. Big data can be combined with predictive analytics, for example, to optimize cargo transport networks based on projected shipping demand.[a] Data exchanged among vehicles and infrastructure will soon be used to automatically optimize vehicle routes and speeds in real time, reducing congestion and emissions. In the Philippines, for example, real-time traffic data shared using open source tools is being used to optimize traffic flows in Manila and Cebu City.[b] In Indonesia, location information from GPS-stamped tweets is being used to reveal commuting statistics in the Greater Jakarta area.[c]

The potential for data-driven intelligent transport systems to transform the world's transportation systems is immense, particularly if the data is combined with new ways to link disparate data sets and creative methods to visualize data.

a. https://www.economist.com/news/briefing/21741139-will-be-bad-news-some-global-logistics-business-going-be-transformed.
b. http://www.worldbank.org/en/news/press-release/2016/04/05/philippines-real-time-data-can-improve-traffic-management-in.
c. https://www.unglobalpulse.org/projects/improving-transport-planning-with-data-analytics.

Figure 3.1 The Sustainable Development Goals

Source: United Nations.

Table 3.1 Examples of artificial intelligence applications for the Sustainable Development Goals

SDGs	Value of artificial intelligence	Case study	Risks and challenges
SDG 1: **No poverty**	Artificial intelligence (AI) can be used to monitor income and track policies to identify progress and successful practices.	**Combining satellite imagery and machine learning to predict poverty in Nigeria, Tanzania, Uganda, Malawi, and Rwanda** Jean et al. (n.d.) combined nighttime maps with high-resolution daytime satellite images to obtain estimates of household consumption and assets. Using survey and satellite data from five African countries—Malawi, Nigeria, Rwanda, Tanzania, and Uganda—the study showed how a convolutional neural network can be trained to identify image features that can explain up to 75 percent of the variation in local-level economic outcomes.	There is a risk of omitting segments of the population that cannot be captured by remote sensing signatures because of their lack of footprint or the given sociocultural context.
SDG 2: **Zero hunger**	AI can be used to maximize yields and improve agricultural practices based on multiple data sources.	**Detecting patterns in big data saves Colombian rice farmers huge losses** A project run by the International Center for Tropical Agriculture mined 10 years of weather and crop data to understand how climatic variation affects rice yields. The project fed the patterns into a computer model and predicted a drought in the region of Córdoba. The center subsequently advised the Rice Producers Federation of Colombia (FEDEARROZ) against planting in the first of two annual growing seasons. This advice saved farmers from incurring significant losses (Palmer 2014).	Overexploitation, based on local optimization, could lead to exhausted lands and lack of resources at the systemic level.
SDG 3: **Good health** **and well-being**	AI can be used to support diagnosis and personalized medical treatment.	**Revolutionizing personalized medicine using AI** Watson, IBM's "cognitive computing" platform uses natural language processing to efficiently and quickly sort through millions of journal articles, government listings of clinical trials, and other existing data sources to help diagnose patients and provide personalized treatment plans. University of Tokyo doctors reported that the artificial intelligence diagnosed a 60-year-old woman's rare form of leukemia that had been incorrectly identified months earlier in less than 10 minutes (IBM 2018).	Overpersonalized medicine could lead to abuse from the insurance industry and other stakeholders based on private personal information.

(continued next page)

Table 3.1 Examples of artificial intelligence applications for the Sustainable Development Goals *(continued)*

SDGs	Value of artificial intelligence	Case study	Risks and challenges
SDG 4: Quality education	AI can be used to tailor the delivery of education based on each student's needs and capabilities.	**Detecting dyslexia in children in Spain** Ten percent of the population has dyslexia, a neurological learning disability that affects reading and writing but does not affect general intelligence. Children with dyslexia can learn coping strategies to deal with its negative effects. Unfortunately, in most cases dyslexia is detected too late for effective intervention. Change Dyslexia is a project that uses cutting edge scientifically based computer games, such as Dytective Test and DytectiveU, that screen and support dyslexia at large scale (Change Dyslexia 2018).	There is the danger that harmful media can be easily accessed by children. For example, the use of YouTube Kids videos optimized with AI and bots that create long, repetitive, and sometimes frightening videos meant to keep children entertained for as long as possible (Robertson 2017).
SDG 5: Gender equality	AI can help correct for gender bias in insights derived from big data and nontraditional data sources.	**Mapping indicators of female welfare at high spatial resolution in Kenya, Nigeria, Tanzania, Bangladesh, and Haiti** A project by Flowminder and WorldPop used geo-located cluster data from the Demographic and Health surveys on rates of literacy, stunting, and use of modern contraception methods to produce high-resolution spatial gender-disaggregated maps, using predictive modeling techniques. The study focused on three countries in Sub-Saharan Africa (Kenya, Nigeria, and Tanzania), one country in South Asia (Bangladesh), and one country from the Western hemisphere (Haiti) (Bosco et al. 2017).	AI applications are at risk of reinforcing existing gender biases present in the data used to train the algorithms.
SDG 6: Clean water and sanitation	AI can predict consumption patterns from sensor data to optimize water and sanitation provision.	**Monitoring coastal water quality in real time in Singapore** Project Neptune is a real-time monitoring and prediction system strategically deployed around Singapore's coastline. The system integrates hydrodynamic and water quality modeling into a forecasting framework that forms the backbone of a central operational management system. Eight specially outfitted buoys act as miniature labs, collecting data on pollutants, including oil and nutrients, and send live updates to the authorities on how they could spread (NUSDeltares 2014).	AI (or simple malware) can be used to attack or disable critical public infrastructure by means of remote warfare.
SDG 7: Affordable and clean energy	AI can be used to make existing infrastructure more intelligent and energy efficient.	**Preventing power supply failures in domestic railway networks in India** Aiming to reduce the risk of signal failure, Indian Railways has trialed remote condition monitoring of the power supply systems, leveraging AI to predict possible outages. The measure is set to be rolled out on two sections of the Western and South-Western railway network (Economic Times 2017).	As noted above, critical network infrastructures may be subject to cybersecurity threats.
SDG 8: Decent work and economic growth	AI can be used to optimize recruitment for both employers and jobseekers.	**Optimizing online job searches** LinkedIn, a well-known business- and employment-oriented social networking service, uses AI and big data to help recruiters automate much of the candidate screening process. The tool is also integrated in different applicant tracking systems and, for example, automatically synchronizes with the different open jobs, ranking candidates against them (LinkedIn 2017).	If algorithms learn hiring practices based on biased data that prefers, for example, Caucasian names rather than others, it can make biased hiring decisions.

(continued next page)

Table 3.1 Examples of artificial intelligence applications for the Sustainable Development Goals *(continued)*

SDGs	Value of artificial intelligence	Case study	Risks and challenges
SDG 9: Industry, innovation and infrastructure	AI can be used to automate and eliminate rote or routine work, freeing up labor to focus on more creative tasks.	**Speeding up toy production in Denmark** A factory in Denmark uses autonomous robots and precision machines to make 36,000 Lego pieces per minute, or 2.16 million pieces every hour.[a]	AI will transform and could eliminate some jobs. McKinsey estimates that some 60 percent of all jobs will see a third of their activities automated (McKinsey Global Institute 2017).
SDG 10: Reduced inequalities	AI can support translation of less-known languages to ensure all voices are accounted for in decision-making processes.	**Accelerating development in Uganda with speech recognition technology** UN Global Pulse and the Stellenbosch University in South Africa used machine learning to develop speech-to-text technology to filter the content of public radio broadcasts for less-known languages spoken in Uganda. Once converted into text, the information can reveal sentiment around topics relevant for sustainable development (UN Global Pulse 2017b).	Advances in robotics and AI could increase inequality within societies, further entrenching the divide between rich and poor.
SDG 11: Sustainable cities and communities	AI can measure traffic in real time, monitor commuting statistics, or improve transportation services.	**Inferring commuting statistics in Indonesia with Twitter** Some estimates for the Greater Jakarta area put the population at more than 30 million. In response to the needs of the authorities, UN Global Pulse—Pulse Lab Jakarta initiated a project to test whether location information from social media on mobile devices could reveal commuting patterns in the area. The results of the research confirmed that geo-located tweets have the potential to fill current information gaps in official commuting statistics (UN Global Pulse 2017c).	AI may lead to cascading failures of interconnected systems in smart cities. Failures in machine learning algorithms need to be accommodated in urban emergency planning.[b]
SDG 12: Responsible consumption and production	AI can improve efficiency of recycling processes, which can eliminate waste and improve yields.	**Supporting smart recycling in the United States with dumpster diving robots** Spider-like robotic arms, guided by cameras and artificial intelligence, are helping to make municipal recycling facilities run more efficiently in the United States. Through deep learning technology, robotic sorters use a vision system to see the material, AI to think and identify each item, and a robotic arm to pick up specific items. The technology could help make recycling systems more effective and profitable (O'Conner 2017).	AI can also be used to increase the scale of extractive or manufacturing industries, creating a larger environmental footprint over time.
SDG 13: Climate action	AI and climate science can help researchers identify previously unknown atmospheric processes and rank climate models.	**Predicting road flooding for climate mitigation in Senegal** Using data from mobile operator Orange, a team from the Georgia Institute of Technology developed a framework to improve the resilience of road networks in Senegal to flooding, including recommendations on how to prioritize road improvements given a limited budget. The results showed how roads are being used, how they are damaged, and how policy makers can allocate budget in the most efficient way to repair them (Data for Climate Action 2017).	Heavy computation required to power AI may lead to increased energy costs (Lee 2017).

(continued next page)

Table 3.1 Examples of artificial intelligence applications for the Sustainable Development Goals *(continued)*

SDGs	Value of artificial intelligence	Case study	Risks and challenges
SDG 14: Life below water	AI can help detect, track, and predict the movement patterns of vessels engaged in illegal fishing.	**Supporting sustainable legal fishing in Indonesia** Indonesia and Global Fishing Watch—a partnership between Google, Oceana, and SkyTruth—are cooperating to deliver a vessel monitoring system for all Indonesian-flagged fishing vessels and generate data that is publicly available. The project aims to promote transparency in the fishing industry (Global Fishing Watch 2018).	The data collected might be incomplete, as some vessels may be undetectable when switching off their transmitters.
SDG 15: Life on land	AI can be used to map and protect wildlife on land using computer vision systems.	**Identifying, counting, and describing wild animals in camera-trap images in Tanzania** The University of Minnesota Lion Project deployed 225 camera traps, across 1,125 square kilometers, in Serengeti National Park to evaluate spatial and temporal dynamics. The cameras accumulated some 99,241 camera-trap days, producing 1.2 million pictures between 2010 and 2013. Members of the general public classified these images via a citizen-science website. The project then applied an algorithm to aggregate the classifications to investigate multi-species dynamics in the local ecosystem (Swanson et al. 2015).	Monitoring technologies can be used by poachers just as easily as conservationists.
SDG 16: Peace, justice and strong institutions	AI can reduce discrimination and corruption and drive broad access to e-government.	**Turning information into knowledge and action in Estonia** In Estonia, government services—legislation, voting, education, justice, health care, banking, taxes, policing, and so on—have been digitally linked across one platform, "wiring up" the nation. Estonia is also exploring ways to leverage AI to improve e-government and other public services (e-Estonia 2017).	Citizen monitoring could be misused to repress political practices (such as voting, demonstrations).
SDG 17: Partnerships for the Goals	AI should be a public good.	**Leveraging partnerships to improve AI for global good** Multisectoral collaboration is essential for the safe, ethical, and beneficial development of AI. The Partnership on AI[c] represents a collection of companies and nonprofits that have committed to sharing best practices and communicating openly about the benefits and risks of AI research. Another example is the annual "AI for Good Global Summit"[d] organized by the International Telecommunication Union, the UN's specialized agency for information and communication technologies.	Collaboration must also result in action.

Note: AI = artificial intelligence; SDG = Sustainable Development Goal.

a. https://www.youtube.com/watch?v=whv-krWnq0g.

b. For example, mapping apps were reportedly directing people fleeing the California wildfires in Los Angeles, in 2017, to areas that were exposed (Price 2017).

c. https://www.partnershiponai.org/partners/.

d. https://www.itu.int/en/ITU-T/AI/Pages/201706-default.aspx.

are now able to translate over a hundred languages (Li 2016). Also, new systems have been developed that perform real-time translations—such as a Skype system that can translate voice calls into 10 different languages in real time (Caughill 2017).

Early models of machine translation used statistical methods that translated words based on a short sequence, that is, within the context of several words before and after the target word, which did not always work for long and complex sentences.[4] New neural network architectures,

Radio remains a primary source of information for communities in many parts of the world, particularly in remote rural areas where coverage and access to other forms of connectivity is limited. Radio is also an accessible medium for the millions who remain illiterate.

In Uganda, where a majority of the population lives in rural areas, radio is a vibrant platform for community discussion, information sharing, and news broadcasting. Radio talk shows and dial-in discussions are popular forums for voicing local needs, concerns, and opinions.

UN Global Pulse collaborated with Stellenbosch University in South Africa to develop speech-recognition technology to automatically convert these radio broadcasts into text for several of the languages spoken in Uganda, including English, Luganda, Acholi, Lugbara, and Rutooro. "Radio mining" consisted of two automated software stages and two human analysis stages. This semi-automated approach allowed a relatively small team of analysts to process many audio recordings quickly and affordably.

Several projects were piloted with UN partners to understand the value of talk radio to provide information on topics relevant to the Sustainable Development Goals, such as health care service delivery, response to disease outbreaks, and the efficiency of public awareness-raising radio campaigns, among others.

Source: Adapted from UN Global Pulse 2017b.

such as long short-term memory, have drastically improved efficiency. Such systems can now learn from millions of examples and are able to translate whole sentences at a time, rather than word by word (Turovsky 2016).

Computer vision, image analysis, and geospatial data

Accurate population information is critical for authorities to plan and deliver quality public services and coordinate crisis-relief efforts. However, collecting related data traditionally is a long-standing challenge for development practitioners and policy makers. For example, gathering national household survey data on poverty is typically time-consuming and expensive, requiring elaborate data collection and analysis techniques. This exercise is particularly challenging in fragile states, where limited capacity and security concerns typically hinder data collection and processing. In this setting, for example, satellite imagery has been used to gain an overview of population density and assess poverty and access to energy—covered by SDG 1 and SDG 7 (see boxes 3.4 and 3.5).

In the health sector—covered by SDG 3—current advances in medical imaging and computer analysis of tumors can complement and refine radiologists' analysis. Mobile phone call records have also been combined with satellite data to build dynamic population maps and estimate cross-border flows of migrants to enable development actors to track the spread of disease. This technique was leveraged in southern Africa to map the movements of cross-border communities to better understand malaria infections patterns (Rango and Vespe 2017).

In the environmental field—SDGs 12, 13, 14, and 15—AI-assisted analysis of satellite imagery can be used to monitor damage to coastal areas due to floods or typhoons, or drought-affected areas, or the retreat of wetlands or encroaching land use in deltas or river basins. Combined with meteorological models and large data sets on changes in ocean temperature and currents, such mapping can help improve forecasting and early warning systems of future major weather events. Moreover, GPS data has been used to analyze traffic patterns to reduce pollution (see box 3.6).

Another AI application getting considerable attention is automated or self-driving cars—a potential solution for optimizing transportation in ways that can minimize car accidents. Debate is ongoing about what a fully automated car really is, but considerable progress has been made toward solving problems of visual recognition, object identification, and reaction processing, which are critical to this endeavor.

Box 3.4 Estimating population counts and poverty in Afghanistan and Sudan

In Afghanistan, the United Nations Population Fund and the UN Country Team collaborated with Flowminder, an organization that collects, aggregates, and analyzes anonymous mobile, satellite, and household survey data to generate population maps. The project used survey data, geographic information systems, and satellite imagery data to estimate populations in areas with no such data.

In Sudan, the United Nations Development Programme used satellite data to estimate poverty by studying changing nighttime energy consumption. The team used data pulled from nighttime satellite imagery, analyzing illumination values over two years, in conjunction with electric power consumption data from the national electricity authority. The study was also informed by desk research, including similar World Bank work in Kenya and Rwanda. Electricity consumption was used as a proxy indicator for income, as poorer households were assumed to be lower energy consumers. The exercise demonstrated how satellite imagery can help measure poverty.

Sources: Rango and Vespe 2017; UNDP and UN Global Pulse 2016.

Box 3.5 Mapping energy access in India

Satellite night-light data has also been leveraged in India. A team from the University of Michigan, the U.S. National Oceanic and Atmospheric Administration, and the World Bank Group's Energy and Extractives Global Practice analyzed the daily light signatures of more than 600,000 villages from 1993 to 2013 (see map B3.5.1).

Map B3.5.1 Night lights in India

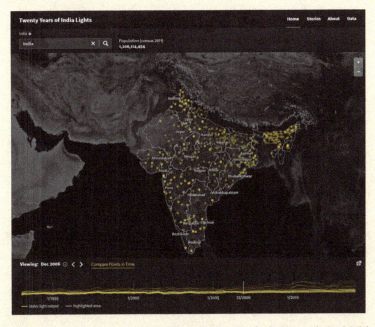

Source: World Bank, Energy and Extractives Global Practice, India Lights Platform (http://india.nightlights.io/).

(continued next page)

Electrification trends were visualized on NightLights.io, an open-source platform for processing big data in a scalable and systematic way. The platform features an application programming interface that enables technical partners to query light output. And its interactive maps allow users to explore light output trends. Through the project, the research team gained a high-level overview of rural electrification, compared villages and plot trends, and shared data, which can help inform government policy.[a]

Source: Gaba and Sánchez-Andrade Nuño 2016.

a. The platform can be freely accessed and explored at http://india.nightlights.io/#/about.

Box 3.6 Cleaning Mexico City's air with big data and climate policy

Mexico City's congestion, among the world's worst, worsens local air quality. City dwellers are exposed to twice the recommended level of ozone and fine particulate matter (PM2.5), as advised by national standards and according to 2016 data, resulting in some 10,850 annual deaths. A team of researchers from the University of California, Berkeley, and the Instituto Nacional de Ecología y Cambio Climático in Mexico used data from Waze, a GPS navigation software, to evaluate various transport electrification options based on their ability to reduce urban air pollution and emissions—including (a) the electrification of the entire city taxi fleet, (b) the electrification of public transit buses, and (c) the electrification of all light-duty vehicles.

The team first measured the number, location, and duration of traffic jams throughout the city, estimating related emissions using the MOVES-Mexico model. The team then used data from Google's "popular times" function to map urban population movement.

Using this information, the team was able to identify the best policy options and optimal locations for electric vehicle charging stations.

Source: Data for Climate Action 2017.

Building on humble beginnings and minor innovations (including cruise control, assisted steering, lane assist, automatic braking, and "Traffic Jam Assist"), the race toward a fully automated car is now underway (box 3.7).

Text mining and text analysis

Also known as text mining, text analytics is the science of turning unstructured text into structured data. Text analytics is focused on extracting key pieces of information from conversations. By understanding the language, the context, and how language is used in everyday conversations, text analytics uncovers the "who"

of the conversation, the "what" or the "buzz" of the conversation, "how" people are feeling, and "why" the conversation is happening. Conversations are categorized and discussion topics identified.

The technology is being leveraged, among other things, to support agricultural development and build food security—covered by SDG 2. Kudu, a mobile auction market application, is using text analysis algorithms to match farmers looking to sell their produce with suitable market traders. The system allows any farmer or trader to send a message by phone. Once matched, compatible buyers and sellers are notified. Kudu not only limits unnecessary travel and

Human error causes about 90 percent of all car accidents. Artificial intelligence (AI) and autonomous driving might therefore help reduce accidents and save lives. Self-driving cars have to identify, assess, evaluate, and respond to fast-changing circumstances, and predict likely events in real time. A fully automated car has to master vehicle dynamics, control systems, and sensor optimization. For example, detecting pedestrians from images or video is a very specific image-classification problem.

Driverless cars require robust data capacity for image processing and recognition. Navigation and mapping data is also essential, with GPS coordinates used extensively. Mercedes, BMW, and Audi purchased the mapping business Here from Nokia for US$2 billion; Here combines "static" mapping data taken from cars with 3D cameras with live information supplied by a network of connected devices, including cars (Bell 2015). In January 2016, Volkswagen partnered with Mobileye, a technology company that develops vision-based advanced driver-assistance systems, to produce its real-time image-processing cameras and mapping service for driverless cars. Ford became the first manufacturer to road test a fully autonomous car in snow on public roads in March 2016 after working with researchers from the University of Michigan to create an algorithm recognizing snow and rain (Ford 2016). Ford has already tested autonomous Fusion cars on public roads in the U.S. states of Arizona, California, and Michigan.

Despite these groundbreaking developments, the move toward autonomous driving is not without its problems. Many worry that a car-centric vision detracts from more sustainable solutions related to public transportation and urban design (covered by Sustainable Development Goal 11). Driverless vehicles are also likely to wipe out millions of jobs, including taxi drivers, couriers, and truck drivers, something new policies must address urgently. Moreover, legal frameworks will need to keep pace and be redesigned. Although a few countries are moving to issue new legal frameworks for autonomous driving, significant legal gaps remain.

dependency on intermediaries, but encourages competition by overcoming critical information gaps. The application was developed by the AI Research Group, which is specialized in the application of AI to problems in the developing world and operates out of the College of Computing and Information Sciences at Makerere University in Kampala, Uganda.[5]

Analysis of text from Twitter feeds has also been used to track food prices in real time in Indonesia. UN Global Pulse worked with the Ministry of National Development Planning and the World Food Programme to "nowcast" food prices based on Twitter data. The outcome was a statistical model of daily price indicators for four commodities: beef, chicken, onion, and chili. When the modeled prices were compared with official food prices, the forecast and actual prices were closely correlated, demonstrating that near real-time social media signals can serve as a proxy for daily food prices (UN Global Pulse 2014).

Similar techniques are being used to analyze a host of other development issues. For example, the ability to monitor public sentiment toward policy measures in real time, via social media, can provide critical information on the impact of policy and how it is playing out in practice, especially for vulnerable groups or households (box 3.8). Data from social media can also help estimate the number of expats around the world (box 3.9).

As mentioned earlier, conducting household surveys is often expensive. New approaches such as monitoring social media could help address data gaps in developing economies. Moreover, these approaches may capture marginalized or migrating communities not always accounted for by traditional means such as national censuses (Rango and Vespe 2017).

Box 3.8 Monitoring public sentiment about policy reforms using social media in El Salvador

In April 2011, the government of El Salvador removed a countrywide subsidy on liquid petroleum gas, the most common domestic cooking fuel. Instead of subsidizing prices at point of sale, eligible households were given an income transfer. The reform triggered considerable public debate and controversy.

UN Global Pulse and the World Bank teamed up to investigate whether social media signals from Twitter could be used to understand public perceptions and social dynamics surrounding the fuel subsidy reform, specifically reactions and concerns about political partisanship, the level of information reaching communities about the reform, and trust in government commitment to deliver the subsidy. A taxonomy of keywords was developed to filter Twitter for relevant content. Regional experts were consulted to ensure slang words and synonyms were included in the taxonomy. Tweets were then filtered to assess relevance and isolate content originating from El Salvador.

The study suggests that social media analysis, using big data and AI, can help inform policy implementation, as the sentiment observed was similar to public opinion measured by household surveys.

Source: Adapted from UN Global Pulse 2015.

Box 3.9 Shedding light on migration patterns using social media information

Data from social media can be used to help estimate migrant populations. For example, studies based on Facebook data yield estimates of approximately 214 million "expats" in the world (people stating that they live in a country other than their self-reported "home country"), close to the 2017 estimated total of 258 million international migrants globally.

Among the issues surrounding the use of social media data to estimate migrant populations are the difficulty in defining who an international migrant is, selection bias, and the reliability of self-reported information. But scholars are working on reducing selection bias via model fitting and results are promising.

Source: Adapted from Rango and Vespe 2017.

From design to responsible use: Ethical challenges with using big data and AI

Although we are only scratching the surface of what is possible in the new age of big data and AI, and how they can be leveraged for social good, we also need to grapple with both the unintended risks and malicious use of the same technology. These benefits and looming risks were aptly articulated by the UN Secretary-General at the 2017 "AI for Good Global Summit":

We face a new frontier, with advances moving at warp speed. Artificial intelligence can help analyze enormous volumes of data, which in turn can improve predictions, prevent crimes and help governments better serve people. But there are also serious challenges, and ethical issues at stake. There are real concerns about cyber security, human rights and privacy. . . The implications for development are enormous. Developing countries can gain from the benefits of AI, but they also face the highest risk of being left behind.

Algorithm-based systems, powered by big data and AI, increasingly both learn from and autonomously interact with their environments, as well as one another.

This tends to generate behavioral patterns that cannot always be predicted or explained. Where this evolution in AI will ultimately take us is not yet clear. Some raise the risk of autonomous weapons or viruses targeting individuals with a particular defective DNA trait as one frightening scenario. And rising concerns about the malicious use of AI, for instance, for profiling, merits a stronger ethical governance and regulatory framework that covers how related methods are developed and deployed. The risk of unintended consequences of AI should be accounted for at each stage of innovation, beginning with design.

Technologies and algorithms by themselves have no intrinsic morality—however, technology can be used for good or bad depending on how it is employed. Looking at existing technologies, ethical considerations need to address questions such as what life-and-death decisions self-driving cars make. Although privacy norms have been long established to protect personal data from misuse and ensure individual privacy in the digital world, ethics has become an additional tool in AI applications used to protect fundamental human rights and help make decisions in areas where law has no clear-cut answers. The UN Special Rapporteur on the right to privacy recommends formal consultation mechanisms be instituted "including ethics committees, with professional, community and other organizations and citizens to protect against the erosion of rights and identify sound practices" (Cannataci 2017). A recent example in which ethics and moral obligations of data handling were included in an official UN document is the "Guidance Note on Big Data for the achievement of the 2030 Agenda" adopted by the UN Development Group (UNDG 2017). The note, the first official document in the UN on big data and privacy, stresses the importance of ensuring that data ethics is included as part of standard operating procedures for data governance (box 3.10).

Data ethics should be treated holistically using a consistent and inclusive framework that considers a diverse set of outcomes instead of an ad hoc approach that only accounts for limited applications (Floridi and Taddeo 2016). Such mechanisms include codified data ethics principles or codes of conduct, ethical impact assessments, ethical training for researchers, and ethical review boards.

Privacy impact assessments, in general, allow developers and organizations to effectively assess the risks posed to privacy by big data and AI, thereby ensuring compliance with privacy requirements, identifying mitigation measures, and effectively classifying the impacts of data and algorithm use. Including issues of ethics and human rights in any impact assessment, including a privacy impact assessment, could prove more effective than developing a separate analysis or ethical review framework.

For example, UN Global Pulse builds ethical considerations into its data practices by conducting a "risks, harms, and benefits assessment," which may help identify anticipated or actual ethical and human rights issues that may occur during a data innovation project (UN Global Pulse 2018). The assessment considers the proportionality of potential benefits compared to risks of harm from data use, as well as risk of harm from the data not being used. If the risks outweigh the benefits, the project does not proceed. In its "Guide to Personal Data Protection and Privacy," the World Food Programme also builds ethics into its procedures through the application of humanitarian principles and risk assessments (WFP 2015). Although ethics may not have clear-cut rules, when assessing the risk of harm along with the benefits "any potential risks and harms should not be excessive in relation to the [likely] positive impacts of data use" (UNDG 2017, 5).

Incorporating *privacy by design* is also crucial for innovation applications that operate with limited human supervision. The rapidly developing nature of AI algorithms can give rise to algorithmic bias and unverified results. Similar to privacy by design is the concept of *AI ethics by design*, which suggests seven principles, including recommendations to proactively identify security risks by using tools such as the privacy impact assessment to minimize potential harm. In addition, ensuring oversight of the entire data innovation process, from design to use, is vital to securing true incorporation of ethics into AI systems (Cavoukian 2017).

Moreover, accountability and transparency are critical ethical principles that must accompany any AI innovation project (UNDG 2017). "[T]ransparency builds trust in the system, by providing a simple way for the user to understand what the system is doing and why" (IEEE 2016). To maintain transparency, the Institute of Electrical and Electronics Engineers recommends developing new standards that describe measurable, testable levels of transparency so systems can be objectively assessed and

1. LAWFUL, LEGITIMATE AND FAIR USE

Data should be obtained, collected, analysed or otherwise used through lawful, legitimate and fair means, taking into account the interests of those individuals whose data is being used.

2. PURPOSE SPECIFICATION, USE LIMITATION AND PURPOSE COMPATIBILITY

Any data use must be compatible or otherwise relevant, and not excessive in relation to the purposes for which it was obtained.

3. RISK MITIGATION AND RISKS, HARMS AND BENEFITS ASSESSMENT

A risks, harms and benefits assessment that accounts for data protection and data privacy as well as ethics of data use should be conducted before a new or substantially changed use of data (including its purpose) is undertaken.

4. SENSITIVE DATA AND SENSITIVE CONTEXTS

Stricter standards of data protection should be employed while obtaining, accessing, collecting, analysing or otherwise using data on vulnerable populations and persons at risk, children and young people or any other data used in sensitive contexts.

5. DATA SECURITY

Robust technical and organizational safeguards and procedures should be implemented to ensure data management throughout the data lifecycle and prevent any unauthorized use, disclosure or breach of personal data.

6. DATA RETENTION AND DATA MINIMIZATION

Data access, analysis or other use should be kept to the minimum amount necessary to fulfill the purpose of data use.

7. DATA QUALITY

All data-related activities should be designed, carried out, reported and documented with an adequate level of quality and transparency.

8. OPEN DATA, TRANSPARENCY AND ACCOUNTABILITY

Appropriate governance and accountability mechanisms should be established to monitor compliance with relevant law, including privacy laws and the highest standards of confidentiality, moral and ethical conduct with regard to data use.

9. DUE DILIGENCE FOR THIRD PARTY COLLABORATORS

Third party collaborators engaging in data use should act in compliance with relevant laws, including privacy laws as well as the highest standards of confidentiality and moral and ethical conduct.

Source: Adapted from the UN Development Group 2017. See the full version at https://undg.org/wp-content/uploads/2017/11/UNDG_BigData_final_web.pdf.

the level of compliance can be determined. Although it is harder and harder to keep algorithms transparent because of heavily interlinked and layered processes of algorithmic programming, the AI ethics by design approach suggests that ensuring the transparency and accountability of algorithms is essential to determining the intended outputs and preventing algorithmic bias.

The overall data ethics program may also include recurring data ethics reviews at every critical juncture, such as review boards. A similar approach already exists in research institutions and is usually referred to as internal review boards. For example, in their published procedures for ethical standards regarding data collection, the United Nations Children's Fund (UNICEF) adheres to mechanisms for review such as internal and external review boards as well as the basic ethics training for researchers. Any UNICEF project involving surveys, focus groups, case studies, physical procedures, games, or diet and nutritional studies is subject to ethical review (UNICEF 2015).

A stakeholder-inclusive approach that features "the proactive inclusion of users" is also desirable. "Their interaction will increase trust and overall reliability of these systems" (IEEE 2016). "[T]he context of data use" should also always be considered, thus requiring human intervention, and at times, context-specific expertise—such as the presence of a humanitarian expert during a humanitarian response or of a transportation planning expert in a project that looks at transportation policy (UNDG 2017).

Finally, ethical approaches to AI should be human-rights-centric, incorporating substantive, procedural, and remedial rights (McGregor 2017). Just as misuse of AI may lead to harm, nonuse of AI may allow preventable harm to occur. Decisions to use or not use applications of AI can infringe on fundamental rights. As suggested by the UN Special Rapporteur on the right to privacy in his recent report to the UN General Assembly, "commitment to one right should not detract from the importance and protection of another right. Taking rights in conjunction wherever possible is healthier than taking rights in opposition to each other" (Cannataci 2016, 6, 10). But undoubtedly, incorporating ethics into every stage of project design and implementation of AI can potentially mitigate harm and maximize positive impact of rapidly developing new technologies, ensuring they are used for social benefit.

A way forward: Harnessing big data and AI to "leave no one behind"

This chapter has detailed a handful of examples of the many innovative applications of big data and AI being used to inform sustainable development and humanitarian work globally (see table 3.1 in particular), illustrating the value of this technology for development actors.

The pervasive nature of big data and the rapidly evolving capabilities of AI hold tremendous promise for social impact and can drive transformation across many domains, ranging from health, to food security, to jobs, and action on climate. Scope therefore exists to expand use of this technology beyond current applications, leveraging big data and AI in new ways that help us achieve the 2030 Agenda. National and international development actors should prioritize operational integration of these digital innovations into policy and practice. Doing so will allow them to craft more agile and responsive programming, to support anticipatory approaches to managing risk, and to find new ways to measure social impact. However, mainstream, scaled adoption by policy makers and communities themselves still faces systemic barriers and pervasive inertia.

Given their broad applicability, big data and AI necessitate new forms of interinstitutional relationships to leverage data and computational resources, human talent, and decision-making capacity. The capabilities of a diverse set of stakeholders can enable the integration of data innovation into ongoing policy processes rather than one-time policy decisions (Maaroof 2015).

Moreover, as adoption of big data and AI increases and the technology evolves, so do the potential risks and issues that need to be resolved. Many question the suitable application of this technology, including malicious use, and highlight the risk of unintended consequences in this rapidly evolving field, where policy makers may struggle to keep pace. Although both the supply of and demand for data are expanding at "warp speed," the data ecosystem, as we know it, is still embryonic—with many advanced potential applications still more theory than practice. As new capabilities and data sources are applied for good—whether to create smarter public services, better early warning systems, or more effective responses to crises—development actors must pause to consider the potential for harm that may arise, for example, from inadequate privacy protection.

To date, no standards exist for the anonymization and sharing of insights from big data in priority industries such as financial services, e-commerce, and mobile telecommunications—although the latter has done work to develop such standards. At the same time, as noted, nonuse of these new capabilities and data sources represents at least as great a risk of harm to the public as that potentially arising from inadequate privacy protections. New frameworks are needed that go beyond privacy and ensure accountability and responsible use and reuse of data for the public good. Principles such as responsibility, accuracy, auditability, and fairness should be core concepts that guide the development of algorithms and AI. The "society-in-the-loop" algorithm concept, for example, proposes to embed the "general will" into an algorithmic social contract in which citizens oversee algorithmic decision-making that affects them.

Developing countries may have the most to gain from the use of new data sources and tools. However, without thoughtful application and critical complements they may also stand to lose the most. To reap the societal benefits of AI—including expected improvements to productivity and innovation—countries must have access to the data, tools, and human expertise necessary to support their application, as well as viable plans to address the likely displacement of workers. The availability of data is to a large degree a by-product of digitization, an area in which developing countries lag far behind. There can be no mass digitization without universal and affordable access to broadband. According to International Telecommunication Union (ITU) statistics, some 3.8 billion people, or just over half the world's population, were still lacking access to the internet in 2017 (ITU 2017).

The way forward must be inclusive. For the big data and AI revolution to benefit the most vulnerable people, current AI research roadmaps must increase attention to methodologies that can work in data-scarce environments, that can be adapted quickly and with few examples—as in crisis scenarios—and that can work with incomplete or missing data (such as "one-shot learning"). Need is also urgent for bridging gender inequalities in big data. More effort must be made to train younger generations, women and men, to ensure gender equality and the inclusiveness of ethnic groups in shaping AI.

As the field of data science accelerates, countries must create robust big data and AI strategies to prevent growing inequalities in access and use of these technologies. In digital advertising, for example, where many of these capabilities were incubated, big data and AI continue to demonstrate their ability to concentrate wealth—and data—in the hands of the few and widen inequalities.

Just as misuse of AI may lead to harm, nonuse of AI may allow preventable harms to occur. The challenge is that misuse of these new tools is already rife online and real harm is being done, while the opportunity cost of failure to use them responsibly is mounting. Clearly, although achievement of the 2030 Agenda and the modernization of humanitarian practices necessitates responsible use of these new tools, it urgently requires a new, rights-centric effort by all stakeholders to ensure innovations meet community needs and no one is left behind. Undoubtedly, assessing the ethical impact of AI in addition to privacy protection measures can mitigate harm, maximize benefit, and lead to use of the new technologies as a force for good.

Notes

1. See https://sustainabledevelopment.un.org/post2015/transformingourworld.

2. See https://www.un.org/sustainabledevelopment/sustainable-development-goals/.

3. See www.dataforclimateaction.org for the Data for Climate Action challenge, an open innovation challenge to channel data science and big data from the private sector to fight climate change, organized by UN Global Pulse with the support of Western Digital Corporation and the Skoll Global Threats Fund.

4. See Microsoft Translator, "What Is Neural Network-Based Translation?" https://microsofttranslator.uservoice.com/knowledgebase/articles/1099027-what-is-neural-network-based-translation

5. See https://kudu.ug/about/.

References

Bell, M. 2015. "BMW, Audi, Daimler Buy Nokia's Mapping Unit: An Autonomous Future Is Nigh." *Car*, December 8. www.carmagazine.co.uk/car-news/industry-news/mercedes-benz/bmw-audi-and-daimler-purchase-nokias-here-system-an-autonomous-future-is-nigh/.

Bosco, Claudio, Victor Alegana, Tom Bird, Carla Pezzulo, Graeme Hornby, Alessandro Sorichetta, Jessica Steele, Cori Ruktanonchai, Nick Ruktanonchai, Erik Wetter, Linus Bengtsson, and Andrew J. Tatem. 2017. Mapping Indicators of Female Welfare at High Spatial Resolution. WorldPop Project and

Flowminder Foundation. http://www.data2x.org/wp-content/uploads/2017/02/Mapping-Indicators-of-Female-Welfare-at-High-Spatial-Resolution.pdf.

Cannataci, Joseph. 2016. "A More In-Depth Look at Open Data and Big Data." Annex 11 in *Report of the Special Rapporteur on the Right to Privacy.* A/HRC/31/64. Geneva: Office of the High Commissioner for Human Rights.

———. 2017. "Report of the Special Rapporteur on the Right to Privacy." Doc. A/72/43103. Office of the High Commissioner for Human Rights, Geneva.

Caughill, P. 2017. "Skype Can Now Translate Your Voice Calls into 10 Different Languages in Real-Time." *Futurism,* April 10. https://futurism.com/skype-can-now-translate-your-voice-calls-into-10-different-languages-in-real-time/.

Cavoukian, Ann. 2017. "Ethical Standards in Artificial Intelligence: AI Ethics by Design." Presentation to UN Global Pulse, December 13.

Change Dyslexia. 2018. "The Best Tool to Detect and Improve Dyslexia Related Skills" (in Spanish). https://www.changedyslexia.org/.

Data for Climate Action. 2017. "Grand Prize Winner: Electro-Mobility: Cleaning Mexico City's Air with Transformational Climate Policies through Big Data Pattern Analysis in Traffic and Social Mobility." http://www.dataforclimateaction.org/meet-the-winners/.

E-Estonia. 2017. "Artificial Intelligence Is the Next Step for E-Governance in Estonia." https://e-estonia.com/artificial-intelligence-is-the-next-step-for-e-governance-state-adviser-reveals/.

Economic Times. 2017. "Railways to Use Artificial Intelligence for Preventing Signal Failures." November 22. https://energy.economictimes.indiatimes.com/news/power/railways-to-use-artificial-intelligence-for-preventing-signal-failures/61747929.

EMC Corporation. 2014. "Digital Universe Invaded by Sensors." Press release, April 9. https://www.emc.com/about/news/press/2014/20140409-01.htm.

Floridi, Luciano, and Mariarosaria Taddeo. 2016. "What Is Data Ethics?" *Philosophical Transactions of the Royal Society A* 374 (2083): 20160360. http://rsta.royalsocietypublishing.org/content/roypta/374/2083/20160360.full.pdf.

Ford. 2016. "From Autonomy to Snowtonomy: How Ford Fusion Hybrid Autonomous Research Vehicle Can Navigate in Winter." https://media.ford.com/content/fordmedia/fna/us/en/news/2016/03/10/how-fusion-hybrid-autonomous-vehicle-can-navigate-in-winter.html.

Gaba, K. M., and B. Sánchez-Andrade Nuño. 2016. "Eyes in the Sky Help Track Rural Electrification." World Bank blog, January 21. http://blogs.worldbank.org/energy/eyes-sky-help-track-rural-electrification.

Global Fishing Watch. 2018. "Vessel Monitoring Data: Indonesia." http://globalfishingwatch.org/indonesia-vms.

IBM (International Business Machines Corporation). 2018. "IBM Watson for Genomics Helps Doctors Give Patients New Hope." https://www.ibm.com/watson/health/oncology-and-genomics/genomics/.

IEEE (Institute of Electrical and Electronics Engineers). 2016. "The IEEE Global Initiative on Ethics of Autonomous and Intelligent Systems: Ethically Aligned Design; A Vision for Prioritizing Wellbeing with Artificial Intelligence and Autonomous Systems V.1." The IEEE Global Initiative on Ethics of Autonomous and Intelligent Systems. http://standards.ieee.org/develop/indconn/ec/autonomous_systems.html.

IOM (International Organization for Migration). 2017. *Fatal Journeys: Improving Data on Missing Migrants.* Part 1, vol. 3. Geneva: IOM. https://publications.iom.int/system/files/pdf/fatal_journeys_volume_3_part_1.pdf.

ITU (International Telecommunication Union). 2017. "ICT Facts and Figures." https://www.itu.int/en/ITU-D/Statistics/Pages/facts/default.aspx.

Jean, Neal, Marshall Burke, Michael W. Xie, Matthew Davis, David B. Lobell, and Stegano Ermon. n.d. "Sustainability and Artificial Intelligence Lab: Combining Satellite Imagery and Machine Learning to Predict Poverty." Stanford University. http://sustain.stanford.edu/predicting-poverty.

Kapoor, S. 2017. "Artificial Intelligence: Re-imagining Big Data's Applicability." CXOtoday.com, July 17. www.cxotoday.com/story/artificial-intelligence-re-imagining-big-datas-applicability/.

Lee, T. B. 2017. *Bitcoin's Insane Energy Consumption, Explained.* https://arstechnica.com/tech-policy/2017/12/bitcoins-insane-energy-consumption-explained/.

Li, A. 2016. "Google Translate Adds 13 New Languages Bringing Total to 103." https://9to5google.com/2016/02/17/google-translate-13-languages.

LinkedIn. 2017. "Brilent, the Intelligent Candidate Recommendation Engine." https://www.linkedin.com/pulse/brilent-intelligent-candidate-recommendation-engine-edouard-murat/.

Maaroof, Abbas. 2015. "Big Data and the 2030 Agenda for Sustainable Development." Report for UN-ESCAP. http://www.unescap.org/sites/default/files/Final%20Draft_%20stock-taking%20report_For%20Comment_301115.pdf.

McGregor, Lorna. 2017. "Ethical Development of AI." Statement at the ITU AI for Good Summit, June.

McKinsey Global Institute. 2017. "Jobs Lost, Jobs Gained: Workforce Transitions in a Time of Automation." https://www.mckinsey.com/~/media/McKinsey/Global%20Themes/Future%20of%20Organizations/What%20the%20future%20of%20work%20will%20mean%20for%20jobs%20skills%20and%20wages/MGI-Jobs-Lost-Jobs-Gained-Report-December-6-2017.ashx.

NUSDeltares. 2014. "Neptune OMS for Singapore Coastal Quality." http://www.nusdeltares.org/projects/neptune/.

O'Conner, M. C. 2017. "Dumpster Diving Robots: Using AI for Smart Recycling." *IQ*, July 5. https://iq.intel.com/dumpster-diving-robots-using-ai-for-smart-recycling/.

Palmer, N. 2014. "Cracking Patterns in Big Data Saves Colombian Rice Farmers Huge Losses." Research Program on Climate Change, Agriculture, and Food Security (CCAFS), Montpellier, France. https://ccafs.cgiar.org/research/annual-report/2014/cracking-patterns-in-big-data-saves-colombian-rice-farmers-huge-losses.

Price, R. 2017. "Mapping Apps Are Reportedly Directing People Fleeing the Southern California Wildfires to Areas That Are on Fire." *Business Insider*, December 7. http://www.businessinsider.com/la-fires-gps-apps-directing-people-areas-fire-lapd-2017-12.

Rango, M., and M. Vespe. 2017. "Big Data and Alternative Data Sources on Migration: From Case Studies to Policy Support." Summary Report, European Commission. https://bluehub.jrc.ec.europa.eu/bigdata4migration/uploads/attachments/cjdelbdgo00hnqazv3u7xi6pd-big-data-workshop-draft-summary-report.pdf.

Robertson, A. 2017. "What Makes YouTube's Surreal Kids' Videos So Creepy?" *The Verge*, November 21. https://www.theverge.com/culture/2017/11/21/16685874/kids-youtube-video-elsagate-creepiness-psychology.

Swanson, Alexandra, Margaret Kosmala, Chris Lintott, Robert Simpson, Arfon Smith, and Craig Packer. 2015. "Snapshot Serengeti, High-Frequency Annotated Camera Trap Images of 40 Mammalian Species in an African Savanna." *Nature. Scientific Data.* https://www.nature.com/articles/sdata201526.

Touger, Glenn Evan. 2018. "What's the Difference between Artificial Learning (AI), Machine Learning, and Deep Learning?" Prowesscorp, August 3. www.prowesscorp.com/whats-the-difference-between-artificial-intelligence-ai-machine-learning-and-deep-learning/.

Turovsky, Barak. 2016. "Found in Translation: More Accurate, Fluent Sentences in Google Translate." Google, November 15. https://blog.google/products/translate/found-translation-more-accurate-fluent-sentences-google-translate/.

UN Global Pulse. 2014. "Nowcasting Food Prices in Indonesia Using Social Media Signals." Global Pulse Project Series, no. 1. https://www.unglobalpulse.org/projects/nowcasting-food-prices.

———. 2015. *Using Twitter Data to Analyze Public Sentiment on Fuel Subsidy Policy Reform in El Salvador.* Global Pulse Project Series, no. 13. www.unglobalpulse.org/sites/default/files/UNGP_ProjectSeries_ElSalvador_Fuel_2015_0.pdf.

———. 2016. "Haze Gazer: A Crisis Analysis Tool." Tool Series, no. 2. http://unglobalpulse.org/sites/default/files/2-pager%20Haze%20Gazer%20-%20Feb%202017_0.pdf.

———. 2017a. "Social Media and Forced Displacement: Big Data Analytics and Machine-Learning." White paper. http://unglobalpulse.org/sites/default/files/White%20Paper%20Social%20Media%203_0.pdf.

———. 2017b. "Using Machine Learning to Analyse Radio Content in Uganda." http://unglobalpulse.org/sites/default/files/Radio%20Analysis%20Report_Preview%20%283%29.pdf.

———. 2017c. "Inferring Commuting Statistics in the Greater Jakarta Area with Twitter." https://www.unglobalpulse.org/projects/inferring-commuting-statistics-greater-jakarta-area-twitter.

———. 2018. "Data Innovation Risk Assessment Tool." Data Innovation for Development Guide. http://unglobalpulse.org/sites/default/files/Privacy%20Assessment%20Tool%20.pdf.

UNDG (United Nations Development Group). 2017. "Data Privacy, Ethics, and Protection: Guidance Note on Big Data and the Achievement of the 2030 Agenda." https://undg.org/wp-content/uploads/2017/11/UNDG_BigData_final_web.pdf.

UNDP (United Nations Development Programme) and UN Global Pulse. 2016. *A Guide to Data Innovation for Development: From Idea to Proof of Concept.* http://www.undp.org/content/undp/en/home/librarypage/development-impact/a-guide-to-data-innovation-for-development---from-idea-to-proof-.html.

UNICEF. 2015. "Procedure for Ethical Standards in Research, Evaluation, Data Collection and Analysis." CF/PD/DRP/2015-001. April 1. https://www.unicef.org/supply/files/ATTACHMENT_IV-UNICEF_Procedure_for_Ethical_Standards.PDF.

United Nations. 2015. *Transforming Our World: The 2030 Agenda for Sustainable Development.* New York: UN Publishing. https://sustainabledevelopment.un.org/post2015/transformingourworld.

Wesolowski, A., T. Qureshi, M. F. Boni, P. R. Sundsøy, M. A. Johansson, S. B. Rasheed, K. Engø-Monsen, and C. O. Buckee. 2015. "Impact of Human Mobility on the Emergence of Dengue Epidemics in Pakistan." *National Academy of Sciences* 112 (38): 11887–92.

WFP (World Food Programme). 2015. *WFP Guide to Personal Data Protection and Privacy.* Rome: WFP. https://docs.wfp.org/api/documents/e8d24e70cc11448383495caca154cb97/download/.

Chapter 4

People and Data

Introduction

How can the data revolution expand economic development opportunities for more people? Can the increasing collection, analysis, and use of data—often from individuals[1] through digital transactions or digital records of offline activities—broadly benefit those individuals and people? And what risks might arise, such as to individual privacy, and how might they be managed?

Conversations about data have become very popular: interest over time in "big data," as indicated by Google searches, for instance, has grown one-hundred-fold since 2010.[2] More data is being generated—by people and machines—and captured, processed, and transferred than ever before. Much of this is because of the increasing use of digital technologies by people and organizations globally; indeed, even most analog processes have digital components (such as a visit to a doctor's office leading to a digital drug prescription).

But while the data revolution can benefit people, this chapter proposes that the structure of data markets might be raising risks and costs to individuals. People bear many of the costs and risks of participating in data markets and, indeed, might not even be aware they are participating. The poorest also face entry barriers, and it is possible that they might not benefit from their participation even when it is possible.

The *benefits* from data include—at the most general level—the ability of data users to make better decisions using the information processed and to enjoy more convenience when interacting with organizations (for instance, easier interchange of data between platforms or service providers). The increasing use of such data by organizations, such as businesses and governments, implies the potential for faster and better decisions by these entities. This can help them improve service delivery, reduce costs and prices, or support process or product innovation, all of which would benefit the people that those organizations serve.

For example, better techniques for tracking how and where people drive their cars can inform traffic planning and management (Shu 2018). Data from people's online activities inform advertising decisions that fund the operation of many widely used internet services that are "free" at the point of use (Richter 2018). And as digital tools proliferate, individuals are increasingly able to benefit directly from access to more and new types of data and the information derived from it. People can take steps to increase their physical activity and improve their health by using digital pedometers, which have now become available on many smartphones apart from watch-like activity trackers (Wang and Gandhi 2014; Lyons et al. 2014). They can analyze market trends and make more informed choices about the products or services they buy, for instance, when buying books (Chevalier and Mayzlin 2006) or purchasing air tickets (Sengupta and Wiggins 2014). And depending on the organizations that use that data, people may benefit indirectly by being better able to navigate the organization's products and services and through an expanded set of choices or opportunities, based on analysis of the preferences exhibited by collating data on consumer and web traffic choices.

The possible *costs* to the user of data collection include the loss of privacy, of agency, and of control. Such costs can undermine people's trust in the organizations that collect, control, and use data. Indeed, at the time of writing, various controversies had broken out over data leaks compromising the privacy of personal data and the biases involved in the use of data to profile individuals; these have underscored the risks emerging in the new data-rich economy. These costs are not always apparent or are distributed in biased ways among participants in data markets. This is because of how those markets have been evolving, with some organizations gaining significant power in defining how such data is collected, used, and shared. Other risks are emerging in this era of data: because of barriers that prevent people—especially the poor—from participating effectively in data markets and analog limitations to the benefits of the data revolution.

The chapter considers several aspects of personal data markets, which run on the personally identifiable data that people generate (figure 4.1 reviews the types of personal data). It looks at how data markets have evolved, highlights the various players in the data market, and then discusses the benefits and costs for participants in data marketplaces

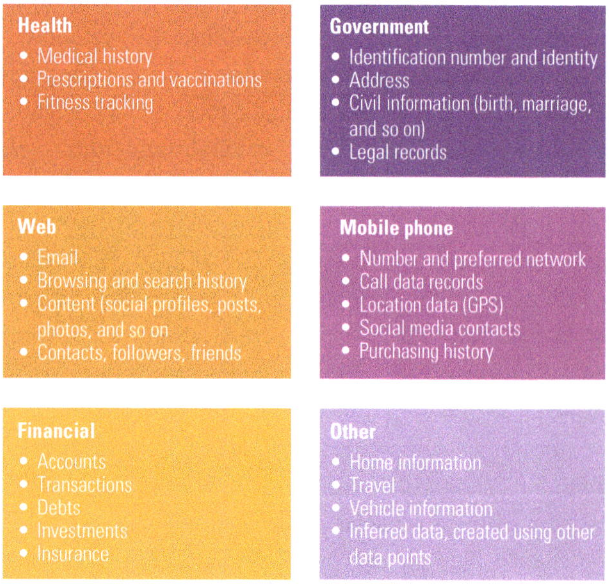

through digital networks and how negative impacts might be reduced.

The chapter concludes with a discussion of public policies that could rebalance the costs and benefits to ensure fairer distribution among participants and understand how data marketplaces can focus more on people. These choices could determine whether data will help people—especially the poor—find economic opportunity. Few best practices exist as models, and hence the chapter will leave the reader not with specific policy prescriptions, but with a better sense of the dynamics at play.

The data market

Technological change and evolving business models

Personal data is generated through an individual's actions (such as making a payment using a credit card), through business processes that digitize analog data (such as medical histories), or through consequent machine response (such as call data records). Such data is now increasingly coming from use of the internet, wireless sensors, and the billions of mobile phones around the world. As the world gets more connected, more people are leaving a digital trail, wherever they go and whatever they do.

This data, which has become more voluminous and granular over time, piqued the interest of various organizations that saw the financial value embedded in it. By the early 1990s, personal data such as telephone numbers and email addresses was widely used for marketing (Seller and Gray 1999). Companies crunched data to predict how likely people would be to buy a product, and began using that knowledge to come up with targeted marketing messages. As more digital data was collected, organizations began to use increasingly powerful computing tools to manipulate and apply that data. Marketing companies built richer consumer profiles to predict future purchases and manufacturing and services companies to design and model new products (Davenport, Cohen, and Jacobson 2005; Accenture 2015).

Companies are now using such data to develop services powered by artificial intelligence (AI), and the bigger the data set, the better the AI (Elgan 2016). These and other innovations have greatly increased the value of data and its potential for being monetized, or bought and sold as a product in its own right. Data continues to gain value as

Figure 4.1 Types of personal data

Health
- Medical history
- Prescriptions and vaccinations
- Fitness tracking

Government
- Identification number and identity
- Address
- Civil information (birth, marriage, and so on)
- Legal records

Web
- Email
- Browsing and search history
- Content (social profiles, posts, photos, and so on)
- Contacts, followers, friends

Mobile phone
- Number and preferred network
- Call data records
- Location data (GPS)
- Social media contacts
- Purchasing history

Financial
- Accounts
- Transactions
- Debts
- Investments
- Insurance

Other
- Home information
- Travel
- Vehicle information
- Inferred data, created using other data points

its potential uses increase. Organizations—including businesses, governments, and others—can derive value from data by applying the insights arising from data's analysis to internal cost and revenue optimization, marketing and advertising, intelligence and surveillance, and automation.[3]

The application of personal data for online advertising has skyrocketed, with the internet now surpassing television as the leading advertising channel. At a forecast US$237 billion in 2018, digital ads are expected to grow from 44 percent of global advertising revenues in 2018 to more than 50 percent by 2020 (Magna Global 2017). Facebook and Google accounted for 84 percent of digital advertising revenue in 2017 (excluding China).[4] In 2016, Facebook's advertising revenues were US$27 billion (up more than 1,300 percent since 2010), accounting for more than 97 percent of its total revenues.[5] Google's advertising revenues—US$79 billion (growing 180 percent since 2010)—accounted for 88 percent of its total revenue.[6] Combined, the advertising revenues of these two online platforms were on par with the gross domestic product (GDP) of Morocco.

Data market actors

Table 4.1, complemented by figure 4.1, identifies the main types of actors operating in the markets built around personal data and the relationships among them. Using these categories of participants, it is possible to illustrate a simple model of the data market, as shown in figure 4.2. People produce personal data, the "raw material," which they "sell" (traditionally at zero price) to other market players who then use that data to derive various benefits. Individuals also provide "free labor" on many of these online platforms—by creating content such as posts and reviews and by uploading photos and videos—that data collectors can "scrape"—extracting data from online sources—to infer personal traits and preferences. This personal data, along with the data that individuals generate from their activities, and that might be inferred from their data (such as their political or culinary preferences), is the main source of data for these organizations.

People do not always directly derive value or benefits from this data (until recently, as discussed later). But people have been deriving indirect benefits from their sale of data in services or products that data-using organizations provide. These benefits are discussed in the next section.

On the other side of the market, the "buyers" are the various organizations that collect and use the data. In some cases, these organizations depend on the data as a necessary input for their operating model, as do online social media, search engine websites, and various information and news sites. Using advertising as a source of revenue, they typically compensate people—producers of the data—with free or highly subsidized access to their services. Hence, data has financial value to those organizations, either immediately when it is sold to other organizations (such as marketing companies) or through the services that an organization offers others (such as a search engine selling advertisements tied to search terms).[7]

In other cases, data is an input into an operating model. Health systems or government services are one example. Their processes are traditionally standardized and have relied in the past on highly abstracted models of user preferences. Data is thus an input into these systems and does not have an immediate financial value but has informational value. This implies that such services are often performed for a fee, whether paid immediately or separately (such as through taxes). However, these interactions do generate significant amounts of data, and thought has increasingly gone into creating more specialized services and choices based on that data (such as in e-government services) or improving the quality of those abstract models to design improved services (such as better medicines or treatments). Businesses can unlock financial value by generating more effective insights from data to launch a new product, reduce waste or costs, enable better decisions, and boost innovations.

One may say that the value of data depends on how and for what the data is used and how well it is prepared (cleaned and organized). In either case, however, data can find its way to other parties. The regulation of those data flows is the responsibility of data protectors, which can include rules pertaining to privacy and sharing of specific types of data (such as health or financial data), as well as rules about electronic transactions. Data could also be held as an "asset" by those who collect it directly or via others, and new rule systems have emerged around concepts such as the "right to be forgotten" by such entities (Kelly and Satola 2017). Hence, data regulators can also protect people by defining and enforcing rules around the use of their data.

In this construction of the generic data market, organizations have an opportunity to capture the value from the data people produce, and they can determine how much of this value returns to those people. As noted, this data has significant financial and political value since it contains

Table 4.1 Typology of actors in the personal data market

Actor	Description	Examples
Data producers	Personal data is generated by individuals as they fill in forms (either online or offline where the latter is digitized), through sensors (such as fitness trackers and home monitors), through using applications and services on mobile phones and the internet, through using credit cards, and from being captured by security cameras and other sensors.	People generate data anonymously through sensors, security cameras, and the like. Individuals generate data using mobile phones, credit cards, internet search,[a] fitness trackers, and so on. In some cases, civil society organizations can help produce data, especially among poorer communities.[b]
Data collectors	Companies and governments collect data in different ways. Businesses collect personal information from their individual customers (Accenture 2015). Similarly, governments collect data from citizens for a wide range of purposes.	• A bank asking for financial and personal information. • An internet service provider recording web sites a user has visited. • An information services company soliciting personal information for an individual to open an email or social media account. • Citizens providing birth, marriage, and death details to governments for civil registries.
Data aggregators (brokers)	Obtain personal data from public and private parties to combine for resale to businesses. Some add additional value through analytics.	Data mining companies, such as Acxiom[c] or notoriously Cambridge Analytica,[d] that collect information from sources such as public records and consumer surveys to provide insights for clients such as banks, car companies, and retailers (Singer 2012).
Data users	Businesses who purchase data aggregators' products. Users of the analyzed data can also play the role of data collectors and aggregators on the market.[e]	Businesses and governments for law enforcement.[f] Alphabet (Google's parent company), Amazon, Facebook, and others are data collectors, data aggregators, and users of the analyzed data. Advertisers are major users of personal data to better target online ads.
Open data providers	Prepare (for example, anonymize) and make relevant personal data open to use and redistribute.	National governments, affiliated agencies, or organizations (such as civil society groups).
Data protectors	Address privacy and control of personal data. Protect the interests of individuals that have generated that data or its derivatives.	National data protection authorities through privacy and computer crime legislation. Companies offer products that provide data security, stronger data protection, or information about personal data that is collected. Many tips are available for protecting personal data. However, the decision to provide personal data in exchange for use of some services is still up to the user.[g]

a. Madrigal 2012.

b. For example, Twaweza's "Uwezo" learning assessments, deployed in East Africa, have informed public debate on education quality in Kenya and highlighted similar issues in the media and among politicians in Tanzania and Uganda. In India, the Society for Education, Action and Research in Community Health provides health care to rural and tribal people in the impoverished Gadchiroli district. Since 1989, it has captured both community-based and hospital-based data as part of its community-based, participatory approach to health care, which has been replicated by other civil society organizations in South Asia.

c. See https://www.acxiom.com/.

d. The Guardian, n.d.

e. Governments are not typically among such users, often due to legal restrictions, though they can obtain data for law enforcement; they would more likely acquire data from primary data collectors.

f. See https://transparencyreport.google.com.

g. Deloitte Review 2013.

information on behavior and preferences. Where people do provide such data voluntarily, it is because they expect to gain some of those benefits—whether it is access to online services or better medical care, or merely the chance to win a competition.

Questions then emerge from the perspective of data producers: are people aware of what data they are providing and under what conditions (or at what cost)? Do they understand the value (monetary and otherwise) of the benefits they receive? Are they able to assign value to the data they provide in a manner that explicitly differentiates between their perception of value and the actual value of the benefits that they already have or could receive? And what might ensure that maximum

Figure 4.2 The personal data market

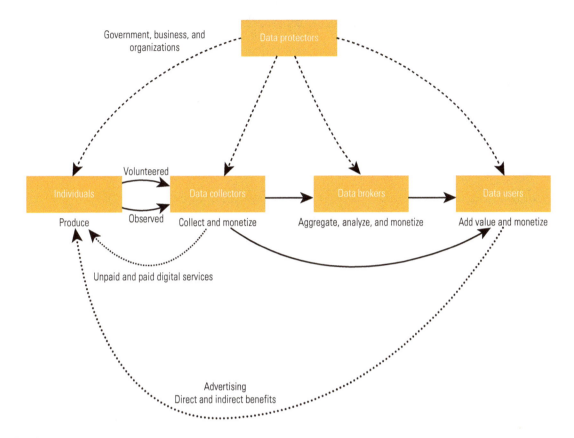

benefits are delivered to those who produce the data? The following section unpacks the benefits and costs that accrue to individuals as they participate in these data markets as data producers.

The benefits, costs, and risks for people

As noted above, the main benefits from the data revolution arise from the information value that personal data can provide to either individuals or to organizations that serve those individuals and from the financial value that it has for organizations. Yet costs and risks to individuals exist in the era of expanding collection, flow, and use of personal data. These include, as noted, privacy, loss of agency or control, and risk of exclusion from benefiting from data's value. This section notes that people are not always aware of the costs or the benefits of their participation in the data marketplace and, even if aware, might be constrained in their ability to improve the tradeoff due to the structure of the market.

Benefits

The data revolution has given more people access to information they can use to make better decisions. This is, first, because people can use data for its *informational value*—either directly or through the organizations that serve them—exposing them to new information or by creating new services or products, both of which help them make or realize better decisions.

Second, it is because their personal data has *financial value*, implicit or explicit, that allows them to exchange (sell or barter) personal data for services or products they might otherwise have had to pay for. Often this includes a range of sophisticated online tools that allow them to be better informed about services or reduce transaction costs (including information sources such as search engines or communication tools such as email services).

Table 4.2 summarizes the two forms of value and provides examples of how they operate in the data market.

Benefits due to informational value

When data is organized and analyzed it creates information, which can be an essential input in economic decision-making

Table 4.2 Benefits from personal data to individual

Data holds	Informational value	Financial value
	Information is derived from the data people produce, which could inform decision-making.	People produce data that has financial value for some other party and exchange their data for products or services.
Effects	**Direct:** Derived when people use their own or others' data to make decisions (such as exercise data from a wearable activity tracker or reviews on a shopping portal).	**Direct:** Derived when people share their data (knowingly or otherwise) with organizations in return for services (for example, people provide data in return for access to information services or social networks online); those services are financed through the sale of the data or its derivates.
	Indirect: People's data goes to organizations (for example, health care companies, urban planners, financial institutions, news organizations) that use it to improve or subsidize their products.	**Indirect:** People provide data that collectors use or sell on to others, generating economic value that could return to individuals through lower prices or income-generating opportunities, or feed into broader economic processes, which could also include innovations that benefit the wider public.
Benefits	• Better decisions • Innovative products • Improvement in public services	• Access to digital services • Wider economic benefits for data users that could spill over into opportunities for data producers

and security; it influences resource allocation, choices about technologies, and political choices and informs them about the markets that they participate in. When farmers have access to market pricing information, they can make better choices about when and where to sell their produce. Similarly, when consumers have better information about the supply, quality, and price of goods or services, they can make better choices about where and when to buy them. When data from weather monitoring systems feeds into complex models and informs governments, businesses, and individuals about potential inclement weather, it allows each to take measures to minimize or respond to damage. When civilians have better information on the events taking place around them and the decisions their political representatives are making, they can make better decisions about where to live, how to get around, how to spend leisure time, and how to vote. And when young people have better information about careers and wages, they can make better choices about what they study.

The data revolution is giving more people increasingly diversified and context-specific information through improvements in data collection, processing, analysis, and distribution, online and offline.[8] Thus far, people have typically benefited *indirectly* from data, as when organizations that collect, process, and use data to make decisions or inferences about people's demands or interests[9] then provide new or better information or expand the set of opportunities available to individuals. For instance—continuing from a previous example—this happens when governments improve disaster preparedness or response or

insurers process claims faster. And when people share their personal data with many of today's online services providers, those companies can attract advertisers, giving more people access to many sophisticated digital tools, from financial planners to cloud-based storage, often free.

Organizations can use personal data for innovation in processes, products, and services. These innovations could lead to economic benefits for people through lower prices and a better match between products and consumer needs (McKinsey Global Institute 2011). For example, TrueCar[10] collects and analyzes individual transaction data to provide an idea of local vehicle-specific prices so that car buyers know what others have paid for the same car. And various companies are using personal data to design more engaging or useful products and services (World Economic Forum 2013). In health care, data collected from large groups of individuals is improving diagnoses and helping to identify treatment options (SAS Institute, n.d.; Warren 2016).

Personal data is being used to improve public service delivery, enhance policy making, strengthen citizen participation, and enhance security. For instance, New York City is planning to use data from devices installed in taxis that use GPS, as well as pick-up and drop-off data from ride-sharing apps, to improve traffic management, identify roads that need to be fixed, and determine where to focus efforts after inclement weather (Marshall 2017). Similarly, in Seoul, the capital of the Republic of Korea, the location of mobile calls and text messages is used to optimize night bus routes.

One popular application gaining use around the world is the use of locational information from smartphones to report problems with local services (Gunawan 2017). Not only does this pinpoint the exact location of annoyances, such as uncollected garbage, potholes, or graffiti, it can also help foster citizen engagement. Social media activity can be "scraped" to alert vulnerable populations, such as informing Brazilian Facebook users about the Zika disease.[11] When personal data is used in ways that improve welfare, people will again be open to sharing it with public agencies and other organizations.

And people now are increasingly able to benefit from such data *directly*, using a wider range of progressively sophisticated tools to process data and derive their own conclusions. This includes making personal finance decisions[12] or modifying health-related behavior (Piwek et al. 2016).

Benefits due to financial value

Personal data has financial value, mainly placed on it by organizations that use that data to market products and services to their customers. This financial benefit is typically not available to the individuals that produce the data, but those organizations could "pay back" the producers of data directly by providing them with access to additional digital services, or indirectly through wider economic benefits,

such as the availability of credit ratings allowing access to credit. For example, most of those online provide personal information for access to advertiser-sponsored digital applications such as search engines, storage, email, and social media. And there is significant personal-data-driven advertising sponsored content online, such as news, health, and education sites of importance to individuals.

Personal data also supports a vast ecosystem of digital companies (see chapter 5), and is beginning to influence firms outside the traditional digital sectors as well. The growth of such businesses—fueled by data—implies economic growth that in turn will benefit individuals. The large information technology and services companies that use and benefit from personal data have created thousands of direct and indirect jobs, for example, and have created platforms that have led to the creation of other businesses. Not all are positive developments, with opportunities for some to generate fake data, for instance (see box 4.1).

Costs and risks

Despite the potential benefits of the data revolution, people, and especially the poor, are often subjected to many costs and risks or even precluded from partaking of the benefits described above. This stems mainly from how individuals

---

Box 4.1 Income-generating opportunities

Some people benefit financially and directly from their ability to earn revenue from the data economy. This includes a handful of services that provide money (or discount coupons) in exchange for personal information.

People can set up websites and receive income from personal-data-driven advertising tools such as Google's AdSense. Freelancers can earn money from jobs in data-related areas on Mechanical Turk (www.mturk.com); Upwork a freelance broker reported that jobs associated with data and artificial intelligence were among the fastest growing in the fourth quarter of 2017 (Upwork 2018).

And potential could exist for outsourcing analytics projects; a data scientist in India, for example, reported earning US$200 an hour for overseas jobs (Leber 2013). But, while individuals could get a financial return for their own personal data, they might also do so with false data. Income can be made from ethically questionable activities such as using fake accounts or reviews to influence social media. For instance, the *#richkidsofinstangram* handle was used by social media influencers to attract unwitting users to invest in dubious online trading schemes.[a] Estimates of fake accounts—also created by governments and criminals—range from almost 50 million for Twitter to about 60 million for Facebook (Confessore et al. 2018).

a. https://www.theguardian.com/news/2018/apr/19/wolves-of-instagram-jordan-belmont-social-media-traders.

have been largely dependent on the organizations that collect or use their personal data as gatekeepers to realize the benefits of those data, and to act on their decisions.

The costs and risks stem from two issues involving these organizations: first, the limitations in how the analog world permits people to benefit from the data revolution, and second, the unequal power relationships between people and these organizations. The first can be discussed briefly, as its resolution requires a shift beyond the data economy itself; the focus instead will be on the second.

Risks arising in the analog world

A key risk in the data economy is that missing analog complements, such as limited literacy, can constrain the extent to which people can realize benefits from digital data markets.[13] For instance, if organizations do not function well or are in uncompetitive markets, the collection of more data might not improve flows of information or decision-making by individuals, nor will it create incentives to deliver the expected benefits. In such a market, people may perceive the value of their data as low, because of information asymmetries, and many may give up their data unknowingly or without expecting an appropriate return.

The poor also face risk of exclusion: the barriers to entry in data markets are often too high for them, as they do not have access to digital technologies or they lack the skills to use data and convert it into relevant or useful information. Although the use of new technologies has exploded across the globe in the past 10 years, the price to access this data is still prohibitive for many. In Bolivia, Honduras, and Nicaragua, for example, a mobile broadband subscription exceeds 10 percent of average monthly GDP per capita, compared with France and Korea, where it is less than 0.1 percent (see figure 5.6). Many people—especially women, people living in the 40 percent of the population with the lowest incomes, or people with disabilities—lack the digital tools or literacy to use technology.[14] People who over-share online data concerning their sexuality, eating and drinking habits, or their taste for high-risk sports may be unwittingly excluding themselves from insurance coverage, or at least raising their premiums.

One consequence is that digitally excluded populations increasingly risk exclusion from data sets created from mining digitally generated information that might be used to enhance their livelihoods. And this makes many developing countries "data poor" themselves; that is, they have substandard data on a population, with entire groups of people invisible, such as unemployed women, indigenous populations, or slum dwellers.

The poor also often face constraints on how they use data—even if they are aware the data exists. This is because growing data flows often do not reach them, due to weak institutions or constraints on the functioning of markets. For example, if government weather data is not made public quickly, it will not benefit them. Or if disaster preparedness and response systems are not in place or fail to operate because alerts do not reach people quickly, even having that data will not expand opportunities in a way that would allow most to benefit from them.

Costs and risks arising from the data market(s) status quo

Costs are embedded in how data is shared and consumed, because of the structure of the markets in which the data is used. These costs might not be transparently disclosed to individuals (data producers), or they might have unintended consequences for the way that the data market functions. Several costs can be identified: loss of privacy, loss of control, loss of agency. When these costs are disclosed or uncovered (especially unintentionally, such as through data leakage, or deliberately through hacking), they could undermine the functioning of the digital ecosystem supported by data markets due to a *loss of trust* in the participants in those markets.

Concerns about *privacy* have been central to discussions about the data economy. Cases exist in which people may provide personal data willingly—to government officials, health care workers, or marketers. For example, they might trade it, knowingly or unknowingly, for access to online information services. Collection of such data allows data-driven services to improve. But this may mean people lose some privacy willingly. And it has also made securing and protecting personal data increasingly important for all kinds of organizations, both data collectors and users. Incidents in 2017[15] and 2018 have shown that the personal data of millions of people could be accessed—legally, accidentally, or illegally—including through means that neither the individuals nor data collectors might have been aware of. Most notable is the use of data collected through personality profile surveys on Facebook for targeted political advertising campaigns (Caldwelladr and Graham-Harrison 2018).

Much personal data, held and used as it is in financial, health, or public services organizations, is sensitive, and privacy has therefore been recognized as a fundamental human right deserving protection.[16] Loss of privacy risks becoming a negative influence on the behavior of others or organizations, such as through exclusion of people from access to services, social threats (bullying and stalking), or employment hiring or firing decisions.[17]

Transparency about what data is being collected, from whom, and about how it could be used is critical. However, much of the data people generate is now automatically created through their actions and often does not request explicit permission for collection or sharing with others (beyond accepting terms and conditions, often wordy and complicated). Because digital data is effectively permanent and can be replicated infinitely, its use can extend far beyond what was earlier possible with analog records. Such loss of control occurs as people give data away unwillingly or unknowingly, and, hence, lose control over it, are not aware of how or when it will be used or by whom, and are unable to engage in its secondary use.

One example is Meitu, a photo-enhancing app that requests access to far more data than needed, such as GPS location, cell carrier information, Wi-Fi connection data, SIM card information, and personal identifiers that could be used to track people's devices and sell the data without them realizing it. Users have control over whether to use an application or not as well as to adjust privacy settings within applications, but the configurations can be complicated or unwittingly bypassed. Often, individuals are unable to deny an organization control of their data, sometimes exclusively, without giving up access to all of its services; no options are available, especially in the online world, where terms and conditions to give up control are frequently "take it or leave it."

Loss of agency happens when algorithms or the input data causes people to lose control over their actions or restrict their ability to determine their own choices. Such loss is reinforced by the development of algorithms that are starting to offer choices to people for everything from what movies to watch, which news sources are relevant, what to buy (Boffey 2017), or which web pages might offer the information they seek (Naone 2011).

Those algorithms are developed based on models of personal preferences, using user data, that are abstractions of individual behavior. Such algorithms may frequently be inaccurate, no matter their sophistication. They model an individual's preferences, discouraging experimentation and reinforcing segmented stereotypes, often hidden from view both in what the sources of data are and how the algorithm itself works. At the time of writing, discussions had grown about how algorithms on some platforms might influence significant choices, such as voting.[18] And even if the more serious of these claims are ultimately unproven, the working of many of these algorithms is not clear (as well as what biases might inadvertently or purposefully exist).

These hidden costs, when they are disclosed, are often then accompanied by significant negative publicity for the organizations involved. This could undermine the provision of such products or digital services—dependent as they are on personal data—because people lose trust in those services. Theft of personal data, its growing accumulation and analysis by companies, and the spread of fake information increasingly targeting specific groups of people lowers trust for governments that people feel are not doing enough to protect them and for companies they feel are misusing their data (Mineo 2017).

Underlying many of these risks is the imbalanced structure of many data markets. Increasingly, private organizations are holding and using data, and these organizations are not subject to democratic pressure (as many public institutions are), and increasingly are subject to winner-takes-all pressure in network industries. As noted, individuals are often unable to negotiate better terms and conditions related to their data or create better trade-offs between their privacy, control, agency, and access to services. Better informed and targeted regulation is part of the solution, given the collective action problem that occurs when large numbers of people engage with such organizations or networks. The next section discusses other protections that might be needed.

Remedies

Vibrant debate is now ensuing about what public policies could help respond to these failures within and outside the data market, and how regulations may be applied in this sector, which up until now has been largely unregulated. Appropriate policies—helped by emerging technologies—could lead the data revolution to expand economic opportunities for more people. Part of this could be achieved by making the costs and benefits transparent and redistributing them more fairly across different players in the market.

Specific remedies could help address or minimize the risks and costs to individuals arising from the ways data markets function today. Areas that a personal data policy could address include overcoming the identified market failures—loss of privacy, control, and agency; exclusion from participation in the market; and unfair distribution of the market benefits among data market participants.

But little consensus exists for now on what remedies will work, and some approaches are yet to be tested. And current data policies are highly fragmented, with diverging global, regional, and national regulatory approaches. Moreover, these remedies do not directly address the unequal power of individual users versus the organizations (global platforms or states), an underlying issue in data markets. This issue might only be addressed through strong regulatory or large-scale user action; but, again, little consensus exists on how these might be achieved.[19] Table 4.3 and the rest of this section outline emerging responses.

Privacy

Privacy protections have been typically ensured through legal frameworks. A global survey, reported by UNCTAD (2017) shows that data and privacy protection legislation has been put in place in more than 100 economies, 66 developing or transitioning (see map ES.1). More than one-fifth of economies, primarily developing ones, had no legislation, and few have developed comprehensive data protection laws.

Key attributes of such a legal framework include protection of personal data collected by organizations, such as effective and appropriate security to protect the data from theft and misuse. It is also generally accepted that organizations need to keep personal data accurate, relevant, and updated. Data subjects must be able to access and correct their personal data. Widely cited frameworks to define the rules around the privacy of personal data include the European General Data Protection Regulation (GDPR) (EU 2018); the APEC Privacy Framework (APEC 2015); and the OECD's Privacy Guidelines (OECD 2013). The Council of Europe's Convention 108 is a foundational data protection initiative, with a treaty that opened for ratifications in 1981 (COE 1981). The treaty intends to "secure in the territory of each Party for every individual, whatever his nationality or residence, respect for his rights and fundamental freedoms, and in particular his right to privacy, with regard to automatic processing of personal data relating to him ('data protection')."[20]

The GDPR, which came into force in May 2018, enables better control over personal data, entitling individual protection of anonymity, pseudonymity,[21] and rights to request and erase personal data ("right to be forgotten"). Another novel feature is data portability, giving individuals the right to request that their data be transferred to another controller and for data controllers to use common formats.

Table 4.3 Risks and remedies

Risk	Remedy	Example
Loss of privacy	Legal frameworks to protect personal data from theft and misuse, to require consent for collection and use, to keep personal data accurate and relevant (where data subjects can access and correct their personal data), to define how such data can flow (including across borders), and to specify the mechanisms to assist individuals if violations occur.	European General Data Protection Regulation (GDPR) (EU 2018); APEC Privacy Framework (APEC 2015); OECD Privacy Guidelines (OECD 2013).
Loss of agency	Informing individuals about when and how data is collected and used, including how their experiences are modified by algorithms based on that and others' data. Allowing users to switch off such algorithms or hold back their data from being used. Clarity about data sources to minimize the risk of fake data or its derivatives influencing decisions.	None, although some companies such as Google do now allow users to "turn off" personalized search results, for example.
Loss of control	Legal frameworks limit the collection of personal data, and limit use and disclosure to specific purposes. Data subjects should be notified about the purpose and disclosure of the data collection and can opt out of data sharing between the data collector and other companies. They can also choose to be forgotten.	Canadian Personal Information Protection and Electronics Documents Act; European GDPR.
Loss of trust	Reducing personal data breaches, business codes of conduct where regulation is weak or vague, acting on feedback from user communities.	Data Science Code of Professional Conduct.[a]
Exclusion	Connecting people to the better-quality, affordable internet.	Universal technology access programs and digital literacy training.

a. See http://www.datascienceassn.org/code-of-conduct.html.

Cross-border personal data flows are also regulated, with onward transmission generally only permitted if the recipient country has adequate data protection laws. Businesses that do not comply with the regulation face significant fines.

The right of an individual to privacy is often balanced with the need to secure the greater public good. For example, even the Council of Europe's Convention 108 permits restrictions in cases when "overriding interests (e.g. State security, defense, etc.) are at stake."[22] In other cases, privacy rules permit irreversibly anonymized data to be used for research or public interest activities (EU 2018, Art. 26). This balances the interests of individuals in safeguarding their privacy with the benefits of being able to use personal data, as described in the preceding sections.

Beyond legal frameworks, however, new approaches are emerging. This helps in areas given institutional capacity limitations, the difficulty in regulating across borders, and the "take-it-or-leave-it" nature of many services. For example, online services that embed privacy into their designs have emerged in messaging or search.[23] A more detailed discussion is found in chapter 6.

Control

To overcome loss of control, collection of personal data should be transparent, and use or disclosure limited to specific purposes. Individuals should be notified about the purpose and disclosure of the data collection. One example is Canada's Personal Information Protection and Electronics Documents Act passed in 2000 (passed by the Privacy Commissioner of Canada). Under the act, individuals have the right to access the information held about them, challenge its accuracy, and give consent for personal information to be collected. Organizations have obligations to ensure data security, limit the data they collect, use personal data only for the purposes consented to by the consumer, and not retain the data when purposes for collection are no longer in effect (Green 2018). The EU's GDPR also enhances individuals' control over personal data by enabling the "right to be forgotten," permitting them to control what personal data is available online or with data users.[24] The rules also allow users to control how personal data is used by those organizations.[25]

Agency

Loss of agency can be averted by educating individuals in data collection methods and in how algorithms modify their experiences based on their data. The Data Privacy Project in New York City trains librarians, in turn, to provide guidance on protecting personal data to the largely vulnerable patrons that utilize libraries' internet services.[26] Some applications allow individuals to switch off predictive algorithms. For example, Google allows its users to delete their past searches or prevent saving of searches[27] or allows users to turn off personalized search results that might create an "echo chamber" for users by limiting their exposure to new sources of information.[28]

Exclusion

Exclusion of individuals from data markets can be overcome in different ways. It is estimated that well over 2 billion people did not use the internet at all in 2016, either because they had no access, could not afford it, or did not know how or want to use it. A significant proportion of these people live in rural areas of developing countries, where levels of internet infrastructure and incomes are often low. Exclusion from the data market can be overcome through introduction of information and communication technology, particularly mobile telephony and the internet, among lower-income groups and connection of more people through inexpensive phones.

Governments need equally to tackle the challenge of people who have the needed infrastructure within reach but do not use the internet because they lack digital literacy. This could be done through creation of awareness about data-driven services (such as social networks, public services, search engines), as the Indian government's Digital India Program of 2015 does. The program helps farmers get access to information about different wholesale markets in their community through digital apps on smartphones and helped cut out middlemen (see Reuters Market Light 2015). Farmers can use this information to make better choices and not be beholden to centuries-old systems (Bergvinson 2017). By the end of 2015 the program had already helped increase farmers' incomes 5–25 percent.[29]

Trust—and the dominance of digital platforms

During the writing of this report, many episodes underscored the scale of the personal data economy, but also undermined the trust that people have in the organizations that have grown significantly in the data market. These episodes have included massive leaks of personal data, discovery of unapproved access to private data, attempts at manipulation of ostensibly neutral information sources, and sharing of personal information. The scale of these episodes is significant, given the reach and popularity of the organizations and platforms that they involve, such as Experian or Facebook.

Debate about the implications of these episodes is only just beginning, and focusing on privacy of personal data, control over who accesses and uses people's data, and the agency of users. In one account, the organizations involved in transgressions might have been unaware themselves of the potential for trouble or unable to prevent it. But such accounts do little to shore up trust in these services. Even so, the scale of organizations' networks and their importance might lead people to continue using them, even if less willingly.

It might be possible to instill greater trust through actions to remedy some of these other risks. It might also be possible to seek ways to manage data more collaboratively, for instance, adopting a code of conduct (such as the Data Science Code of Professional Conduct of the Data Science Association) (Data Privacy Project 2018), and with more transparency, in how data is managed and used. As the next section discusses, this may involve moving toward a more balanced personal data market in which users regain control over their data.

Toward a more balanced data market

Emerging trends suggest new opportunities for individuals to regain control of their personal data, giving people more power as actors in the data market. People are looking for ways to keep their data secure and to monetize it and to get better value in exchange for the personal information they provide (Whitler 2016). Newer business models—driven by technological advances and people's greater awareness of the transactions and value of data markets—are prompting creation of a more balanced market for personal data. However, scope remains for greater coordination or even aggregation of data streams and sources to maximize value.

Emerging business models allow people to control and directly sell their data to businesses. Companies such as Datacoup[30] enable users to sell their personal data for a monthly fee, for example, data generated through social media activity and credit card transactions (Simonite 2014). Another example of this is Alphabet's Project Baseline, which collects laboratory results and real-time health data from individuals wearing a special wristband. Participants in the study share their health data for two years and receive US$410 per annual visit, US$30 per visit for quarterly assessments, and US$10 for filling in questionnaires (Lomas 2017).

Businesses are finding that their customers are becoming more informed about the use of their data and the potential monetary value of it, and expect value in return for data used to target marketing and for data sold to third parties (Morey, Forbath, and Schoop 2015; Accenture 2015). Companies may also begin to find that they lose customers when they fail to keep data secure; however, the winner-takes-all nature of many of the platforms and services in use today might mean that an exodus might not occur often or easily.

For individuals, the biggest benefit is regaining control of personal data. A second gain could be more accurate data, as individuals would have a greater incentive to keep it up to date to better monetize it. This protects people in instances in which out-of-date information might be used against them (such as applying for loans or insurance). More comprehensive information could also expand the scope of applications and services. Third, personal information would be centralized and simplified using personal data management software. Individuals would have fewer passwords to keep track of.[31]

Thus, it should be possible for people to act as data-producing entrepreneurs—having a data profile, personal data management software, and an online wallet—and exchange the data for money, discount coupons, or free applications and services. The World Economic Forum (2011) has proposed the concept of a data bank account, in which an individual's data would "reside in an account where it would be controlled, managed, exchanged and accounted for."

One challenge lies in determining the value of personal data. In Italy, a team of researchers monitored a study group that auctioned off smartphone data for two months, with the median bid across all data categories of €2 (US$2.72) (MIT Technology Review 2014). One individual sold his personal data on a crowdsourcing site for US$2–US$200 (depending on the amount and frequency of the information), earning US$2,733 from 213 backers in one month, or an average of US$12.83 per backer (see Zannier, n.d.). Another study uses operating metrics from Experian and Facebook, companies whose revenues are largely generated from personal data, finding that the average revenue per user of both was about US$6 a year (Roosendaal, van Lieshout, and van Veenstra 2014). Another perspective on personal data valuation is total global digital advertising revenue

(US$178 billion; see Magna Global 2017) divided by the number of internet users around the world (3.4 billion),[32] for an average of US$53 in 2016.

Personal data does not have a uniform value and varies according to several variables, such as type of information and income of user. Data from Facebook confirms the latter, with the company having different average revenue per user depending on the region. In the end, the value of personal data will be determined by what purchasers are willing to pay. This will become more apparent with the emergence of global, regional, and national markets for personal data, in which data collectors would review the data available and purchase directly from individuals or third parties they have entrusted the data to. Personal data management software that individuals can operate themselves or where firms act as trusted custodians for users who lack the skills are already on the market (Lehtiniemi 2017).

It is certain that large internet companies will resist individuals' greater control over personal data. Collecting personal data is at the center of these companies' business models, driven by the willingness of individuals to sacrifice personal data for unpaid services. Developed and developing countries also appear to be split over the threat to businesses of individuals monetizing their personal data. In developed nations, it is less of a threat to businesses, with bigger worries in government regulation, cyberattacks, and personal data protection applications. But in Brazil, China, and India, individuals charging for their personal data is among the top business concerns.

However, the unbalanced personal data market could lead to greater disenfranchisement among individuals. This in turn could lead a growing number of individuals to opt out of the existing arrangement.

Tools are already available that give people greater control over their personal information. For example, a Swedish company claims, in a few clicks, to be able to find and delete accounts created using Gmail (see Neal 2016). Stricter policies about sharing personal information are available with free email,[33] office applications,[34] and browsers.[35] Scope also exists for paid tools with tighter privacy controls, as users might pay for applications and services that protect different types of personal information. One study found that individuals in the United States would pay most to protect government identification, those in India for credit card information, and in Germany and the United Kingdom, for medical records (Morey, Forbath, and Schoop 2015).

Products also exist for individuals to protect at least some personal information from internet service providers (Kalia 2017). In addition, cookie controls (Brandom 2017) and ad blockers will allow users to block online marketing generated from their personal information (Rosenwald 2015).

Some individuals have consciously decided to restrict sharing of personal data. Ironically, many people involved in the social media or technology industries limit their use of these services or systems because of concerns about psychological and other dangers caused by services using their personal data (Lewis 2017). These trends may initially lack the scale of the large internet companies, but could grow as more individuals weigh the tradeoff between sacrificing personal data for unpaid services.

Looking to the future

It is possible that the future would lead to greater democratization of access and use of personal data. This could lead to more data sharing and, eventually, transform individuals from consumers of data to both consumers and suppliers of data. As data suppliers, individuals would be able price the data they produce and share with businesses or governments.

The market power of private organizations, especially data collecting platforms and networks, possibly, could also be moderated. This is possible through the emergence of competition (such as new social networks or online service providers), regulation by governments or the platforms themselves,[36] and shifts in consumer preferences *en masse*, which could privilege privacy or control over access. Any such shift will emerge out of negotiation among market players, but should ideally seek to balance innovation by these firms with respect for individuals' rights.

Recent trends are shifting the value distribution to the producers of data, in terms of such things as better health care (cancer research, medical treatment, or diagnosis) and better public services (such as traffic and road planning, water planning). Technologies such as micropayments may also lead to innovation in this area, as noted, possibly allowing people to directly sell their data to businesses and governments in the future. The rise of AI and the Internet of Things will help individuals trade personal data and receive personalized services based on personal data.

Apart from the technological aspects and drivers of this change, the personal data market that may emerge would benefit from more consistent structuring and organizing of data. This is because such organizations—focusing on the benefits to people rather than to organizations alone—could help aggregate or combine data across platforms and permit portability.

Already, data can be accumulated and cross-referenced across various financial services and platforms to detect opportunities to maximize returns on investment. For instance, online personal finance tools have begun to link people's bank, securities, retirement, and credit card accounts to provide ideas and offer products or services to budget better, increase access to credit, or identify investment opportunities.[37]

But we could go further: linking personal data about physical movement collected through phone location or health tracking, combined with data about transportation use, could be combined to provide people looking to exercise with ideas about adopting a routine that increases walking. Shopping patterns across various stores could be combined to provide better choices or insight to people about ways to save by changing the locations or timing of their purchases. The potential opportunities to merge data sources and improve decision-making holds promise, again, with the caveat that the costs and risks need to be managed.

People as a focus for data markets

The data revolution holds great promise. When better data is available to people, they can make better decisions and find the information needed to improve their economic and social lives. The technological tools to realize these benefits exist today and will develop further. As more people connect to the internet and new ways of collecting, managing, and analyzing personal data become commonplace, more people, including the poor, will participate in the growing data economy.

But these changes will not come without their risks and costs. Without measures in place to protect privacy, agency, and control over data, the risk is that businesses and organizations will benefit the most and few of these improved opportunities will pass on to individuals generating these vast troves of data. If the data economy does not become more inclusive, with wider access to the digital tools and the skills to use them, it is likely that the data economy will not benefit the poor.

Finally, as noted, better data will only go so far to improve opportunity; institutions, infrastructure, and rules will need to be in place to ensure that people can use the information generated through the exponentially growing streams of data. The digital data revolution might be upon us, but people will also need reform in the analog world to effect real change in their lives.

Notes

1. The other major source of data is machine generated, which accounts for an increasing share of the global total. This includes data that is generated automatically, without human intervention.

2. See https://trends.google.com/trends/explore?date=all&q=big%20 data,open%20data,data%20analytics.

3. See https://www.mckinsey.com/~/media/McKinsey/Business %20Functions/McKinsey%20Analytics/Our%20Insights /The%20age%20of%20analytics%20Competing%20in%20 a%20data%20driven%20world/MGI-The-Age-of-Analytics -Full-report.ashx.

4. See "Ad Spend Forecast Update 2018: DOOH, Google and Face-book Drive Growth" at http://www.jcdecaux.com/blog/ad-spend -forecast-update-2018-dooh-google-and-facebook-drive-growth.

5. See https://s21.q4cdn.com/399680738/files/doc_presentations /FB-Q4'16-Earnings-Slides.pdf, slide 8.

6. See https://abc.xyz/investor/pdf/2016_google_annual_report .pdf, page 22.

7. For one example, see Google's AdWords service at https://en .wikipedia.org/wiki/AdWords.

8. For example, financial transactions are being increasingly digitized—through mobile money and credit cards—or sensors in buildings, roads, or wearable devices are collecting massive troves of increasingly high-resolution data about our movements or activities in the offline world.

9. For example, Dewey (2016).

10. For information, see https://www.truecar.com/.

11. See "A Case Study: Data and Social Media Can Lead to Healthier Lives" at http://neo-assets.s3.amazonaws.com/news /FB-UNICEF-Big.png.

12. See https://www.investopedia.com/personal-finance/personal -finance-apps/.

13. "Analog complements" are thoroughly discussed in World Bank (2016, 2). As it notes, "to get the most out of the digital revolution, countries also need to work on the 'analog complements'—by strengthening regulations that ensure competition among businesses, by adapting workers' skills to the demands of the new economy, and by ensuring that institutions are accountable."

14. See http://www.cepal.org/publicaciones/xml/5/48385/leo2013 _ing.pdf.

15. For example, see Dave 2017.

16. See, for example, (a) Universal Declaration of Human Rights, Article 12 (United Nations, 1948), (b) Convention for the Protection of Human Rights and Fundamental Freedoms, Article 8 (European Court of Human Rights, 1950), http://www.coe.fr/eng/legaltxt/5e.htm, (c) Convention for the Protection of Individuals with Regard to Automatic Processing of Personal Data, ETS No. 108 (Council of Europe, 1981), http://www.coe.fr/eng/legaltxt/108e.htm, (d) International Covenant on Civil and Political Rights (United Nations, 1966), http://www.hrweb.org/legal/cpr.html, and (e) Regulation (EU) 2016/679 of the European Parliament and of the Council of 27 April 2016 on the Protection of Natural Persons with Regard to the Processing of Personal Data and on the Free Movement of Such Data, and Repealing Directive 95/46/EC (General Data Protection Regulation), to become effective May 25, 2018.

17. See http://www2.mitre.org/public/jsmo/pdfs/03-01-employer-liability.pdf.

18. For information, see https://www.theguardian.com/technology/2018/mar/17/facebook-cambridge-analytica-kogan-data-algorithm; https://slate.com/technology/2018/04/the-cambridge-analytica-scandal-suggests-algorithms-are-the-new-campaign-donation.html; https://www.newamerica.org/future-tense/events/the-tyranny-of-algorithms/.

19. It appears that even when many users are provoked, scale does not materialize. For instance, following the revelations of the Cambridge Analytica scandal, a "#DeleteFacebook" movement got significant coverage in the media, but had limited impact. As of May 2018, user growth continues at Facebook and advertising revenues also increased. See Hsu (2018); Romano (2018); Murdock (2018); and Sloane (2018).

20. See http://ec.europa.eu/justice/data-protection/article-29/documentation/opinion-recommendation/files/2014/wp228_en.pdf.

21. Separating personal data from direct identifiers so it is not possible to identify the individual (see https://iapp.org/news/a/top-10-operational-impacts-of-the-gdpr-part-8-pseudonymization/).

22. See https://www.coe.int/en/web/conventions/full-list/-/conventions/treaty/108.

23. For more information, see https://en.wikipedia.org/wiki/Comparison_of_instant_messaging_clients#Secure_messengers; and Field 2018.

24. See European Commission, "Can I Ask A Company or Organization to Stop Processing My Personal Data?" at https://ec.europa.eu/info/law/law-topic/data-protection/reform/rights-citizens/my-rights/can-i-ask-company-organisation-stop-processing-my-personal-data_en.

25. See https://ec.europa.eu/info/law/law-topic/data-protection/reform/rights-citizens/my-rights/can-i-ask-company-organisation-stop-processing-my-personal-data_en.

26. See the Data Privacy Project at https://dataprivacyproject.org.

27. See https://support.google.com/websearch/answer/4540094?co=GENIE.Platform%3DDesktop&hl=en.

28. See https://en.wikipedia.org/wiki/Google_Personalized_Search.

29. See https://www.mygov.in/sites/default/files/user_comments/Digital%20India-Agriculture.pdf.

30. See https://datacoup.com/.

31. One survey found an average of more than 100 online accounts per email address in 2015, and the average number of forgotten passwords to be 37; see Le Bras 2015.

32. See the ITU World Telecommunication/ICT Indicators Database.

33. See https://protonmail.com/security-details for details.

34. See https://www.openoffice.org/privacy.html for details.

35. See https://www.mozilla.org/en-US/privacy/firefox/.

36. For discussions on this topic, see http://www.europarl.europa.eu/RegData/etudes/BRIE/2017/607323/IPOL_BRI(2017)607323_EN.pdf; https://www.eff.org/deeplinks/2018/04/platform-censorship-wont-fix-internet; and http://www.oecd.org/competition/rethinking-antitrust-tools-for-multi-sided-platforms.htm.

37. See https://www.pcmag.com/article2/0,2817,2407617,00.asp.

References

Accenture. 2015. "Guarding and Growing Personal Data Value." https://www.accenture.com/t20150821T065218__w__/us-en/_acnmedia/Accenture/Conversion-Assets/DotCom/Documents/Global/PDF/Dualpub_15/Accenture-Guarding-and-Growing-Personal-Data-Value-Narrative-Repo.

APEC (Asia Pacific Economic Cooperation). 2015. *The APEC Privacy Framework*. Singapore: APEC Secretariat.

Bergvinson, David. 2017. "Digital Agriculture Empowers Farmers." *Business Today*, January 15. https://www.businesstoday.in/magazine/features/digital-agriculture-empowers-farmers/story/242966.html.

Boffey, Daniel. 2017. "Google Fined Record €2.4bn by EU over Search Engine Results." *The Guardian*, June 27. https://www.theguardian.com/business/2017/jun/27/google-braces-for-record-breaking-1bn-fine-from-eu.

Brandom, Russell. 2017. "Apple's New Anti-tracking System Will Make Google and Facebook Even More Powerful." The Verge, June 6. https://www.theverge.com/2017/6/6/15747300

/apple-safari-ad-tracking-cookie-blocker-google-facebook
-privacy

Caldwelladr, Carole, and Emma Graham-Harrison. 2018. "Revealed: 50 Million Facebook Profiles Harvested for Cambridge Analytica in Major Data Breach." *The Guardian*, March 17. https://www.theguardian.com/news/2018/mar/17 /cambridge-analytica-facebook-influence-us-election.

Chevalier, Judith, and Dina Mayzlin. 2006. "The Effect of Word of Mouth on Sales: Online Book Reviews." *Journal of Marketing Research* 43 (3): 345–54. https://msbfile03 .usc.edu/digitalmeasures/mayzlin/intellcont/chevalier _mayzlin06-1.pdf.

COE (Council of Europe). 1981. "Convention for the Protection of Individuals with Regard to Automatic Processing of Personal Data." ETS No. 108. http://www.coe.fr/eng /legaltxt/108e.htm.

Confessore, Nicholas, Gabriel J. X. Dance, Richard Harris, and Mark Hansen. 2018. "The Follower Factory." *New York Times*, January 27. https://www.nytimes.com/interactive/2018/01/27 /technology/social-media-bots.html.

Data Privacy Project. 2018. "Code of Conduct: Data Science Code of Professional Conduct." http://www.datascienceassn.org /code-of-conduct.html.

Dave, Paresh. 2017. "Credit Giant Equifax Says Social Security Numbers, Birth Dates of 143 Million Consumers May Have Been Exposed." *Los Angeles Times*, September 7. http:// www.latimes.com/business/technology/la-fi-tn-equifax-data -breach-20170907-story.html.

Davenport, Thomas H., Don Cohen, and Al Jacobson. 2005. "Competing on Analytics." Babson Executive Education: Knowledge Research Center. http://www.babsonknowledge .org/analytics.pdf.

Deloitte Review. 2013. "Data as the New Currency: Government's Role in Facilitating the Exchange." *Deloitte Review* 13. https://deloitte.wsj.com/riskandcompliance/files/2013/11 /DataCurrency_report.pdf.

Dewey, Catherine. 2016. "98 Personal Data Points That Facebook Uses to Target Ads to You." *Washington Post*, August 18. https://www.washingtonpost.com/news/the-intersect /wp/2016/08/19/98-personal-data-points-that-facebook-uses -to-target-ads-to-you/?utm_term=.8e8b6b4fb92b.

Elgan, Mike. 2016. "Artificial Intelligence Needs Your Data, All of It." *ComputerWorld*, February 22. https://www.computerworld .com/article/3035595/emerging-technology/artificial-intellige nce-needs-your-data-all-of-it.html.

EU (European Union). 2018. "The EU General Data Protection Regulation (GDPR)." https://www.eugdpr.org.

Field, Matthew. 2018. "DuckDuckGo: The Private Search Engine Standing Up to Google." *Technology Intelligence*, April 23. https://

www.telegraph.co.uk/technology/2018/04/23/duckduckgo -tiny-private-search-engine-standing-google/.

Green, Andy. 2018. "Canada's PIPEDA Breach Notification Regulations Are Finalized!" *Varonis*, May 3. https://blog.varonis.com /canadas-pipeda-breach-notification-regulations-finalized/.

The Guardian. n.d. "The Cambridge Analytica Files." https://www .theguardian.com/news/series/cambridge-analytica-files.

Gunawan, Imana. 2017. "App Helps Indonesian Capital Get 'Smart' to Improve Public Services." *Humanosphere*, January 6. http://www.humanosphere.org/social-business/2017/01 /app-helps-indonesian-capital-get-smart-to-improve-public -services/.

Hsu, Tiffany. 2018. "For Many Facebook Users, a 'Last Straw' That Led Them to Quit." *New York Times*, March 21. https:// www.nytimes.com/2018/03/21/technology/users-abandon -facebook.html.

Kalia, Amul. 2017. "Here's How to Protect Your Privacy from Your Internet Service Provider." Electronic Frontier Foundation, April 3. https://www.eff.org/deeplinks/2017/04/heres-how -protect-your-privacy-your-internet-service-provider.

Kelly, Michael, and David Satola. 2017. "The Right to Be Forgotten." *University of Illinois Law Review* 1. https://papers.ssrn .com/sol3/papers.cfm?abstract_id=2965685.

Le Bras, Tom. 2015. "Online Overload—It's Worse Than You Thought." Infographic, Dash Lane Blog, July 21. https://blog .dashlane.com/infographic-online-overload-its-worse-than -you-thought/.

Leber, Jessica. 2013. "In a Data Deluge, Companies Seek to Fill a New Role." *MIT Technology Review*, May 22. https://www .technologyreview.com/s/513866/in-a-data-deluge-companies -seek-to-fill-a-new-role/.

Lehtiniemi, Tuukka. 2017. "Personal Data Spaces: An Intervention in Surveillance Capitalism?" *Surveillance and Society* 15 (5). https://ojs.library.queensu.ca/index.php/surveillance-and -society/article/view/6424.

Lewis, Paul. 2017. "'Our Minds Can Be Hijacked': The Tech Insiders Who Fear a Smartphone Dystopia." *The Guardian*, October 6. https://www.theguardian.com/technology/2017 /oct/05/smartphone-addiction-silicon-valley-dystopia.

Lomas, Natasha. 2017. "Form an Orderly Queue! Google Wants Your Blood (and Other Bodily Fluids). Oh and Your Medical Records." TechCrunch. https://techcrunch.com/2017/04/21 /form-an-orderly-queue-google-wants-your-blood-and -other-bodily-fluids-oh-.

Lyons, Elizabeth, Zakkoyya Lewis, Brian Mayrsohn, and Jennifer Rowland. 2014. "Behavior Change Techniques Implemented in Electronic Lifestyle Activity Monitors: A Systematic Content Analysis." *Journal of Medical Internet Research* 16 (8). http://doi.org/10.2196/jmir.3469.

Madrigal, Alexis C. 2012. "I'm Being Followed: How Google—and 104 Other Companies—Are Tracking Me on the Web." *The Atlantic,* February 29. https://www.theatlantic.com/technology /archive/2012/02/im-being-followed-how-google-151-and-104 -other-companies-151-are-tracking-me-on-the-web/253758/.

Magna Global. 2017. "Advertising Forecasts: Winter Update (Dec 4, 2017)." https://www.magnaglobal.com/wp-content /uploads/2017/12/MAGNA-Global-Forecast_Winter-Update _Final.pdf.

Marshall, Aarian. 2017. "The Secret Uber Data That Could Fix Your Daily Commute." *Wired*, February 3. https://www.wired .com/2017/02/ubers-coughing-data-nyc-fix-commute/.

McKinsey Global Institute. 2011. *Big Data: The Next Frontier for Innovation, Competition, and Productivity.* https://www .mckinsey.com/~/media/McKinsey/Business%20Functions /McKinsey%20Digital/Our%20Insights/Big%20data%20 The%20next%20frontier%20for%20innovation/MGI_big _data_full_report.ashx.

Mineo, Liz. 2017. "On Internet Privacy, Be Very Afraid." *Harvard Gazette*, August 24. https://news.harvard.edu/gazette /story/2017/08/when-it-comes-to-internet-privacy-be-very -afraid-analyst-suggests/.

MIT Technology Review. 2014. "Researchers Test Personal Data Market to Find Out How Much Your Information Is Worth." July 9. https://www.technologyreview.com/s/528866 /researchers-test-personal-data-market-to-find-out-how -much-your-information-is-worth/.

Morey, Timothy, Theodore Forbath, and Allison Schoop. 2015. "Customer Data: Designing for Transparency and Trust." *Harvard Business Review*, May.

Murdock, Jason. 2018. "Mark Zuckerberg Says 'Delete Face-book' Protest Had No Meaningful Impact on His Busi-ness." *Newsweek*, April 5. http://www.newsweek.com /zuckerberg-says-deleting-facebook-has-no-meaningful -impact-his-business-872876.

Naone, Erica. 2011. "How Useful Is Personalized Search?" *MIT Technology Review*, April 11. https://www.technologyreview .com/s/423596/how-useful-is-personalized-search/.

Neal, Dave. 2016. "Swedish Deseat Software Will Help You Delete Yourself from the Internet." *The Inquirer*, November 25. https://www.theinquirer.net/inquirer/news/2478419/swedish -deseat-software-will-help-you-delete-yourself-from-the -internet.

OECD (Organisation for Economic Co-operation and Develop-ment). 2013. "The OECD Privacy Framework." OECD, Paris. http://www.oecd.org/internet/ieconomy/oecd_privacy _framework.pdf.

Piwek, Lukasz, David A. Ellis, Sally Andrews, and Adam Johnson. 2016. "The Rise of Consumer Health Wearables: Promises and Barriers." *PLOS*, February 2. http://journals.plos.org /plosmedicine/article?id=10.1371/journal.pmed.1001953.

Reuters Market Light. 2015. "Addressing Farmers Problems through Digital India Initiative." https://www.mygov.in/sites /default/files/user_comments/Digital%20India-Agriculture .pdf.

Richter, Wolf. 2018. "Online Ad Revenues Are Surging, but 2 Companies Are Getting Most of the Spoils." *Business Insider*, April 27. http://www.businessinsider.com/online-ads -revenues-going-to-google-and-facebook-the-most-2017-4.

Romano, Aja. 2018. "How Facebook Made It Impossible to Delete Facebook." *VOX*, March 22. https://www.vox.com /culture/2018/3/22/17146776/delete-facebook-difficult.

Roosendaal, Arnold, Marc van Lieshout, and Anne Fleur van Veenstra. 2014. "Personal Data Markets." TNO Innovation for Life. http://publications.tno.nl/publication/34612412/riZsP9 /TNO-2014-R11390.pdf.

Rosenwald, Michael. 2015. "The Digital Media Industry Needs to React to Ad Blockers . . . or Else." *Colombia Journalism Review*, September/October. https://www.cjr.org/business _of_news/will_ad_blockers_kill_the_digital_media_indus try.php.

SAS Institute. n.d. "Big Data Analytics." https://www.sas.com /en_us/insights/analytics/big-data-analytics.html.

Seller, Marianne, and Paul Gray. 1999. "A Survey of Database Marketing." Center for Research on Information Technology and Organizations, University of California at Irvine. https:// escholarship.org/uc/item/36z642kj.

Sengupta, Anirban, and Steven N. Wiggins. 2014. "Airline Pricing, Price Dispersion, and Ticket Characteristics On and Off the Internet." *American Economic Journal: Economic Policy* 6 (1): 272–307.

Shu, Catherine. 2018. "Waze Signs Data-Sharing Deal with AI-Based Traffic Management Startup Waycare." *Tech Crunch*, April 26. https://techcrunch.com/2018/04/26/waze -signs-data-sharing-deal-with-ai-based-traffic-manage ment-startup-waycare/.

Simonite, Tim. 2014. "Sell Your Personal Data for $8 a Month." *MIT Technology Review*, February 12. https://www.technol ogyreview.com/s/524621/sell-your-personal-data-for-8-a -month/.

Singer, Natasha. 2012. "Mapping, and Sharing, the Consumer Genome." *New York Times*, June 17. https://www.nytimes .com/2012/06/17/technology/acxiom-the-quiet-giant-of -consumer-database-marketing.html.

Sloane, Garett. 2018. "What Facebook Crisis? Ad Sales Skyrocket to $11.8 Billion, Users Don't #delete." *AdAge*, April 25. http:// adage.com/article/digital/privacy-concerns-facebook-ad -sales-hits-11-8-billion/3s13271/.

UNCTAD (United Nations Conference on Trade and Development). 2017. *Information Economy Report: Digitalization, Trade and Development*. Geneva: UNCTAD. http://unctad.org/en /PublicationsLibrary/ier2017_en.pdf.

Upwork. 2018. "Upwork Releases Q4 2017 Skills Index, Ranking the 20 Fastest-Growing Skills for Freelancers." Press release, February 7. https://www.upwork.com/press/2018/02/07 /q4-2017-skills-index/.

Wang, Teresa, and Malay Gandhi. 2014. "The Future of Biosensing Wearables: A Review of the Current Landscape and Future of Biosensing Wearables." Rock Health. https:// rockhealth.com/reports/the-future-of-biosensing-wear ables/.

Warren, Mark. 2016. "The Cure for Cancer Is Data—Mountains of Data." *Wired*, October 19. https://www.wired.com/2016/10 /eric-schadt-biodata-genomics-medical-research/.

Whitler, Kimberly A. 2016. "The Personal Data Revolution: Why It's Time for Marketers to Care." *Forbes*, September 18. https://www .forbes.com/sites/kimberlywhitler/2016/09/18/the-personal-data -revolution-why-its-time-for-marketers-to-care/#488b46db5681.

World Bank. 2016. *World Development Report: Digital Dividends*. Washington, DC: World Bank.

World Economic Forum. 2011. "Personal Data: The Emergence of a New Asset Class." World Economic Forum, Geneva. http:// www3.weforum.org/docs/WEF_ITTC_PersonalDataNew Asset_Report_2011.pdf.

———. 2013. "Unlocking the Value of Personal Data: From Collection to Usage." World Economic Forum, Geneva. http:// www3.weforum.org/docs/WEF_IT_UnlockingValuePersonal Data_CollectionUsage_Report_2013.pdf.

Zannier, Federico. n.d. "A Bite of Me." https://www.kickstarter .com/projects/1461902402/a-bit-e-of-me/description.

Chapter 5

Firms and Data

Introduction

Data is becoming crucial to the competitiveness of nations, regions, cities, and companies. This chapter highlights the implications of the transition to a data-driven economy for firms, especially in emerging markets. The emergence of the data economy has stimulated development of new business models and is transforming many of the key functions of private sector firms, including product development, customer relationships, supply chains, and core enterprise functions such as marketing, human resources, and finance. Governments in emerging markets are keen to explore and implement the right policies to allow private sectors to enhance competitiveness and benefit from new opportunities in the digital economy while mitigating risks.

The chapter examines the impact of data on firms from three distinct perspectives. The first part of the chapter introduces an assessment framework for digital platforms—a dominant aspect of data economies—and features case studies of selected digital platforms in emerging markets. Next, the chapter looks at how data affects firms, highlighting the tension between data as an equalizer, but also as a key competitive differentiator. Finally, the chapter looks at how data affects small and medium enterprises (SMEs)—and their specific needs.

Digital platforms

Defining digital platforms

Digital platforms might be defined as "multisided marketplaces with business models that enable producers and users to create value together by interacting with each other" (Still et al. 2017), and by facilitating matching, searching, exchanging, transactions, and so on (Evans 2013a, 2013b). Marketplaces rely on information to adjust prices and impose rational order, but information is frequently uneven and incomplete. Digital platforms offer advantages over traditional marketplaces through scale and network effects that increase the information flow and interaction between participants. Participants derive benefits from communications networks that increase as others join the system (Rohlfs 1974). For marketplaces that bring together suppliers (or advertisers) and users (or information consumers), economies of scale become even more important (Rochet and Tirole 2003). Multisided platforms benefit from positive network externalities, as the utility of each side increases as participants increase on the other side. For example, the utility of a car-sharing platform for each side increases with the increase of drivers and riders. The scale effects are not uniformly positive, however, and policy makers must recognize risks such as dominance and anticompetitive behavior.

Digital platform enablers

Digital platforms typically combine physical (and virtual) and behavioral (and market) enablers. *Physical enablers* (figure 5.1) include digital infrastructure (fixed and mobile broadband networks), smartphones, payment tools, geolocation, cloud-based services, security, and ancillary enablers (such as distribution, logistics, and intermediary goods). *Behavioral* or *market enablers* (figure 5.2) nudge consumers toward buying goods or accessing services in a peer-to-peer economy in which platforms increasingly mediate interactions, typically coordinated by peer-based trust relationships. This development is sometimes called collaborative consumption (Constantinou, Marton, and Tuunainen 2017).

Figure 5.1 Physical and virtual enablers

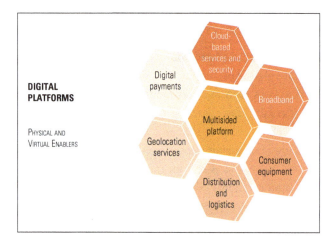

Figure 5.2 Market and behavioral enablers

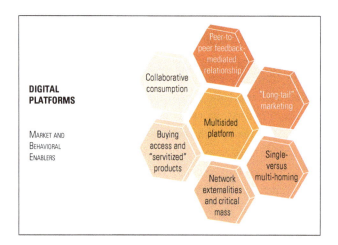

Platform enablers have important implications for economic development. Emerging and transitioning economies often lack pervasive broadband internet infrastructure (Kelly and Rossotto 2012), and present wide disparities in internet access among population groups (these differences relate to, among other things, urban versus rural, gender, age, education, and income differences). Equally important divides affect access to devices such as smartphones and laptops (World Bank 2016). Overcoming the digital divide is thus essential to developing digital platforms in emerging markets. In the Middle East and North Africa region, the ride-hailing platform Careem emphasizes the social value proposition of not only creating jobs, but fostering social value by allowing drivers to become micro-entrepreneurs, including by equipping them with smartphones.

The development of the physical and virtual enablers of digital platforms in developing countries may require dedicated policies, technical assistance, and investment. Digital infrastructure may also require a combination of telecommunication market liberalization, regulatory reform, and better targeting of subsidies to extend the commercial viability of broadband infrastructure (Kelly and Rossotto 2012) or public-private partnerships (Ragoobar, Whalley, and Harle 2011). Increasingly, as shown in chapter 3, these physical enablers are software based, such as artificial intelligence, the Internet of Things (IoT), machine learning, and autonomous vehicles (Lal Das et al. 2017; Schwab 2017). They may also require harmonized data protection and privacy standards to facilitate the development of cross-border operations (ITU 2015). The development of technology enablers has been crucially important, for instance, for Alibaba's ecosystem development (Tan et al. 2015) to bring together the trading platform, payment system, and logistics network that forms the basis for its e-commerce business platform (Tsai 2016; see figure 5.3).

The study of the market and behavioral enablers of digital platforms constitutes a research agenda by itself. In many cases, participant behavior and market development in emerging markets closely mirror that in high-income markets. For example, digital platforms to match labor supply and demand are popular in emerging markets: the Philippines, the Russian Federation, and Ukraine are among the top 10 countries providing skilled labor on Upworks' digital platform. Alibaba is a serious global competitor for eBay and Amazon, and Alipay's transactions are a multiple of those of Paypal.

Figure 5.3 Geographical concentration of digital multinational enterprises with revenue in excess of US$1 billion, by region, 2016

| 63: $2.8 trillion | 42: $670 billion | 27: $161 billion | 3: $61 billion |

● Publicly listed   ● Privately owned

Source: UNCTAD 2017, citing Van Alstyne 2016.

But ability to scale up and reach critical mass is limited to a relatively few emerging markets. Plus, platforms often exclude many economic actors, such as consumers outside the reach of mobile broadband coverage or without smartphones and SMEs without access to technology. SME owners can be encouraged to participate in platforms through tax breaks or subsidies or be given training or access to technology (Badran 2014). Incentives to global platforms to localize businesses by partnering with local businesses could also be an option, as shown, for example, by the Uber-Yandex agreement in Russia.

Business models for digital platforms

Emerging business models for multisided platforms are based around the bargaining power of different participants to drive revenues and organize dispersed information to make it available to market participants (Rochet and Tirole 2003). By using platforms, firms can drastically slash transaction costs, creating new markets (Henten and Windekilde 2016). By using social networks combined with such digital platforms, firms can leverage a "long tail" of market participants, that is a large number of customers with specific product preferences, or a large number of products that sell in small quantities (Enders et al. 2008). So-called long-tail effects on digital platforms give users more choice, enabling them to search for less common items or services from foreign countries, such as Indian music (Booth 2017) or Latin American cultural artifacts (Suominen 2017). The value to advertisers of capturing long-tail marketing data fosters marketplaces, such as Jumia in Africa (see box 5.1) and MercadoLibre in Latin America. Other differentiators may include price discrimination, delivery, geographic reach, and wholesale versus retail (Täuscher and Laudien 2018).

Platforms in emerging markets share many of the characteristics of business models encountered in high-income markets. Regional matching platforms like Laimoon.com (matching labor supply and demand in Arab countries) and Arabmatrimony.com seem to mirror the models, respectively, of Upworks and Match.com, taking cultural differences into account. Successful platform models that worked in advanced economies were also adopted by local platforms, as the case of Careem shows. Careem is a transport network company based in Dubai, with operations in 53 cities in the Middle East, North Africa, and South Asia. The company was valued at about US$1 billion as of 2017.

Jumia is an African online shopping website, primarily for electronics and fashion goods, developed through a strategy of envelopment and service diversification. Jumia launched in Lagos, Nigeria, in June 2012 with initial funding from Rocket Internet (Germany), MTN (South Africa), and Millicom (Luxembourg). It has grown through acquisitions and foreign expansion and, in fiscal year 2017, it generated some €93.8 million in revenue (US$111.4 million), although it continues to post substantial losses. It had 2.2 million customers across 14 countries in Africa, though it also offers sales elsewhere.[a]

As in most of Africa, Nigeria mostly uses cash, with 99 percent of transactions cash related. When launched, according to MasterCard,[b] some 59 percent of the Nigerians questioned the safety of online transactions and 43 percent were concerned about the quality of the products delivered and would rather buy from stores where they could physically inspect products.

To address these constraints, Jumia uses a cash-on-delivery mode of payment. Consumers can pay by cash or with a point-of-sale terminal and receive their receipt on the spot. This method addressed consumers' concerns, giving them the human contact associated with visiting a physical shop while building customer trust as well. Some earlier e-commerce ventures, such as kasuwa.com and sabunta.com, had failed and the incubator investor, Rocket Internet, merged and rebranded them as Jumia in 2012. Just a year after introducing the cash-on-delivery option in six Nigerian cities, Jumia.com.ng had become the most popular and fastest-growing online merchant in the country and accounted for 92 percent of total orders.[c]

In the Kenyan market, which Jumia entered in March 2013, the company also offers the facility to pay through mobile money. In addition, it has launched offline "experiential centers" to help consumers overcome their doubts about the look and feel of the products they are purchasing.[d] A major constraint on home delivery is the lack of formal street addresses in many African cities, or detailed mapping, and Jumia has had to develop its own maps for delivery.

For the moment, the global e-commerce majors, such as Amazon and Alibaba, have not developed a strong presence in Africa, though Amazon is building a fulfillment center in Cape Town[e] and Alibaba has established a fund for young African entrepreneurs.[f] It remains to be seen whether local African e-commerce companies, such as Takealot (South Africa), Kilimall (Kenya), Konga (Nigeria), as well as Jumia, can build sufficient scale to resist the global majors when they do arrive.

a. Financial information extracted from Rocket Internet financial report at https://www.rocket-internet.com/sites/default/files/investors/2017_FY%20Rocket%20Internet%20and%20Selected%20Companies%20Results.pdf.

b. Mastercard 2012.

c. Jumia, "Africa's Jumia and Zando Receive Significant Funding from J. P. Morgan Asset Management," Press Release, October 9, 2012 (https://blog.jumia.com.ng/wp-content/uploads/2012/10/J.P.-Morgan-Invests-in-Jumia2.pdf).

d. TechMoran 2017.

e. BusinessTech 2018.

f. See http://disrupt-africa.com/2017/07/alibabas-jack-ma-launches-10m-african-young-entrepreneurs-fund/.

As platforms have evolved, four main business models have emerged for revenue:

- Commission-based revenue

- Subscription-based and service-based

- Advertisement-based

- Tertiary services developed based on the data from the network (for example, supplier financing that many platforms provide to their sellers based on their transaction history on the platform)

Täuscher and Laudien (2018) introduce a taxonomy of platform business models in which, in addition to the four revenue models, other dimensions of the revenue source are also captured (such as price discrimination and source), in addition to the delivery dimensions (consumer to consumer, business to business, business to consumer, global, regional, and local, among others). Digital platforms may be primarily wholesale (business to business) or retail (business to consumer). Platforms may mutate the scope and breadth (reach, timeliness) of markets or lower entry barriers (or both), thereby affecting competitive dynamics.

Organizational science has introduced additional elements, adding new dimensions to this taxonomy, including the degree of standardization of output (product) and (input) and how they shape different organizational mechanisms.

The biggest obstacle to the development of certain digital platform models is the relative underdevelopment of the advertising industry in many emerging markets. This factor may limit the ability of platforms in those markets to subsidize a side of the business and limit the range of possible business models. One outcome is to encourage the development of "transactional" models to the detriment of commission-based platforms. A real estate owner in a high-income country, for instance, can choose whether to list a property on a pure, local marketplace (whose business model is purely advertising based) or to use a foreign, commission-based platform like Airbnb. But absent a mature advertising market, the consumer may have a more limited choice of platforms.

Digital platform dynamics

Platform dynamics have business and policy implications. The dominance of a platform, arising from network effects (winner-takes-all), raises competition concerns, although some argue that dominance can benefit consumers through greater convenience. Often, the achievement of critical mass drives platform dynamics (Evans 2013a, 2013b; Ruutu, Casey, and Kotivirta 2017).

Some authors propose a system dynamics simulation model of platform competition (Ruutu, Casey, and Kotivirta 2017), highlighting three cases. In the "chicken-and-egg" scenario, no platform achieves critical mass. In the "winner-takes-all" scenario, a vendor locks the participants into one dominant platform. The final scenario—"winner takes some"—is characterized by the "collaboration and competition scenario in which several platforms coexist in balanced competition" (Ruutu, Casey, and Kotivirta 2017, 128).

Various models have focused on the conditions for multiple platforms to grow first, and then to coexist in a competitive market. Both considerations matter in developing countries, and have policy and regulatory implications (Kenney and Zysman 2016; Frieden 2017). Network effects,

"critical mass" factors, and reversibility of participation create entry barriers and are likely to be more pronounced in developing countries (Evans and Schmalansee 2016).

Competition among multisided platforms depends on several factors, including network effects, and "single-homing" versus "multi-homing" scenarios (Armstrong 2006). If an agent uses only one platform, the agent is said to be single-homing; if the agent uses multiple multisided platforms, the agent is multi-homing. Network effects may lead to situations in which a proprietary platform may be socially desirable, as it partially internalizes two-sided indirect network effects and direct competitive effects on the producer side. Ruutu, Casey, and Kotivirta (2017, 128) indicate that "if platform adopters are able to react quickly, achieving a critical mass may be difficult because the platform firms cannot accumulate enough resources for sufficient platform development."

Competitive dynamics can be altered by "platform envelopment," a strategy through which an entrant platform can rapidly gain market share by entering another platform market and harnessing its network effects by offering a multiplatform bundle (Eisenmann, Parker, and Van Alstyne 2011). An example would be Google's offer of various services around its core search platform, including Google Translate (translation software), Google Checkout (online payment), Chrome (browsing), and Google Docs (productivity software). The services are often offered free of charge to the user (that is, paid by advertising), whereas other competitive service offerings may require payment.

The initial growth phase can be accelerated through open interfaces (that reinforce cross-side network effects), as well as by the ability to transfer user data among competing platforms. These tactics may lead to the envelopment of local service offerings in developing countries. They thus raise competition policy concerns as local companies in these countries often lack economies of scale to respond in kind. This may explain, in part, why the largest internet companies are so clustered in the United States and Asia (see figure 5.3).

Different dynamics can emerge and mutate over time. In the U.S. market for online platforms for books, for example, eBay acquired half.com, eliminating its most direct competitor. However, it did not prevent other platforms, notably Amazon .com (new and second-hand books, and a wide range of other products and services), from dominating the same market segment, deploying a different business model.

Will competition among platforms in emerging markets follow a similar dynamic? The choices may be more limited.

Network effects and critical mass considerations may skew competition toward foreign platforms. The huge size of the domestic Chinese e-commerce market was a factor leading to the emergence of Alibaba and Alipay as global leaders (Tsai 2016), while the ability to cater to domestic demand allowed Yandex to retain two-thirds of the addressable market in Russia. But few developing countries have such economies of scale, and there are many cases in which local platforms do not emerge as winners. As noted, the fear of a winner-takes-all scenario dominated by foreign platforms seems to be a major concern in many markets.

Partnership is another business strategy undertaken by digital platforms, especially in emerging markets. Incentives for global platforms to localize their businesses by partnering with a local business partner can also be an option. In China, Uber decided a better strategy was to sell out to its local partner, Didi Chuxing (Kharpal 2016), and in Southeast Asia it is selling to Grab in exchange for a stake in the combined company (Sherman 2018). The common shareholding in all three companies of Japan's Softbank, now the Visions Fund, seems to have played a part here (*The Economist* 2018a).

Access to user data is of vital value for online platforms to keep advertisers onboard and is a crucial tool for competing. Owning the end customer's data is akin to owning the market. This is one reason traditional freight forwarders are being squeezed by vertically integrated e-commerce companies.[1] Online platforms have an interest in locking out rivals that may threaten their market dominance. This makes data portability—the ability to transfer a user's data from one platform to another—a critical policy issue (Graef, Wahyuningtyas, and Valcke 2015). Data portability benefits users and secondary players in the market, but will most likely be opposed by the dominant players.

Digital platforms in developing countries

A study of digital platforms in emerging markets provides significant insights into business leaders and policy makers. Broadband and smartphone access will have a direct impact on network effects and platform diffusion; the maturity of the advertising market can exclude or boost advertising-based platform models; conversely, the maturity of digital payments, such as mobile money, in emerging markets may allow firms to determine the development of transaction-based models. The interplay of rapidly changing enabling conditions in emerging markets and rapidly changing business models (figure 5.4) will affect the three main drivers of platform dynamics: network effects, localization, and envelopment. To some extent, it will also determine whether winner-takes-some or winner-takes-all trends dominate.

Firms in the data economy

The Organisation for Economic Co-operation and Development (OECD), in its submission to a Group of Twenty conference, provides useful background about the opportunity of the data economy: "As the cost of data collection, storage and processing continues to decline dramatically, ever larger volumes of data will be generated from the IoT, smart devices, and autonomous machine-to-machine communications" (OECD 2017, 63). This will require a new approach to thinking about infrastructure in the twenty-first century, with the definition expanded to encompass broadband networks, cloud computing, and data itself, which drives productivity growth (OECD 2017).

In the United States, for instance, Brynjolfsson, Hitt, and Kim (2011) estimate that output and productivity in firms that adopt data-driven decision-making are 5 percent to 6 percent higher than what would be expected from their other investments in and use of information and communication technologies (ICTs). A study of 500 firms in the United Kingdom found that firms in the top quartile of online data use are 13 percent more productive than those in the bottom quartile (Bakhshi, Bravo-Biosca, and Mateos-Garcia 2014). Overall, these firm-level studies suggest that firms' use of data and data analytics raises labor productivity faster, by 5 percent to 10 percent (OECD 2015).

Other studies (such as Täuscher and Laudien 2018) identify several characteristics of digital business that create "dynamic competition and high consumer surplus" (Täuscher, n.d., 10). Many of these characteristics depend on data as their fundamental lever.

Product and service design

In many industries, data has become the new product, rather than the physical goods that firms traditionally sold. When you buy a custom-fitted suit, you often become an unwitting participant in a data economy in which "clothing companies now see body measurements (data) as one of their most prized currencies" (Harwell 2018). Stitch Fix, for example, which had nearly US$1 billion in sales last year, is really a data company in disguise (it gathers dozens of data points

Figure 5.4 A methodological approach to assessing digital platforms in emerging markets

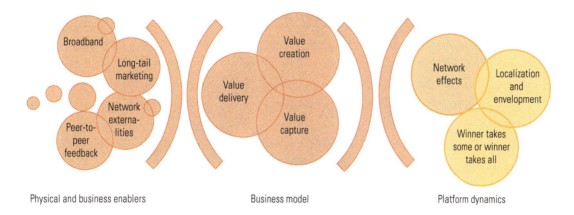

Physical and business enablers   Business model   Platform dynamics

on each customer, including weight, jobs, and past pregnancies). Similarly, the moment you buy a car, you start making money for companies like Otonomo, which sells driving data to third parties. The company has raised US$40 million in investments (Etherington 2017) designed to "move from the age of data mobilization, to the age of data monetization." And finally, when the world's top-ranked tennis player Simona Halep fell out with her clothing sponsor before the Australian Open "she took to the internet to find a design she liked, then ordered it from a seamstress in China. Twenty-four hours later, it was in her hands" (Matthey 2018).

Take a simple example from daily life: smartphone speech recognition can help write text messages three times faster than human typing (Carey 2016), a dramatic improvement over just a few years ago when speech recognition was considered an irritant (or an amusing novelty at best). The availability of more and better data (that feeds artificial intelligence) is the single most important reason for this enhancement, and firms that can successfully utilize the ever-increasing amounts of data at their disposal are beginning to separate themselves from their competitors by delivering new products and services that both depend on and generate vast amounts of data.

If data is to be the new oil, then firms must invest heavily in data refineries and new capabilities (see chapter 2). In 2016, Amazon, Alphabet, and Microsoft together spent nearly US$32 billion in capital expenditure and capital leases, up by 22 percent from the previous year. Firms are also investing significantly in developing analytical tools that can make sense of this data in real time and convert this data into artificial intelligence or "cognitive insights." Unfortunately, as the

scale of investments required to run data-driven businesses has grown substantially, the marketplace has begun to tilt in favor of large-scale incumbents (Surowiecki 2016). Other reports have likewise concluded that the rise of big digital businesses may be squelching competition (Casselman 2017) by using the power of their (data-driven) platforms.

This uneven growth between startups and incumbents is not limited to developed countries and there are still very few examples of scaled up data-driven firms in the developing world (see figure 5.3). Firms in the developing world face several additional data-specific challenges that create a tilted field in the marketplace:

- Low "datafication" of the economy (for instance, government records and archives may not be digitized)

- Limited data talent pool

- Restrictive data policies (localization, poorly developed privacy and consumer protection laws)

- Underdeveloped data ecosystem

- Generally, a higher unit price for data relative to affordability (see map 5.1)

Data-driven supply chains

Supply chains are a vital way for companies to create value and deliver products and services.[2] Technology-based supply chain innovation initially gave firms such as Walmart, which invested heavily in radio frequency identification chip technology, tremendous competitive advantage (FlashGlobal 2018). But firms like Amazon, which

Map 5.1 Average price of 1 gigabyte of mobile data per month, by country, 2016

a. Percent of per capita GDP

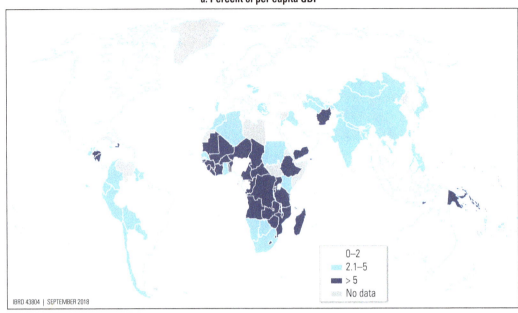

	0–2
	2.1–5
	> 5
	No data

IBRD 43804 | SEPTEMBER 2018

b. US dollars

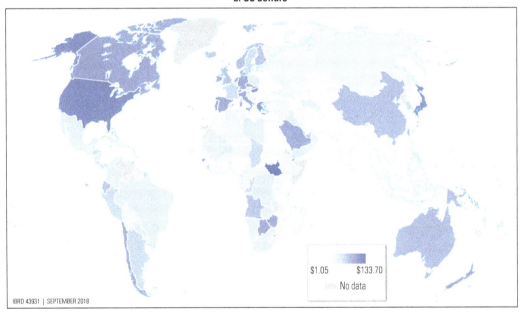

$1.05 $133.70
No data

IBRD 43931 | SEPTEMBER 2018

Source: ICTdata.org.

Note: The maps use International Telecommunication Union methodology (see table DN.1).

have mastered data and digital innovation (Burson 2016), are now showing the way. Koçoğlu et al. (2011) describe integration with customers, integration with suppliers, and interorganizational integration as the key value drivers in supply chain integration. Information or data sharing (with customers, suppliers, internal functions, and across organizations) is a core component across the entire supply chain and is being remade significantly as businesses digitalize ever more.

That said, McKinsey Global Institute (2018) found that as companies have begun to digitize products and services rapidly, supply chain digitization has lagged,[3] (yet the same firms expect the digitization of supply chains to have the highest impact on revenue in the near future). Progress has been especially slow in the management of supply chain data, according to McKinsey Global Institute (2017).[4] Challenges include the development of data infrastructure to manage vast amounts of data (what Ernst and Young [2016] called the "out-of-control data growth trap"), the ability to link disparate sources of data, and the development and utilization of tools to analyze data productively. These challenges have been heightened by the growth of data-fueled disruptive technologies—such as the IoT, artificial intelligence, robotics, and blockchain—that are fast becoming essential elements of supply chain management technology but are frequently beyond the capabilities of SMEs and their customers. Digital and data technologies that have integrated millions of firms and their suppliers in common global value chains are also gradually beginning to separate them.

Amazon is an illustrative example of a firm that has used its mastery of supply chain data to distance itself from competitors but also begin to erode the space of its suppliers and sellers on the platform. With its granular visibility into the operations of both the buyers and sellers on the platform, Amazon has realized that it can manufacture and distribute many products on its platform cheaper than other suppliers can (via the Amazon Basics program). Streamlining of the manufacturing, distribution, and retail of these products, combined with its mammoth scale and superior data smarts, gives Amazon tremendous competitive advantage. Can its competitors without access to any equivalent market data, such as Jumia (see box 5.1), compete?

Marketing and customer relationship management
Customer acquisition, management, and retention are core functions of business and digital and data technologies are transforming this landscape. In many ways, data and digital are the ultimate equalizing force. Firms using digital tools and platforms theoretically have equal access to customers around the world (local laws permitting), can use communication tools and platforms to stay engaged online in real time, and take advantage of a variety of payment systems and platforms plus logistics services to deliver products and services worldwide. This is how Uber was able to reach riders around the world, for instance, and how Instagram became a global rage. If these firms could acquire millions (and even billions) of customers and scale globally quickly, then so can other firms if they can create appropriate products and services.

There is an element of truth to this theory, but data confers several advantages on incumbents (indeed, it may be argued that several disruptors succeeded because the incumbents were not yet digitally or data savvy). Some of these examples include the following:

- *Personalization.* Incumbent firms can often deliver more personalized products and services to customers given the vast amount of data they have collected about them.

- *Predictive analytics.* Firms can use their vast data troves to predict the movies you like, the books you are likely to buy, and your likelihood of trying rival products and services. This gives them a significant advantage against competition.

- *Prescriptive analytics.* Data-smart firms are able to react to events in real time to resolve customer management issues (for instance, vouchers to compensate for a delayed flight [Brahm, Cheris, and Sherer 2016], rather than a routine customer survey, for instance).

Data-poor firms are at an inherent disadvantage in these scenarios.

SMEs in the data economy

Although the digital economy is increasingly dominated by a handful of tech majors, a multitude of innovative SMEs nevertheless are the drivers of the mobile and digital industries, particularly in newly emerging market segments such as data for self-driving vehicles or mobile applications. Opportunity exists therefore for tech-based SMEs to play a major role in the data-driven economy. The mobile ecosystem in Nigeria, for instance, was worth an estimated US$8.3 billion in 2017 (Boateng et al. 2017), and the digital industry may contribute 7 percent of Mali's GDP (da Silva 2014).

However, equally important is the impact of the data economy on SMEs in nontech sectors. It is estimated that half of all job opportunities in middle- and low-income countries are generated by local SMEs (Matthee and Heymans 2013). As a result, SMEs are instrumental in eradicating poverty, creating economic growth, and empowering citizens to become productive economic agents. But SMEs typically lag larger firms in the adoption of certain digital technologies (Andrews, Criscuolo, and Gal 2016). Although SMEs are just as likely to use broadband internet as larger firms, gaps still exist in adopting more sophisticated digital tools. The growing complexity of new technologies requires investment in new skills, and where these skills are lacking it is slowing technology diffusion among smaller and younger firms (Andrews, Criscuolo, and Gal 2016).

SME advantages, drivers, and constraints of data adoption

SMEs try to absorb new technologies and innovation, but are often constrained by limited availability of skilled workers, particularly in emerging markets, in turn limiting potential for growth and job creation. Starting in the 1990s, many SMEs in developing countries began to adopt modern ICTs, increasing profitability and productivity (Badran 2014). In addition, ICT made training and education more accessible for workers. This could eventually raise the employability of low-skilled workers.

SMEs are characterized by potentially advantageous features that distinguish them from other businesses. Their relatively small market size allows them to adapt quicker to changing market conditions, and they are less likely to have stranded assets, both of which increase their chances of success. Increasing digitization dramatically reduces transaction costs for collecting information, communication, and data controlling (World Bank 2016). Through easier access to information and the use of complex data analytics, firms may analyze the interdependency and buying patterns of users to pursue targeted advertisement, and adjust their inventory accordingly. SMEs can exploit low entry barriers to benefit from the potential disruption of data on existing models. Moreover, SMEs' digital technology adoption barriers can be lowered by the transition from hard infrastructure investments to platform-based digital services. The increasing availability and range of cloud-based tools for enterprise management is particularly relevant to SMEs.[5]

Data analytics allows firms to establish new forms of customer engagement, exploit digital distribution channels, and serve new customers. Data analytics, combined with voice and vision recognition, enables firms to complement or substitute for human labor with machines (such as automated call answering and recording to reduce call center employees). Leveraging data can also affect competition, with SMEs transforming processes, facilitating innovation, and addressing key challenges. Access to data can revolutionize decision-making with enhanced visibility of firm operations and improved performance measurement techniques.

Innovative data-driven business models for SMEs

The use of alternative data to build credit histories by scanning users' mobile phones for their history or credit charges, for instance, is spurring new business models for SMEs to provide credit to the underserved. Even in sectors unrelated to financial products and services, firms are developing new data-centric business lines and alternative revenue streams out of the data they collect from customers. Firms in Sub-Saharan Africa, such as M-KOPA Solar (Kenya),[6] Off Grid Electric (Tanzania),[7] PEG Africa (Ghana),[8] and BBOXX (Côte d'Ivoire),[9] have not only revolutionized energy access, but are also starting to support financial inclusion. Through "pay-as-you-glow" business models, these providers allow low-income, mostly rural consumers to have solar energy at home. On the basis of the data collected on the timeliness of repayments they accumulate for the home solar systems they offer, these energy companies can allow customers to build a credit history and thus access credit and loans.

However, challenges to the use of data and data analytics exist, particularly in emerging markets, which are more acute for SMEs than for larger firms, as discussed below.

First is *financial and access constraints*. SMEs tend to have limited access to financial resources, which makes it hard to invest in new technologies and maintain them. Limited financial resources also cause SMEs to lack a formal risk management practice, even for those that do have an information technology department (Priyadarshinee et al. 2017). In addition, SMEs in emerging markets often face obstacles accessing data relevant to their business. Larger firms gain access to that same data, often owned by the government, or are able to pay for it from private sources, thanks to larger financial resources or networks of contacts not available to SMEs.

Second is *limited awareness*. SMEs also tend to lack awareness of the opportunities offered by digitized business and operations, which affects their ability to adapt and compete in a fast-evolving business environment. A 2014 survey among 1,000 SMEs in Germany revealed that for 70 percent of enterprises with annual revenue below €500 million, the digitization of processes was still seen as irrelevant. Making the situation worse is that many available ICT products and information do not necessarily take the specific needs of SMEs into account.

Third, *human capital limitations* are a constraint. Investments in new technologies often require investments in complementary knowledge-based assets. SMEs frequently lack the skilled people to benefit from new digital

Digital technologies can change farm practices and agricultural structures and, hence, contribute to the prosperity and resilience of farming systems. Agribusiness supply chains are increasingly becoming data driven, which raises the need to move toward higher levels of data integration along production chains. Farmers and agribusinesses can benefit from enhanced data usage for improved sustainability, food safety, resource efficiency, and reduced waste. Over the last decade, information and communication technology (ICT) use in the farm sector has increased significantly. The World Bank (2017) highlights a range of areas in which ICT has been successfully applied (such as the use of GPS for farm field management, sensor data on crops and cattle to predict diseases, weather data, logistics tracing and tracking, online shops, agricultural market pricing data, and many others). Food supply chain players have been making advanced use of ICTs, with the next steps related to small and medium enterprise (SME) capabilities to unlock the potential generated by ICT applications. Farm data is still hardly shared with sectoral stakeholders, analyzed by intelligent software, or combined in regional analysis and advice. Hence, food supply chains may not fully take advantage of the large amounts of potential data, especially to smallholder farmers (figure B5.2.1).

Agribusiness is a sector with many small firms whose need will increase to invest in software and combine it with data seamlessly available to business partners and government agencies—as large firms already do internally in their enterprise resource planning systems. However, the limited interoperability of data and information systems makes it more complicated. This holds for SME-to-SME and SME-to-government communication as well as SME-to-big-company communication. For instance, consider the challenge for a large avocado cooperative that wishes to exchange digital data with thousands of farmers spread across Peru, or a dairy manufacturer that wants to monitor operational data from Ethiopian farmers. As such, business-to-business digital platform applications, and data common standards, become crucial to foster data usage in heavy supply chain sectors, like agribusiness.

Figure B5.2.1 How more data contributes to current business models in the food chain

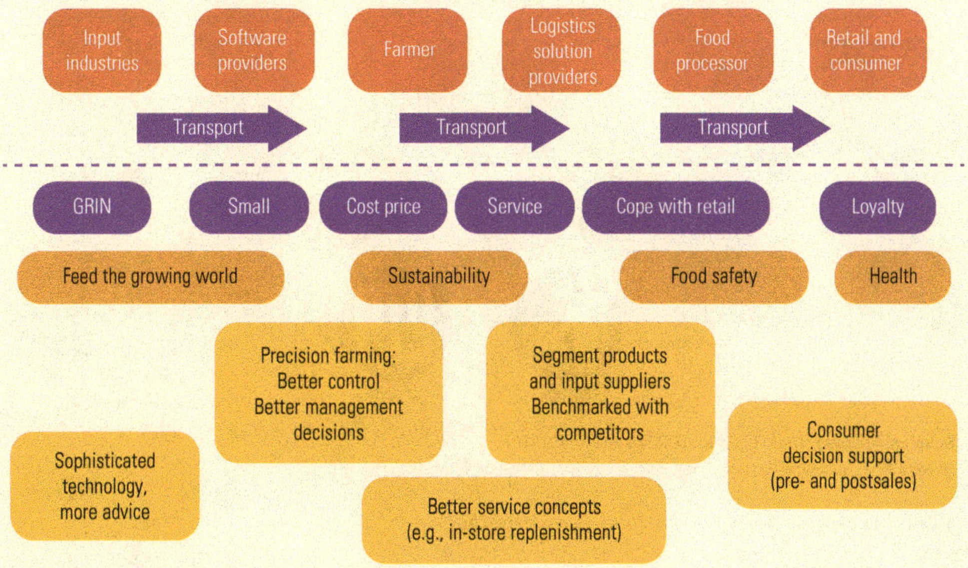

Source: Poppe et al. 2013.
Note: GRIN = Genetics, robotics, information, and nanotechnologies.

Alibaba, the world's largest e-commerce platform by sales volume, supports an estimated 10 million jobs, or 1.3 percent of China's workforce.

One of the most valuable assets Alibaba and other e-commerce operators accumulate is data. Data connects small and medium enterprises (SMEs), many of which are in the 2,000 plus so-called Taobao villages,[a] to Alibaba's ecosystem, and ultimately to consumers. Each transaction contributes to improved knowledge about the economy and consumer behavior. This information, coupled with data analytics, supports new business lines and product innovation, such as extending credit to small firms based on automated evaluations of creditworthiness (figure B5.3.1).

Chinese companies selling on Alibaba, in large part SMEs, reach an average of 3 and in some cases up to 100 different export destinations, up from an average of 1 and a maximum of 50 export destinations for offline firms. Alibaba further guarantees the on-time delivery of money from foreign buyers and has implemented a system to verify sellers on its website for business-to-business transactions. Firms can acquire a "gold" supplier status by paying for a third-party verification company to conduct on-site quality control. Alibaba is promoting its model abroad, with recent memoranda of understanding with both the Malaysian and Mexican governments, to provide SMEs in developing countries the skills to benefit from cross-border trade.

Figure B5.3.1 Alibaba's physical and virtual enablers

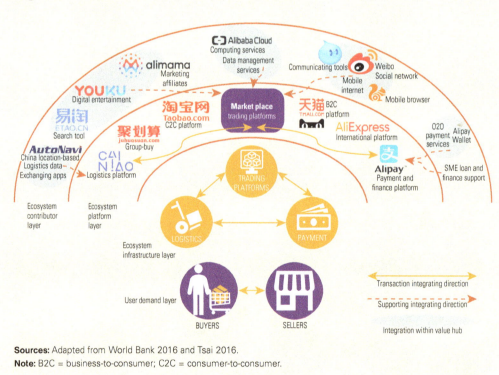

Sources: Adapted from World Bank 2016 and Tsai 2016.
Note: B2C = business-to-consumer; C2C = consumer-to-consumer.

a. See https://sampi.co/taobao-villages-china-rural-ecommerce/.

According to a recent report by the Mohammed Bin Rashid School of Government, more than 96 percent of users in the Arab States region said they personally had experienced a positive impact from digital platform apps, with some 55 percent saying it saved them time, 33 percent that it saved money, and 8 percent that it had personally generated income from delivering services on sharing economy apps. On the other hand, 3 percent of users reported negative impacts on the income of the users, mainly because these services hurt their existing sources of income (for example, taxi drivers and hotel owners). Digital platforms include transport applications, the most popular type of sharing economy services in the Arab world. Slightly more than half reported using the Careem and Uber apps, and a quarter use accommodation apps, such as Airbnb. Local alternatives, such as Tirhal and Mishwar, were also popular in some countries.

Sources: GSMA 2017; Salem 2017.

technologies, the resources to train these workers, or the management that can help them make the most of the new technologies. The lack of availability of skilled labor inhibits the adoption of data analytics, complex data integration, and model building in SMEs, especially in developing countries. That SMEs in emerging markets have a harder time competing for scarce skilled labor against larger firms, both local and foreign, compounds this challenge.

Fourth, *new data sources may require remodeling of existing systems, such as SME warehouse systems.* This is particularly true considering the volume and variety of structured and unstructured data becoming available from different sources, including social media. Organizational challenges also exist, such as internal resistance to adopting data analytics as a new way of doing business (Bain and Company 2013). On the other hand, wider access to different tools can help SMEs "turn digital" and help mitigate the challenges SMEs face.

Fifth, *infrastructure* constrains many SMEs in emerging markets because of challenges in accessibility, affordability, and quality of connectivity, particularly outside major urban centers (map 5.1). SMEs scattered across territories, particularly microenterprises and entrepreneurs, face a digital divide that could hinder the benefits of data for SMEs.

Sixth, *lack of trust.* This is mainly due to the increased digital security risks perceived by potential SME adopters, which is partly also the result of the increasing sophistication of digital security threats. In addition, the lack of data governance frameworks in many countries, or a lack of awareness of them or an understanding of how to comply,

affects the ability of SMEs to adopt digital-data-generating tools. These frameworks should include privacy policies, intellectual property, data security, and access rights. Emergent practices also risk reducing confidence in the digital economy and the incentives to adopt ICT. Discrimination enabled by data analytics, based on profiling customers by where they live, for example, may create greater efficiencies and innovation but also limit individual freedom (OECD 2015). On the other hand, disruptive technologies that tackle data governance aspects, such as distributed ledger technologies like blockchain, are emerging rapidly, facilitating inclusion. These could ease SME access to digital payments, loans, supply chains, land titles, contracts, or even ID.

Policies for SMEs in the data-driven economy

In an interconnected world, access to and use of digital technologies and data tools has become key to SME competitiveness, affecting the very chances to survive and develop. Cloud computing, in particular, allows smaller firms to overcome the barriers associated with the high fixed costs of ICT investment, and can help smaller firms rapidly scale up, providing high-power computing resources flexibly via a pay-as-you-go model.

SMEs tend to struggle to navigate the web of regulations and policies pertaining to data and understanding the legal and administrative frameworks governing cross-border data flows, data protection, data privacy, and personal data, to name a few. Data regulatory frameworks are complex, and many SMEs struggle to find the time and resources to fully comprehend their implications. SMEs may thus limit their utilization of data.

Evidence shows that the lack of appropriate (open) standards and fear of vendor lock-in, often due to proprietary solutions, can be strong barriers to adoption. This is particularly true for SMEs, which often lack the negotiating power and know-how about advanced ICTs such as cloud computing, data analytics, and the IoT (see OECD 2017).

Recent analysis suggests that small firms are often much more affected by poorly designed regulatory frameworks than large and incumbent firms, limiting their growth and reducing overall business dynamism. Policy action to boost the growth prospects of start-ups and SMEs is thus essential. The available data also point to systematic differences in the adoption of other complex digital technologies across firms.

The following policies can help SMEs benefit from the opportunities of the data-driven economy:

- *Implement a national digital transformation strategy for SMEs.* Enhancing competition in broadband internet to increase speed and reduce costs, promoting nationwide cloud service markets, or reducing import duties and taxes on information technology equipment are national policies with widespread impact that are particularly likely to benefit SMEs. In addition, specific strategic choices need to address the needs of SMEs. For example, digital public procurement has caused an increase of participation of digital SMEs. Awareness and technical training may be necessary to enable compliance with data policies and fully grasp the benefits of big data. A national strategy should also implement awareness-raising initiatives for SMEs to better understand the value of upgrading their technology and fully exploit the potential of digital data. Such an initiative could include, as appropriate, capacity-building programs specifically directed to SMEs.

- *Encourage technology adoption and complementary investments.* It is crucial not only to facilitate the access of SMEs to the technology itself, but also to help them make the necessary complementary investments, for example, in process and product innovation and in ICT services or in skills. SME engagement with competency centers or technology diffusion extension services can also be helpful.

- *Implement data security strategies, with SMEs as a specific segment.* Data security strategies often look just at the critical information infrastructure, but they should also address the specific needs of SMEs by providing them with practical guidance and the appropriate incentives for adopting good practices (see EU Digital SME Alliance 2017). For example, interest is increasing in tailored standards and certification schemes developed by or in cooperation with business and in leveraging digital risk.

- *Implement open data for business initiatives.* Some open government data initiatives focus on transparency and accountability and often tend to neglect its economic value. Disproportionate benefits exist from open data

Box 5.5 Open data for SMEs: The European Union and Colombia

In 2015, the European Union launched the Open Data Incubator for Europe, an incubator for open-data entrepreneurs across Europe that supports the next generation of digital businesses and fast-tracks development of products. Within the six-month incubation program, companies receive up to €100,000 (US$120,000) in equity-free funding, mentoring, business and data training, high-quality media, visibility at international events, and introductions to investors. Over the course of the 20-month project, the incubator has funded 57 companies. Each has contributed to the development of an open-data ecosystem underpinned by economic, social, and environmental benefits.

Colombia's Emprende con Datos is a project that provides support to entrepreneurs through mentoring and advice for the construction of sustainable business models and digital products and services; Colombian entrepreneurs, public entities, and small information and communication technology companies interested in resolving issues of public and social interest can participate in the use of open government data. Support is provided to selected entrepreneurs for 12 to 20 weeks, during which mentors work hand in hand with the entrepreneurs to strengthen their initiatives.

Sources: IDC 2017; and Government of Colombia 2018.

to SMEs, sowing the seeds of further growth and innovation. Even when government data does not have a price tag, the availability of data can depend on "who you are and who you know"; often, the relevant official must be persuaded to supply data and sometimes a personal visit to the office is necessary. As such, open data democratizes access and levels the field with respect to incumbents with established relationships and resources. In 2017, the World Bank's Open Data for Business assessment in Kenya found that small businesses could benefit from the release of government procurement, budget, and geospatial data, and that this would help address structural disadvantages in information access relative to larger, more established, companies.

- *Promote data cooperatives among SMEs and value chains.* These collaborative pools of data can facilitate access and use, and pave the way for moving beyond simply sharing information to a livelier exchange across public-private boundaries.

Looking ahead

Data inequalities, as noted, increasingly dominate in global economies, but they need not be permanent. Available policy options,[10] discussed further in chapter 6, include the following:

- Developing data infrastructure, though competitive market entry

- Closing the data talent gap

- Anticipating disruption, which may require, for instance, more frequent policy reviews and allowing new experimental approaches to flourish without preemptive regulation

- Further clarifying and improving the policy and regulatory environment

- Promoting data innovation and entrepreneurship

Develop data infrastructure

Recognition is growing within many governments that in the digital economy, as an infrastructure asset, data is on par with more traditional infrastructure like transport and public utilities. Indeed, stock exchanges place a much higher value on control of a customer's data than control of infrastructure (see chapter 1). Recent interest has

therefore been in crafting policy that recognizes data as an infrastructure asset.[11] These government policies typically focus on management of the data assets (collection, access, reuse, sharing, preservation, security) and data governance (ownership, funding), though some also address storage (data localization, data center management). The same principles apply to private sector firms gearing up to develop data assets. In addition, governments need to facilitate the development of physical infrastructure to manage data from nontraditional sources that the current telecom infrastructure is not designed to support (IoT, for instance, or call data records).

Close the data talent gap

The shortage of data skills may be the most serious systemic factor holding back data-based innovation and productivity in several countries. Research suggests that 90 percent of jobs within developed economies already require a measure of digital and data skills (UN Broadband Commission 2017), while less than one-third of the population possesses adequate skills. This is a gap that governments must close quickly. A few good practice examples include the Skills Plus program in Norway;[12] the Tech Partnership[13] (a network of employers focused on developing digital skills) and Doteveryone (an independent think tank focused on the digital society) in the United Kingdom;[14] the Intel-backed "She Will Connect"[15] initiative in Nigeria and Kenya; and the e-schools program in Estonia.

Count on disruption

The current wave of digital disruption has produced many winners that dominate the economic landscape (described by *The Economist* [2018b] as "Big, Anti-competitive, Addictive and Damaging to Democracy" or BAADD). The disruptors may soon become the disrupted, however, especially as even newer types of data sources emerge and firms with next-wave data skills develop new products and services. Other threats include the disruption of the current advertising-based models (Bershidsky 2017), which may suffer if more restrictive data policies become the norm and data ownership is relitigated in different societies. Others have theorized that decentralized technologies like blockchain might ultimately be the death knell for firms like Google or Facebook (Munster 2017). None of this is inevitable and it would be foolish to count the incumbents out, but the age of disruption is not over.

Notes

1. See https://www.economist.com/news/briefing/21741139 -will-be-bad-news-some-global-logistics-business-going-be -transformed.

2. See https://ac.els-cdn.com/S2351978917303918/1-s2.0 -S2351978917303918-main.pdf?_tid=0493ba6c-09e4–11e8 –9ef4–00000aacb360&acdnat=1517773737_248e32a343563 316344887ea19da9f17.

3. See https://www.mckinsey.com/business-functions/digital -mckinsey/our-insights/the-case-for-digital-reinvention.

4. See https://www.mckinsey.com/business-functions/operations /our-insights/digital-transformation-raising-supply-chain -performance-to-new-levels.

5. For more information, see https://www.capterra.com/customer -service-software/.

6. See http://www.m-kopa.com/.

7. See http://offgrid-electric.com/.

8. See https://www.pegafrica.com/.

9. See http://www.bboxx.co.uk/.

10. For more information, see World Bank 2017.

11. See https://theodi.org/what-is-data-infrastructure.

12. See https://www.kompetansenorge.no/English/Basic-skills /Competenceplus/.

13. See https://www.thetechpartnership.com/.

14. See https://doteveryone.org.uk/.

15. For more information, see Intel 2013.

References

Andrews, D., C. Criscuolo, and P. N. Gal. 2016. "The Best versus the Rest: The Global Productivity Slowdown, Divergence across Firms and the Role of Public Policy." Productivity Working Paper 5, OECD Publishing, Paris. https://www.oecd .org/global-forum-productivity/library/OECD%20Produc tivity%20Working%20Paper%20N%C2%B05.pdf.

Armstrong, Mark. 2006. "Competition in Two-Sided Markets." *RAND Journal of Economics* 17 (3): 688–91.

Badran, Mona Farid. 2014. "Access and Use of ICTs in Female-Owned SMEs in Selected Arab Countries and Brazil: A Comparative Study." Working Paper 2014/12, Maastricht School of Management. https://www.msm.nl/resources /uploads/2014/05/MSM-WP2014-12.pdf.

Bain and Company. 2013. "Big Data: The Organizational Challenge." https://www.bain.com/insights/big_data_the_organizational _challenge/.

Bakhshi, Hasan, Albert Bravo-Biosca, and Juan Mateos-Garcia. 2014. "Inside the Datavores: Technical Report." Nesta. https://www .nesta.org.uk/report/inside-the-datavores-technical-report/.

Bershidsky, Leonard. 2017. "Google and Facebook Too Can Be Disrupted." *Bloomberg*, December 8. https://www.bloomb erg.com/view/articles/2017-12-08/google-and-facebook-too -can-be-disrupted.

Boateng, Richard, Joseph Budu, Alfred Sekyere Mbrokoh, Eric Ansong, Sheena Lovia Boateng, and Augustus Barnnet Anderson. 2017. "Digital Enterprises in Africa: A Synthesis of Current Evidence." http://believeoverhope.org/pearlrichards /index.php/2017/08/20/digital-enterprises-in-africa-a-syn thesis-of-current-evidence/.

Booth, Gregory D. 2017. "A Long Tail in the Digital Age: Music Commerce and the Mobile Platform in India." *Asia Music* 48 (1): 85–113.

Brahm, Chris, Aaron Cheris, and Lori Sherer. 2016. "What Big Data Means for Customer Loyalty." Brief, Bain and Company, August 7. http://www.bain.com/publications/articles/what -big-data-means-for-customer-loyalty.aspx.

Brynjolfsson, Erik, Lorin M. Hitt, and Heekyung Hellen Kim. 2011. "Strength in Numbers: How Does Data-Driven Decision Making Affect Firm Performance?" Unpublished. https:// papers.ssrn.com/sol3/papers.cfm?abstract_id=1819486.

Burson, Forrest. 2016. "6 Ways Amazon Is Changing Supply Chain Management in 2016." Software Advice. https://www.software advice.com/resources/amazon-supply-chain-management/.

BusinessTech. 2018. "A First Look at Amazon's New Offices in Cape Town." https://businesstech.co.za/news/business/227745/a -first-look-at-amazons-new-offices-in-cape-town/.

Carey, Bjorn. 2016. "Smartphone Speech Recognition Can Write Text Messages Three Times Faster Than Human Typing." *Stanford News Services*, August 24. https://news.stanford.edu/2016/08/24 /stanford-study-speech-recognition-faster-texting/.

Casselman, Ben. 2017. "A Start-Up Slump Is a Drag on the Economy; Big Business May Be to Blame." *New York Times*, September 20. https://www.nytimes.com/2017/09/20/busi ness/economy/startup-business.html.

Constantinou, Ioanna, Attila Marton, and Virpi Kristiina Tuun-ainen. 2017. "Four Models of Sharing Economy Platforms." *MIS Quarterly Executive* 16 (4): 231–51. http://misqe.org /ojs2/index.php/misqe/article/viewFile/798/474.

da Silva, Issa Sikiti. 2014. "Mali Digital Plan 2020 to Reorganise Economy." *Biztech Africa*, December 9. http://www.biztech africa.com/article/mali-digital-plan-2020-reorganiseecon omy/9327/.

The Economist. 2018a. "A Bold Scheme to Dominate Ride-Hailing." May 10. https://www.economist.com/briefing/2018/05/10/a -bold-scheme-to-dominate-ride-hailing.

———. 2018b. "The Techlash against Amazon, Facebook and Google—And What They Can Do." January 20. https://www .economist.com/briefing/2018/01/20/the-techlash-against -amazon-facebook-and-google-and-what-they-can-do.

Eisenmann, Thomas R., Geoffrey Parker, and Marshall Van Alstyne. 2011. "Platform Envelopment." *Strategic Management Journal* 32 (12): 1270–85.

Enders, Albrecht, Harald Hungenberg, Hans-Peter Denker, and Sebastian Mauch. 2008 "The Long Tail of Social Networking: Revenue Models of Social Networking Sites." *European Management Journal* 26 (3): 199–211.

Ernst and Young. 2016. "Digital Supply Chain: It Is All About That Data." https://www.ey.com/Publication/vwLUAssets/Digital _supply_chain_-_its_all_about_the_data/%24FILE/EY-digit al-supply-chain-its-all-about-that-data-final.pdf.

Etherington, Darrell. 2017. "Otonomo Raises $25m to Help Auto-makers Make Money from Connected Cars." *TechCrunch*, April 7. https://techcrunch.com/2017/04/07/otonomo-raises-25m -to-help-automakers-make-money-from-connected-cars/.

EU Digital SME Alliance. 2017. "European Cybersecurity Strategy: Fostering the SME Ecosystem." https://www.cyberwatching.eu /news-events/news/european-cybersecurity-strategy-fostering -sme-ecosystem.

Evans, David S. 2013a. "Economics of Vertical Restraints for Multi-sided Platforms." Working Paper, Coase-Sandor Institute for Law and Economics, Chicago. https://chicagounbound.uchicago.edu /cgi/viewcontent.cgi?article=1187&context=law_and_economics.

———. 2013b. "Some Empirical Aspects of Multi-sided Platform Industries." *Review of Network Economics* 2 (3): 191–209.

Evans, David S., and Richard Schmalansee. 2016. *Matchmakers: The New Economics of Multisided Platforms.* Boston: Harvard Business Review Press.

FlashGlobal. 2018. "Walmart: 3 Keys to Successful Supply Chain Management Any Business Can Follow." April 12. https:// flashglobal.com/blog/supply-chain-management-walmart/.

Frieden, Rob. 2017. "The Internet of Platforms and Two-Sided Markets: Legal and Regulatory Implications for Competition and Consumers." Working paper, College of Communica-tions, Pennsylvania State University, State College, PA. https:// ssrn.com/abstract=3051766.

Government of Colombia. 2018. "Emprende con Datos Finalizó con Más 60 Equipos Apoyados" [Start with Data Finished with More Than 60 Teams Supported]. Ministry of ICT. http://www.mintic.gov.co/portal/604/w3-article-73884.html.

Graef, Inge, Sih Yuliana Wahyuningtyas, and Peggy Valcke. 2015. "Assessing Data Access Issues in Online Platforms." *Telecommunications Policy* 39 (5): 375–87.

GSMA. 2017. *Embracing the Digital Revolution Policies for Building the Digital Economy.* Digital Transformation Report 2017. GSMA. https://www.gsma.com/publicpolicy/wp-content /uploads/2017/02/GSMA_DigitalTransformationReport2017 _Web.pdf.

Harwell, Drew. 2018. "Companies Race to Gather a Newly Prized Currency: Our Body Measurements." *Washington Post,* January 16. https://www.washingtonpost.com/business /economy/companies-race-to-gather-a-newly-prized-cur rency-our-body-measurements/2018/01/16/5af28d98-f6e8 -11e7-beb6-c8d48830c54d_story.html?noredirect=on&utm _term=.4eb7f0e18af4.

Henten, Anders, and Iwona Windekilde. 2016. "Transaction Costs and the Sharing Economy." *Info* 18 (1): 1–15.

IDC (International Data Corporation). 2017. "Impact Assessment of Odine Program: Open Data Incubator Europe." https:// opendataincubator.eu/.

ITU (International Telecommunication Union). 2015. "Interoper-ability in the Digital Ecosystem." GSR Discussion Paper, ITU, Geneva. https://www.itu.int/en/ITU-D/Conferences/GSR /Documents/GSR2015/Discussion_papers_and_Presenta tions/Discussionpaper_interoperability.pdf.

Intel. 2013. "Intel: She Will Connect Initiative." https://www.intel .com/content/www/us/en/corporate-responsibility/social -impact-and-educational-initiatives/she-will-connect.html.

Kelly, Tim, and Carlo Maria Rossotto. 2012. *Broadband Strategies Handbook.* Washington, DC: World Bank. https://openknow ledge.worldbank.org/handle/10986/6009.

Kenney, M., and J. Zysman. 2016. "The Rise of the Platform Economy." *Issues in Science and Technology* 32 (3): 61–69.

Kharpal, Arjun. 2016. "5 Reasons Why Uber Sold Its China Busi-ness to Didi Chuxing." CNBC, August 1. https://www.cnbc .com/2016/08/01/5-reasons-why-uber-sold-its-china-busi ness-to-didi-chuxing.html.

Koçoğlu, İpek, Salih Zeki İmamoğlu, Hüseyin İnce, and Halit Keskin. 2011. "The Effect of Supply Chain Integration on Informa-tion Sharing: Enhancing the Supply Chain Performance." *Procedia—Social and Behavioral Sciences* 24: 1630–49. https:// www.sciencedirect.com/science/article/pii/S1877042811015448.

Lal Das, Prasanna, Stephan Beisswenger, Srikanth Mangalam, and Rasit Yuce. 2017. "Internet of Things: The New Government to Business Platform—A Review of Opportunities, Practi-ces, and Challenges." World Bank, Washington, DC. http:// documents.worldbank.org/curated/en/610081509689089303 /Internet-of-things-the-new-government-to-business-plat form-a-review-of-opportunities-practices-and-challenges.

Mastercard. 2012. "Nigerians Enjoy the Convenience, Pricing and Choice of Online Shopping—MasterCard Survey." Press release, May 1. https://www1.mastercard.com/content/intel ligence/en/research/press-release/2012/Nigerians-enjoy -the-convenience-pricing-and-choice-of-online-shopping .html.

Matthee, Marianne, and André Heymans. 2013. "How South Afri-can SMEs Can Become Better Candidates for Export Finance." *Managing Global Transitions* 11 (4): 391–407.

Matthey, James. 2018. "There's Something Unusual about Simona Halep's Australian Open Dress." News.com.au, January 26. https://www.news.com.au/sport/tennis/australian-open/there

s-something-unusual-about-simona-haleps-australian-open
-dress/news-story/28d7ce2da03fb00a9ad2bd5a79093156.

McKinsey Global Institute. 2017. "Digital Transformation: Raising
Supply-Chain Performance to New Levels." https://www.mckinsey
.com/business-functions/operations/our-insights/digital-transform
ation-raising-supply-chain-performance-to-new-levels.

———. 2018. "Digital Reinvention: Unlocking the 'How.'" https://
www.mckinsey.com/~/media/McKinsey/Business%20Func
tions/McKinsey%20Digital/Our%20Insights/Digital%20
Reinvention%20Unlocking%20the%20how/Digital-Reinven
tion_Unlocking-the-how.ashx.

Munster, Brett. 2017. "Could Blockchain Disrupt Facebook and
Google's Business Model?" *Medium.* https://medium.com
/road-less-ventured/could-blockchain-disrupt-facebook
-and-googles-business-model-fda614de492d.

OECD (Organisation for Economic Co-operation and Development). 2017. "Key Issues for Digital Transformation in the
G20." G20 Germany Presidency and OECD Conference,
January 12. https://www.oecd.org/g20/key-issues-for-digital
-transformation-in-the-g20.pdf.

Poppe, Krijn J., Sjaak Wolfert, Cor Verdouw, and Tim Verwaart.
2013. *Information and Communications Technologies as
a Driver for Change in Agri-Food Chains.* https://s3.ama
zonaws.com/academia.edu.documents/40043142/542e8
ba40cf277d58e8ebffd.pdf20151115-68247-1ccjezq
.pdf?AWSAccessKeyId=AKIAIWOWYYGZ2Y53UL3A
&Expires=1537343545&Signature=ZMUDN6eXwMB17wL
KmsIDXAZzfR4%3D&response-content-disposition
=inline%3B%20filename%3DInformation_and
_Communication_Technology.pdf.

Priyadarshinee, Pragati, Rakesh Raut, Manoj Jha, and Bhaskar B.
Gardas. 2017. "Understanding and Predicting the Determin-
ants of Cloud Computing Adoption: A Two Staged Hybrid
SEM-Neural Networks Approach." *Computers in Human
Behavior* 76: 341–62.

Ragoobar, Tricia, Jason Whalley, and David Harle. 2011. "Public
and Private Intervention for Next-Generation Access
Deployment: Possibilities for Three European Countries."
Telecommunications Policy 35 (9): 827–41.

Rochet, Jean-Charles, and Jean Tirole. 2003. "Platform Competition in Two-Sided Markets." *European Economic Association*
1 (4): 990–1029.

Rohlfs, J. 1974. "Theory of Interdependent Demand for a
Communications Service." *Bell Journal of Economics and
Management Science* 5 (1): 16–37.

Ruutu, Sampsa, Thomas Casey, and Ville Kotivirta. 2017. "Develop-
ment and Competition of Digital Service Platforms: A System
Dynamics Approach." *Technological Forecasting and Social
Change* 117: 119–30.

Salem, Fadi. 2017. *The Arab World Online: Digital Transformations
and Societal Trends in the Age of the 4th Industrial Revolution.*

Vol. 3. Dubai: Mohammed Bin Rashid School of Government.
https://img0bm.b8cdn.com/images/uploads/article_docs
/arab_world_online_2017_4ir_d_fadi_salem_34792_EN.pdf.

Schwab, Klaus. 2017. *The Fourth Industrial Revolution.* New York:
Crown Business.

Sherman, Alex. 2018. "Uber Is Preparing to Sell Southeast Asia Unit
to Grab in Exchange for Stake in Company: Sources." CNBC
News, February 16. https://www.cnbc.com/2018/02/16/uber
-preparing-to-sell-southeast-asia-unit-to-grab.html.

Still, Kaisa, Marko Seppänen, Heidi Korhonen, Katri Valkokari,
Arho Suominen, and Miika Kumpulainen. 2017. "Business
Model Innovation of Startups Developing Multisided Digital
Platforms." In *2017 IEEE 19th Conference on Business Informat-
ics (CBI 2017)*, Vol. 2, 70–75. http://ieeexplore.ieee.org/stamp
/stamp.jsp?tp=&arnumber=8012942&isnumber=8012382.

Suominen, Kati. 2017. "Accelerating Digital Trade in Latin America
and the Caribbean." Working paper, Inter-American Development Bank, Washington, DC. https://publications.iadb.org
/bitstream/handle/11319/8166/Accelerating-Digital-Trade
-in-Latin-America-and-the-Caribbean.PDF.

Surowiecki, James. 2016. "Why Startups Are Struggling."
Technology Review, June 15. https://www.technologyreview
.com/s/601497/why-startups-are-struggling/.

Tan, Barney, Shan Ling Pan, Ziangua Lu, and Lihua Huang. 2015.
"The Role of IS Capabilities in the Development of Multi-sided
Platforms: The Digital Ecosystem Strategy of Alibaba.com."
Journal of the Association for Information Systems 16 (4): 248–80.

Täuscher, Karl. n.d. "Business Models in the Digital Economy:
An Empirical Study of Digital Markets." Working paper,
Fraunhofer MOEZ, Fraunhofer Center for International
Management and Knowledge Economy, Leipzig. https://
www.imw.fraunhofer.de/content/dam/moez/de/documents
/Working_Paper/Working_Paper_Digital_Marketplaces
_final.pdf.

Täuscher, Karl, and Sven Laudien. 2018. "Understanding Platform
Business Models: A Mixed Methods Study of Marketplaces."
European Management Journal 36 (3): 319–29.

TechMoran. 2017. "Jumia Launches Offline Experiential Centers in
Kenya." September 14. https://techmoran.com/jumia-launches
-offline-experiential-centers-in-kenya/.

Tsai, Wen-Chun. 2016. "Analyzing the Emergence of Alibaba
Group from Business Ecosystem Perspective." *Journal of
International Management Studies* 11 (2): 53–64.

UN Broadband Commission. 2017. "Working Group on Education: Digital Skills for Life and Work." Report, Broadband
Commission for Sustainable Development. http://unesdoc
.unesco.org/images/0025/002590/259013e.pdf.

UNCTAD (United Nations Conference on Trade and Development).
2017. *Information Economy Report 2017: Digitalization, Trade
and Development.* Geneva: UNCTAD. http://unctad.org/en
/PublicationsLibrary/ier2017_en.pdf.

Van Alstyne, M. 2016. "Platform Shift: How New Biz Models Are Changing the Shape of Industry." Video. https://www.youtube.com/watch?v=8OFRD66pI0Y.

World Bank. 2016. *World Development Report 2016: Digital Dividends.* Washington, DC: World Bank. doi:10.1596/978-1-4648-0671-1.

———. 2017. "Internet of Things: The New Government to Business Platform—A Review of Opportunities, Practices, and Challenges." Washington, DC. http://documents.worldbank.org/curated/en/610081509689089303/Internet-of-things-the-new-government-to-business-platform-a-review-of-opportunities-practices-and-challenges.

Chapter 6

Policies for the Data Economy

Introduction

As seen throughout this report, data is at the heart of the digital economy—it is the raw material for the development of new products and services and refinement of existing ones. It is also a new asset class, worth billions of dollars. Data is also a policy area that has been evolving very rapidly in the past few years because of the rapid changes in technologies and their effects on relevant data policies. Policy makers struggle to keep up, despite efforts to issue technology-neutral data policy frameworks. As nontraditional sources of data become more common, and data is used in entirely novel ways, questions arise about who owns what data, who can do what with it, and what protections are afforded to whom.

One overarching message is that data policies can achieve greater impact using a dynamic ecosystem approach. Governments need to play a multidimensional role and create new partnerships with a wide range of stakeholders to achieve them. This chapter discusses four dimensions of this question.

First, the chapter briefly reviews policies for building strong data infrastructure to support making data available, including those for management of data assets and data governance. It focuses on open data and principles for data sharing between government, businesses, and individuals.

Second, the chapter considers policies geared toward building consumer trust and principles for setting limits on what can be done with data, such as data protection and privacy (including cross-border data flows and data localization) and data security. Trust encourages governments, the private sector, and users to innovate and benefit from the data revolution.

Third, data security is examined. The lack of a secure and trusted environment could delay both the adoption of data-enabled services and products and, potentially, their offering by the private sector. This could put emerging market economies at a disadvantage in participation in global innovation, educational, and commercial networks. Finally, the chapter covers complementary policies that facilitate building a data economy. Those include policies to support innovation, and those that help build digital skills and entrepreneurship.

As a rapidly evolving area of policy, the examples presented here focus on recent changes. Many come from the European Union (EU), as the European Commission (EC) is moving faster and farther than most in this area. The potential ease of transferring data, including through accessing websites across borders, gives the standards an international dimension (figure 6.1). Thus, new regulations such as the General Data Protection Regulation (GDPR) are of interest for the principles they espouse and for the practical issues they raise for anyone digitally interacting with them, including developing countries.

Figure 6.1 A framework for data policies

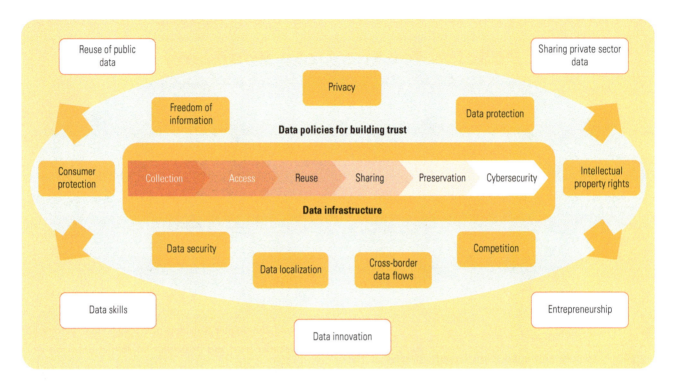

Policies for building data as an infrastructure asset

Data as infrastructure has recently become a prominent topic for discussion in policy circles. Recognition is growing within many governments that, in the digital economy, data is a critical new infrastructure asset that enables new, often more efficient and inclusive delivery of other activities, particularly services. The value of the data and the potential for use expands with quantity and quality. Interest has surged in crafting policies to support wider use of data, while also recognizing the new risks and challenges it poses. This first section looks at policies to expand the sharing of data and the next looks at how to balance that with addressing concerns about privacy and security.

Greater access to data also has beneficial spillovers, and data can be used and reused to open up significant growth opportunities or to generate benefits across society in ways unforeseen when the data was created. The Organisation for Economic Co-operation and Development (OECD) therefore recommends that policy makers aim for an innovation policy mix that encourages investments in data (its collection, curation, and reuse), while addressing the low appropriation of

returns to encourage data sharing (OECD 2015). This calls for ensuring a relevant legal framework exists, with policies aiming for the extensive sharing, use, and development of public data sources and research data infrastructure. Policies governing business-to-business and business-to-government data also need to encourage appropriate sharing of data, spurring innovation while avoiding stifling competition.

Governments increasingly recognize government data as a strategic resource (the data management policy of Qatar's Ministry of Information and Communications Technology [2015], for instance, explicitly identifies it as such). The New Zealand data and information management principles provide a useful set of principles stating that information should be open, readily available, well managed, reasonably priced, and reusable, unless there are necessary reasons for its protection (Government of New Zealand 2011). Personal and classified information will remain protected. Government data and information should also be trusted and authoritative.[1]

In supporting strong data infrastructure, governments should consider policies focused both on management of data assets and on data governance. The next section considers these issues for three types of data sharing—the reuse of certain government data, business-to-business data, and business-to-government data.

Policies on the reuse of public sector information

Many now recognize public data in user-friendly formats freely available online for anyone to use and for any purpose as a major resource to aid economic growth. While social media, companies, and nongovernment organizations can all be sources of open data, the term is usually applied to data that comes from government and government-supported institutions—open government data. The data governments collect or generate, when freely available, is more than just a tool to hold governments accountable. It also drives innovation that can help launch new businesses, optimize existing companies' operations, create jobs, and improve the climate for foreign investment (World Bank 2014). Increased availability of data can fuel the private sector through access to new types of public and publicly funded data, including data held by utility companies and the transport sector, and research data.

The benefits connected to reusable public data, especially open government data, are diverse and yet largely untapped. Positive outcomes range from greater transparency, efficiency, and economic growth to broader social welfare. Although some countries are applying the "open-by-default" principle to public data sharing policies, particularly advanced economies, this does not imply that all data sets should be made available to the public. When thinking of open data policies, governments can consider that the same limits apply to open data as to access to information. In other words, the protection of privacy, personal data, or national security are common limits. In addition, for governments just beginning to open their data, opening certain data sets over others holds more potential value. Geospatial data, or data on weather, transport, and roads, can be particularly critical, and among the first any government should consider opening.

The Open Data Charter sets out six principles developed in 2015 by governments, civil society, and experts around the world to represent a globally agreed-on set of aspirational norms for how to publish data (table 6.1). So far, 57 national and local governments have adopted it for the development of open data policies. However, a vast amount of public information is still made available (if at all) in non-user-friendly formats (that is PDFs and JPEG), making this data suboptimal for creating value-added services and products.

Transparency has been an objective of many open data initiatives in the past decade, based on the principle that sunlight is the best disinfectant.[2] The most important data sets that help enable the growth of an anticorruption culture have now become clearer: corporate registers, public contracting information, information on public officials, land registration information, government budget and spending data, and courts data are all helpful for this agenda. Moreover, the modalities of the publication of this data are also important. Data published in user-friendly, machine-readable formats helps governments fight corruption more effectively as it enables civil society to analyze and support government efforts to identify irregularities. Promotion of common standards, such as the Open Contracting Data Standard, enables sharing of toolsets so that local activists can build on the work of those in other jurisdictions.

Although anticorruption has been an objective of many open data initiatives in the past decade, the supply of data alone is seldom sufficient[3]—civil society actors who will use the data, as well as government willingness to respond, are needed; with these in place, a "virtuous circle" can be created in which some initial pressure leads to initial improvement and release of more data.

Data access policies are increasingly expanding to cover data generated by publicly funded research. "Open science" efforts rely on the premise that scientific information resulting from public funding should be accessible and reusable, with as few restrictions as possible. The opening of research processes, designs, workflows of dissemination of results, and methodologies can expand quality, avoid duplication, and facilitate reuse, which ultimately can help maximize the societal role of science. Research data policies need to ensure coherence and complementarity between open access and open data policies.

Governments can also promote business opportunities by mainstreaming the use of application programming interfaces (APIs) for more automatic access to dynamic data. This has important implications in supporting data ecosystems, as it saves costs and time to access data, facilitating practical usage. Sharing data through secure APIs can produce value added for data assets across the data value chain, particularly where potential is often unexploited by data holders. However, current public sector use of APIs is limited,

Table 6.1 Open data principles

	1. Open by default This can represent a real shift in how governments operate and how they interact with citizens. The presumption is that governments need to justify data that is kept closed, for example, for security or data protection. To make this work, citizens must also feel confident that open data will not compromise their right to privacy.
	2. Timely and comprehensive Open data is only valuable if it is still relevant. Getting information published quickly and in a comprehensive way is central to its potential for success. As much as possible, governments should provide data in its original, unmodified form. Maintaining historical data is important for keeping track of changes and evaluating the impact of reforms.
	3. Accessible and usable Ensuring data is machine readable and easy to find will make it go further. Portals are one way of achieving this. But it is also important to think about the user experience of those accessing data, including the file formats in which information is provided. Data should be free of charge, under an open license, for example, those developed by Creative Commons.
	4. Comparable and interoperable Data has a multiplier effect. The more quality data sets you have access to, and the easier it is for them to talk to each other, the more potential value you can get from them. Commonly agreed-upon data standards play a crucial role in making this happen.
	5. For improved governance and citizen engagement Open data has the capacity to let citizens (and others in government) have a better idea of what officials and politicians are doing. This transparency can improve public services and help hold governments to account.
	6. For inclusive development and innovation Finally, open data can help spur inclusive economic development. For example, greater access to data can make farming more efficient or it can be used to tackle climate change. Finally, we often think of open data as just about improving government performance, but a whole universe exists of entrepreneurs making money from open data.

Source: Open Data Charter.

Box 6.1 Defining a policy framework for open data: Mexico's experience

In 2015, Mexico aimed to make government public data available to all citizens in user-friendly formats on the data.gob.mx platform. In 2013, the Open Data Readiness Assessment was conducted, laying the foundations for implementing the country's open data initiative. The steps taken resulted in (a) the implementation of a national Open Data policy; (b) the establishment of the Consultative Council composed of representatives from the private sector, civil society organizations, and academia; (c) the launch of the single data catalog; (d) implementation of programs for data use in the elaboration of public policies; (e) identification and implementation of the reuse sector; and (f) creation of the Data Squad for preparation and publication of data among public officials. With these measures, Mexico ranks first among the Latin American and the Caribbean countries in three out of four of the Open Data Barometer's evaluations of the country's preparedness for open data.

---

particularly in developing countries—expanding use requires awareness raising and training.

Policies for private sector data as a driver of innovation and competitiveness

Data can be shared to support the creation of more than one new product, service, or production process. This can allow companies to connect in different data-sharing engagements with larger companies, small and medium enterprises (SMEs), and start-ups, or even the public sector. This way, data value can be maximized on several fronts simultaneously.

Data-sharing models have emerged to promote fair and competitive markets for products and services that rely on nonpersonal machine-generated data created, and to assist public agencies in accessing private sector data, to guide policy decisions or improve public services. The EC (2018) defines a set of key principles to be taken into account to improve data sharing for all parties involved, in business-to-business (B2B) and business-to-government situations. Access to and reuse of private sector data also constitute major cornerstones of a common data economy.

Business-to-business data sharing

An ever-increasing amount of data is created automatically by objects or processes based on disruptive technologies, such as sensors and the Internet of Things. These mainly relate to nonpersonal data generated by machines and open a new discussion and a dilemma around the privileged position of the producers of those devices in determining the access to and usage of the data they generate.

An EC public consultation with private sector stakeholders showed consensus that more B2B data sharing would be beneficial (EC 2018), where data can be reused without losing data quality or competitive advantage. The critical point in B2B data sharing might not rely on ownership, but on how data access is structured, managed, and approached. It could be argued that, at this initial stage of the development of data economies, it is too early for legislation requiring B2B data sharing. However, governments can consider nonregulatory measures to promote B2B data sharing:

- *Fostering the adoption and use of APIs* for easier and more systematic access to data. APIs can open up a data ecosystem of startups, exploiting unused data sets and supporting host organizations to adopt and create new data services and products. This has happened in the financial sector, leading to the emergence of financial technology ecosystems and new products and services that are already showing a relevant impact on banking the unbanked. The configuration and utilization of APIs requires the consideration of several principles: security, use of standards, user-friendliness, stability, and sustainability over time.

- *Providing key guiding principles for good practices in B2B sharing agreements* to ensure fair and competitive markets and to avoid excluding SMEs. Those crafted by the EC are an example, including (a) transparency, clearly identifying who will have access, to what type of data, at which level of detail, and usage purposes;

(b) respect for the commercial interests of data holders and users; (c) ensuring undistorted competition when sharing sensitive data; and (d) minimizing data lock-in to enable data portability as much as possible.

- *Promoting the development of trusted and secure platforms and privacy-minded analytical techniques* to secure sharing of proprietary industrial data and personal data and ensure compliance with relevant legislation (data protection, IP rights, and so on). Data collaboratives have emerged as a potentially viable response to the data challenges companies face. They provide access to "verified" and useful data (open data or otherwise) from public and private sources, commercial models that reward data producers and consumers, legal and regulatory protections and guidance, data security infrastructure, network connectivity, analytics infrastructure, and literacy programs.

Business-to-government data sharing

Data that companies collect and produce—cellular data, utility companies, shared carpooling services (such as Uber), or social media—can lead to improved traffic, better urban planning, and so on. As with B2B data sharing, governments can consider using key principles to guide these exchanges. The EC has defined the following key principles: (a) proportionality in the use of private sector data justified by clear and demonstrable public interest—the cost and effort required for the supply and reuse of private sector data should be reasonable compared with the expected public benefits; (b) purpose limitation of business-to-government collaboration; (c) "do no harm"—protection of trade secrets and other commercially sensitive information; (d) conditions for data reuse; and (e) mitigate limitations of private sector data such as potential inherent bias—companies supplying the data should offer reasonable and proportionate support to help assess the quality of the data.

Data policies for building trust

What is at stake?

Policies ruling the data governance framework require as much attention as is given to the need for robust management of data infrastructure. This section focuses on data protection and privacy, as well as data security policies. Countries are struggling with how to build trust in the digital data economy. Policy considerations in many cases are similar to those posed by "analog data." Personal data, whether machine generated or not, is subject to the same privacy rules in Europe as analog, for instance. The World Intellectual Property Organization argues that no additional intellectual property protection should be awarded to machine-generated data beyond the traditional ones (Burns 2017), nor should it be awarded less. A recent (2018) paper by the World Bank and the Consultative Group to Assist the Poor (CGAP), looking at the use of alternative data to build credit histories for greater financial inclusion, frames many policy questions that, at their core, do not vary much from those posed by the use of other kinds of data. If countries can tackle key aspects of trust policies, they will be well on their way to creating a better environment for the digital data economy.

Data protection and privacy are critical policy issues for the data economy and are key to building consumer trust. These are two separate but intertwined concepts. Data protection refers generally to the protection of personal data, though it may also be used in the context of commercially sensitive data. A common definition of personal data was cemented by the EU in its 95/46 Directive,[4] as data that identifies a person, or allows such identification by cross-referencing it with other available data. Privacy is a broader concept, which has sometimes been defined as the right to be let alone (Warren and Brandeis 1890), and it refers not only to data, although it partially covers it. What is at stake for either goes beyond keeping personal or embarrassing information from others. Big issues are how the data will be used and the risks that it will exclude people (such as, for example, by making people ineligible for insurance or credit) or be used for price discrimination, to suppress competition, or to manipulate people (such as, for example, through the crafting of news that could swing elections). This chapter uses "data protection" and "privacy" interchangeably.

Big data provides an example of the massive challenge to privacy in widespread use of technology. Big data preserves privacy by detaching information from individuals and repurposing it. However, by taking multiple, anonymized data sets and triangulating them, you can begin to break down that anonymity. For instance, take information about all the journeys that people have taken over the past year from a taxi service. This data alone is not necessarily sensitive, but if you combine it with venue information and social media, you could conceivably make assumptions about an individual who ended or began journeys at a known lesbian, gay, bisexual, and transgender (LGBT) destination. In countries where this is condemned by law, this information could result in people being sent to prison or worse.

The struggle between the need to protect privacy and allowing big data to continue to improve the way we live without quashing innovation is unlikely to be resolved easily. It remains to be seen how effective new laws, such as the GDPR, will be in achieving either of these aims. One certainty is that data production will not slow down and neither will the development of new ways to use it—legislators face an uphill battle to keep pace.

Trends in principles in protecting data privacy

Data protection laws have been in place for a while, with privacy rights protected as early as in ancient Roman times. Even though the right to privacy was not recognized as such by Roman law, several privacy violations, such as the invasion of the sanctity of one's home, were covered under the law. However, the numerous issues brought up by the sheer volume of data that can be collected about a person through online personas and questions about who can do what with those data, or who "owns" that data, have brought privacy concerns to the forefront of the news and therefore to the desks of policy makers.

Technological developments are pushing policy makers to either amend existing privacy legislation or pass new legislation. The EU 95/46 Directive was replaced in May 2018 by the GDPR. Even international standards, such as the OECD Privacy Guidelines (OECD 1980, Rev. 2013), or the APEC Privacy Framework (APEC 2015), were recently revised or expanded to accommodate these developments.

The GDPR is likely to have a trickle-down effect as other countries revise data protection legislation, and it is already having extraterritorial reach in private sector behavior. Consumers around the world are getting notices of revised privacy policies by global companies in compliance with the GDPR, and some content websites outside Europe have refused access to European consumers because they could not ensure compliance with the GDPR (Noack 2018).

Among the regulatory trends in the privacy space, the more salient are focused on a *risk-based approach to compliance* and on *proactive measures to protect privacy*, as opposed to measures in reaction to a breach. "Privacy-by-design" standards require companies to embed technological measures protecting privacy in their product and service design, for instance, to ensure anonymity of users. The concept of privacy by design was developed by Ann Cavoukian, former Information and Privacy Commissioner in the Canadian Province of Ontario.

The GDPR takes this one step further by carving out the related concept of "privacy by default." With privacy by default, the expectation is that companies and those processing or controlling the data will put in place mechanisms to ensure that only those items of personal information needed for each specific purpose are processed "by default." The main principle is to be proactive rather than reactive and preventive instead of remedial. This is a practical approach for emerging markets to consider, since it can help enforcement, give the private sector a more proactive role, and help prevent privacy violations and data breaches. The capabilities of the local private sector would need to be considered, as well as a plan that would help them ease into this approach should they not have the necessary resources or skills to do so.

Another trend is a strong focus on data security, preventive as well as once a data breach has occurred, on breach notifications. This important corollary to privacy protections is discussed in more detail below.

A legal framework is increasingly a necessity, not a luxury

The need for a legal privacy framework is no longer questioned, even in emerging markets that perhaps are used to seeing privacy at some point as a "luxury" right. According to the United Nations Conference on Trade and Development (UNCTAD 2018), 108 countries either had data protection laws or some kind of law that deals with data, whether in force or not, as of April 1, 2018. However, levels of protection, particularly enforcement, vary widely, even within countries with legal frameworks. In the nearly 30 percent of countries with no laws in place, personal data receives little or no protection, reducing trust and confidence in a wide range of commercial activities. A lack of or weak regulation put these countries at risk of being cut off from international trade opportunities, because many trade transactions require cross-border data transfers that comply with minimum legal requirements.

The GDPR brings additional incentive to strengthen data protection regimes for countries without one or with weak regimes. With a clear objective for extraterritoriality beyond EU borders, the GDPR introduces fines of up to €20 million, or 4 percent of global turnover, whichever is higher, for firms that are data processors or controllers and found not to be compliant. Firms in emerging markets may be subject to those fines if they are found not compliant. This could happen, for instance, to firms with no or little physical presence in the EU, but whose advertisements target EU consumers. Enforcement could be done through the branch office or subsidiary located within the EU of the firm from the emerging market.

Issues to consider when enacting or updating a legal framework

Follow the principles

Numerous countries have identified the need for coordination and cooperation in privacy and data protection. Most have used regional bodies, such as the EU or Asia-Pacific Economic Cooperation, as the vehicle for that cooperation rather than international agreements. These bodies have enacted guidelines or regulations and, not surprisingly, many principles are common among them. Countries considering enacting or updating privacy legal frameworks can reference those common principles. These include principles shared by the European Convention on Human Rights,[5] the OECD Privacy Guidelines, the APEC Privacy Framework, and the GDPR.

Raise awareness, highlight key issues, engage relevant stakeholders early on

At least 35 countries are currently drafting data protection laws to address this gap (UNCTAD 2018; map ES.1). A number of economies are also considering reforms to legal frameworks, including to the extent that it may be affected by extraterritorial application of the EU's GDPR. However, drafting and implementing data protection laws is time consuming and challenging. Surveys by UNCTAD of government representatives in 48 countries in Africa, Asia, and Latin America and the Caribbean (UNCTAD 2016) point to the need to build awareness and knowledge among lawmakers and the judiciary to formulate informed policies and laws in data protection and to enforce them effectively. More than 60 percent of respondents reported difficulty understanding legal issues related to data protection and privacy. Similarly, 43 percent noted a lack of understanding among parliamentarians and 47 percent among police or law-enforcement bodies, which can delay adoption and enforcement of data protection laws.

Another study, covering 22 of the globe's largest information and communication technology (ICT) firms, found that none of them disclosed adequate information about privacy practices and how user information is collected, shared, retained, and used.[6] Requests by governments for access to such data are growing, with most emanating from the United States (figure 6.2).

As with any other legal issue, when developing a legal framework, it is important to engage the main stakeholders early on. This will allow countries to understand potential issues and to get their buy-in and build capacity for implementation. Some countries, like Mexico, have put together a comprehensive effort to raise awareness of these issues with the different government branches, including at the state level. With the support of a World Bank project (World Bank 2008), the Ministry of Economy in Mexico commissioned a thorough review of existing legal issues and gaps and put together a training package for the judiciary, parliamentarians, and state government officials. This helped Mexico not only to identify issues, but also to prepare for implementation.

Other countries, particularly in Eastern Europe, have benefited from twinning programs with an existing data protection agency in another country that has provided technical assistance in the setting up of both the legal framework and their counterpart agency. It is also important to identify potential issues and concerns for private sector stakeholders at an early stage. Countries in the Latin American region support each other in such initiatives through the Ibero-American Data Protection Network.[7] Seychelles is reviewing its data protection framework and

is conducting stakeholder consultations. This will help its government put together a framework taking into account potential obstacles for implementation, including those that could come from a lack of private sector capacity or other country-specific issues.

Consider the legal culture

As seen in chapter 4 and figure ES.4, the level of tolerance for giving up one's privacy varies from country to country, and from individual to individual, with some citizens putting greater value on protecting their credit card information and others placing greater value on protecting their health information. For any country considering enacting a new privacy framework, this cultural dimension will be critical. A reflection of these cultural issues can be seen in the different approaches to privacy taken by the EU and the United States. In the EU, the right to privacy, but also the right to have one's personal data protected, are considered fundamental and are recognized in the Charter of Fundamental Rights of the European Union (2012, Articles 7 and 8). This approach has resulted in the EU having an umbrella data protection framework that does not distinguish between data being held by private or public actors, and which contemplates only a few exceptions, such as in the area of national security. But the EU is not alone in considering privacy a fundamental right. Even in India, where this was no explicit right to privacy, India's Supreme Court found recently that privacy is a fundamental right protected

Figure 6.2 Government requests for user data

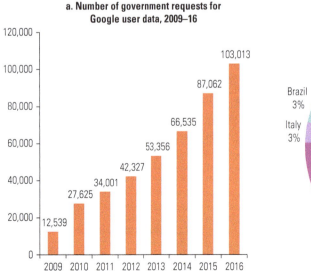

a. Number of government requests for Google user data, 2009–16

- 2009: 12,539
- 2010: 27,625
- 2011: 34,001
- 2012: 42,327
- 2013: 53,356
- 2014: 66,535
- 2015: 87,062
- 2016: 103,013

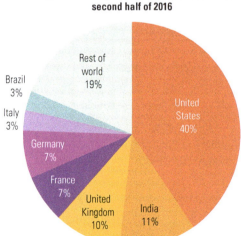

b. Government requests for Facebook user data, second half of 2016

- United States 40%
- Rest of world 19%
- India 11%
- United Kingdom 10%
- France 7%
- Germany 7%
- Brazil 3%
- Italy 3%

Sources: Adapted from Google, *Transparency Report;* Facebook, *Government Requests Report.*

by the constitution (Agrawal 2017). In the United States, by contrast, privacy is not recognized as a fundamental right. Although constitutional limits on the government's intrusion into individuals' right to privacy can be found in the Fourth Amendment, and to some extent in the First and Fifth Amendments, the right to privacy is more of a balancing act against other rights, including very strong rights to free speech and freedom of information. This has led to a more segmented approach to privacy protection, with, for instance, a Privacy Act for children,[8] and for the health sector (Health Insurance Portability and Accountability Act).[9] These deal with data held by government entities and are complemented by different pieces of legislation for data held by commercial entities. The international trend has been toward more comprehensive privacy frameworks, however, and even in the United States several bills have been introduced for "omnibus privacy laws," although they have not yet been adopted.

A prime example of the cultural debate is whether privacy laws should protect personal data, even in the absence of harm. Most jurisdictions can agree that, when an invasion of privacy results in financial harm to a consumer, reason exists for government to intervene. Most jurisdictions would also agree that harm can go beyond financial loss. Injury from loss of privacy can take many forms, and can include medical identity theft or "doxing," which is stalking or extortion coming from the dissemination of private facts. The U.S. Federal Trade Commission (FTC) recently brought a case against MyEx.com,[10] a porn site that allowed users to seek revenge on their ex by posting their intimate pictures. Victims could pay to remove intimate images and personal information. But beyond that, many people lost jobs or job opportunities, and were threatened, stalked, and harassed (Ohlhausen 2017).

In some countries, the use of alternative sources of data (such as credit history downloads from a mobile phone) has revolutionized financial inclusion, allowing consumers with little to no credit history to access credit, but could also further raise the bar for others to ever be able to access credit. However, the use of those same data can lead to price discrimination on the basis of race or gender, or to denial of credit because of data inaccuracy. Questions arise about where to draw the line and whether the basis for government action should only be preventing harm. For those who view privacy as a fundamental right, there is no need of injury for a government intervention, while the definition of injury can be as broad as contravening a person's expectations with regard to respect for their privacy.

Other considerations: Extraterritoriality, trade issues, and cross-border data flows

A key privacy policy issue with potential for big effects on a country's economy is the regulation of cross-border data flows. McKinsey Global Institute (2016) estimates that flows of data and information now generate more economic value than the global goods trade. Although many of these data flows are concentrated in a handful of large companies, some, such as eBay, Amazon, and Alibaba, are really platforms allowing SMEs all over the world to becoming mini-exporters, with an impact across multiple economies. And individuals are not being left behind. About 900 million people have used international connections on social media to connect to networks to find a job, and 360 million take part in cross-border e-commerce (McKinsey Global Institute 2016).

Data transfer policies

Companies need to transfer many different kinds of data across borders in the regular course of business. Those may include data related to commercial transactions, their own internal operations, monitoring supply, human resources data of global employees, and product support in real time. Countries that regulate data leaving their borders often do so on the basis of privacy and data security concerns. Already in the 95/46 Directive, the EU regulated data transfers outside of the EU, and transfers were only allowed to countries the EC determined had adequate data protection. So countries with lower standards risk cutting off opportunities for firms or individuals in their countries from using platforms, websites, or activities involving the transfer of data with EU countries. Governments contemplating restrictions on data transfers outside their borders based on privacy and data security, above those of existing international standards, may discover that global companies decide that it is simpler to block consumers in a particular jurisdiction from accessing services than to try to comply with the data protection rules of that country. This is the recent example of U.S. advertising technology companies. Having data policies out of line with larger regional players is a particular problem for small markets in developing countries that are not part of a wider trade bloc.

Self-regulation, if it complies with required international standards, is another option. Given the reality of global commerce, even the EC has allowed the use of some self-regulatory tools to ensure adequate protection of data outside of its borders under the 95/46 Directive. Global companies could issue binding corporate rules or policies that are internal to a group of companies and become binding once approved by the relevant data protection authorities. They could also use model contracts with their subsidiaries that would ensure adequate protection of personal data. The GDPR expands existing mechanisms and introduces new tools for international transfers. It offers, among other things, adequacy decisions, standard contractual rules, binding corporate rules, certification mechanisms, codes of conduct, and so-called derogations. Countries considering these options have to consider enforceability of instruments like the codes of conduct, and what happens if an institution does not follow its code.

Beyond self-regulation, another option could be specific bilateral agreements between countries, whereby smaller countries offer mutual recognition of rules applied in larger trade blocs, such as the EU, similar to the approach used in type approval (that is, homologation) of customer premises equipment. The EC signed an agreement on International Safe Harbor Privacy Principles,[11] whereby certain companies subject to the FTC's jurisdiction would commit to protect data abiding by the same principles spelled out in the directive. This allowed many companies in the United States, which did not have an "adequacy" finding from the EC, to still transfer data to and from Europe. The Safe Harbor agreement has now been replaced by the Privacy Shield agreement.[12]

But even if countries do not impose particular restrictions on data flows, having to comply with different sets of data protection rules in different countries becomes costly for companies, and a de facto trade barrier. This has led some companies to apply the EU standards to their worldwide operations, as they are considered some of the most stringent, hoping to minimize compliance costs.

Data localization

Data localization policies, in addition to data transfer policies, affect cross-border data flows, international trade, and access to global markets (Chander and Lê 2015). Data localization rules require firms to locate data servers or data centers within the borders of a country to store and process information. Studies show that data localization and other barriers to data flows impose significant costs: reducing U.S. GDP by 0.1–0.36 percent; causing prices for some cloud services in Brazil and the EU to increase by 10.5 percentage points to 54 percent; and reducing GDP growth from 2.4 percent to 1.7 percent in Brazil, China, the EU, India, Indonesia, the Republic of Korea, and Vietnam,

which have all either proposed or enacted data localization policies (ITIF 2017).

In Rwanda, the regulatory body, the Rwanda Utilities Regulatory Authority, went a step further and imposed a fine of US$8.5 million in May 2017 on the mobile operator MTN for storing customer data in Uganda (Reuters 2017). This is equivalent to about 10 percent of its annual revenue, and the decision is likely to have a chilling effect on foreign investment into the country, as well as deterring foreign firms from offering services there.

Defenders of localization laws cite national security, protection of personal data, local cultural and historical context, and economic nationalism as arguments; opponents see such laws as a major barrier to trade and competitiveness. Localization creates its own set of winners and losers in the domestic market. It has been argued that localization laws benefit larger firms at the expense of smaller firms that often do not have in-house data skills and must often pay more per unit of data stored at local firms than might have been available from international data hosting services.

On the other hand, localization laws can shelter local firms to develop skills and capacity without the threat of competition from international firms. Opponents also cite issues such as poor data security (Pfeifle 2017) (as many countries with localization laws lack the skills to handle data securely) and the risk that localization requirements can soon become more pervasive and expand to include other types of data.

Balancing other rights

Data protection and privacy are not absolute rights and need to be balanced against other rights. Some of those rights are access to information, freedom of speech, and the protection of national or personal security interests. Different countries place different emphasis on different values. For access to information, the benefit or the public good of divulging certain information needs to be balanced against an individual's right to privacy. It is generally accepted in many jurisdictions that individuals with a public persona have a lesser expectation of privacy than others. For instance, there is legitimate public interest in knowing whether a lawyer who is prosecuting a case of sexual harassment is practicing what they preach (BBC 2018). But even here, public figures are increasingly bringing cases involving the violation of privacy and sometimes winning compensation for alleged defamation of character (*USA Today* 2017).

Implementation issues

Enforcement

As with any laws, when considering privacy laws, enforcement is a key issue. Whatever the framework, it is only as worthy as its enforcement. Even absent a specific privacy framework, a strong enforcement agency can still protect people's rights through an interpretation of other existing laws. This has been the case for the U.S. FTC. The FTC has been a strong enforcer of privacy rights by implementing a more general statue, the Federal Trade Commission Act, which gives them jurisdiction to protect consumers from deceptive or unfair acts or practices.[13] Examples of recent cases include privacy cases against Uber, Lenovo, VTech, and Venmo.[14]

The reverse is also true. Countries with strong legal frameworks on paper that are nonetheless not enforced remain at the same level as countries with no framework at all. Countries considering institutional arrangements for their laws can look at different models of good practices around the world. The EU GDPR calls for the establishment of independent data protection authorities. Following this model, some economies have chosen to establish a standalone data protection authority, including Canada, Mauritius, and South Africa. Other countries have chosen to merge that independent authority with the authority protecting access to information rights, such as Mexico and the United Kingdom. Other countries, such as the United States, have jurisdiction spread among several agencies, with the consumer protection agency as one of the main enforcers. Yet another model brings the enforcement powers for privacy laws under the Ministry of Justice, such as in Argentina.

No absolute right or wrong way to think about enforcement exists, as long as the end results are there and the law is enforced. Important considerations are identified in the OECD Privacy Guidelines, and include encouraging and supporting self-regulation, whether in the form of codes of conduct or otherwise; providing for reasonable means for individuals to exercise their rights; providing for adequate sanctions and remedies in case of failure to comply with privacy frameworks; and ensuring no unfair discrimination against data subjects (OECD 1980, Rev. 2013).

Emerging market economies need to consider what is feasible within their own contexts, taking into account the budget and skills required. Enforcement alliances, both with other local enforcement agencies, including criminal, as well as with international enforcement agencies, can help greatly.

Enforcers can also have a role in continuous awareness raising, both for the data subjects and for those who manipulate the data.

Data security

On March 22, 2018, the U.S. city of Atlanta was hit by the dreaded SamSam ransomware attack, which brought the city's ICT systems to a halt. Utilities could not collect bill payments, citizens could not pay traffic tickets, the police had to note complaints by hand—the city's digital apparatus essentially stopped functioning and many departments and agencies lost several years of data (Wright 2018). Unfortunately, this was not an isolated incident. In India, a journalist was able to obtain unauthorized data from Aadhar,[15] the national digital identification system. And in Mexico, web users were surprised to discover that the voter data of more than 93 million Mexican citizens was easily accessible online even though the information was classified as confidential (Chang 2016).

It is evident that "not all data is created equal" (Fell and Barlow 2016). Most data is likely of low value, with more limited amounts of medium value, let alone high value. And risk varies across types of data assets too. From a business's perspective, it makes little financial sense to spend as much protecting all assets regardless of their value or the risks they face. Such a requirement could impose a crippling financial burden. At the same time, most organizations lack the skills to properly audit their data assets and thus end up with "orphan assets" littered across systems whose value is less than the cost of controls to protect them. What organizations should focus on, at a minimum, are their "extraordinary assets" critical to them (Kaminski et al. 2017) as well as data for which costs or breaches of privacy rights could be significant should the data become public. If protecting everything equally is not an option, taking this risk management approach should safeguard against deprioritizing sensitive data that is of low financial value to a firm that holds it.

A recent report found significant vulnerabilities in more than three-quarters of applications used by the federal government in the United States (Hesseldahl 2015). Numerous reasons appear to explain this:

- Poor data management processes (Virtu 2015)—including inconsistent response, unresolved issues, notification practices, and lack of data encryption practices

- Legacy systems and old software—still in use in many government organizations[16]

- Poor capacity and skills—due to government's inability to attract top-drawer data-security talent

- A low priority afforded to security when making technical infrastructure investments—in a recent study, respondents showed a marked preference for investments in network security and end-point security over investments in data-at-rest security.[17]

Data security is not only about ICT; it should also cover "analog" aspects of security (such as vetting of staff and physical access to control buildings). Countries use policies as a tool to manage risks and help respond to actual incidents. Data security policies can be in different kinds of laws, including cybersecurity and data protection laws. Governments have to consider leading by example and applying themselves to strong data security measures, in addition to what they expect from the ICT industry.

The OECD identified the main common principles for information security in their Guidelines for Information Security and Networks in 2002 and updated them in the OECD Recommendation on Digital Security and Risk management (OECD 2015); these principles were further spelled out in the Madrid Declaration.[18] They emphasize risk management, awareness raising, having a preparedness and continuity plan to respond to incidents, and adoption of security measures to avoid data corruption, loss, misuse, or unauthorized access. They also highlight stakeholder cooperation, including across borders, given that most incidents have a multi-country footprint. Robust cybersecurity policies,[19] targeting the vulnerability of IT systems, infrastructure, and networks beyond data, should complement data security policies. Different international initiatives have produced or are producing guidelines on cybersecurity.[20]

For consumers, one of the rising trends is to request data breach notifications. Breach notifications can be useful to consumers when their data has been compromised or lost, since a notification allows them to take corrective action as needed. Different countries have different requirements for breach notification, and the main differences are the triggers and timeline for notification. The triggers determine what level of breach is required in order to notify consumers and can rely, for instance, on the sensitivity of the information accessed and the likelihood that it will be misused.

In a report on data-driven innovation, the OECD (2015) recommends that organizations establish a systematic framework of digital security risk management processes and weld it together with the data value cycle (figure 6.3). In this framework, the criteria for determining the level of security are based on the acceptable level of risk to the economic and social activities at stake (OECD 2015) and not the likelihood of threat. Such an approach is premised on the primacy of data as a socioeconomic asset that justifies the move from a culture of security to a culture of risk management.

Policies for maximizing the data economy

In addition to policies for the management and governance of data itself, a number of complementary data-related policies exist that governments can pursue to support the development of the data ecosystem and ensure that access to opportunities is inclusive. Digital skills and data for innovation and entrepreneurship are discussed here.

Data skills

To take advantage of the data economy, more people need to have the requisite digital skills. Educational programs that employ rapid skill training are increasingly demanded to develop data skills and capabilities for the use of data tools for innovators, entrepreneurs, SMEs, other private sector entities, and government agencies. According to Cisco (2015), a shortage of 1 million people to fill data security jobs will exist over the next five years, and demand for data scientists between 2011 and 2013 alone increased about 40 percent. Data skills and tools have become crucial among firms, governments, and, particularly, entrepreneurs.

Data literacy is increasingly considered a core skill, with some research suggesting that 90 percent of jobs within advanced economies already require a measure of digital or data skills (EC 2018), while less than one-third of the population possesses adequate skills. The gap in developing countries is even wider. This is a gap that governments must close quickly.

Governments have employed different models to promote digital literacy. Examples include the following:

- *Inclusion of digital literacy as part of government-supported basic skills programs,* such as the Skills Plus program in Norway.[21]

Figure 6.3 Digital security risk management cycle

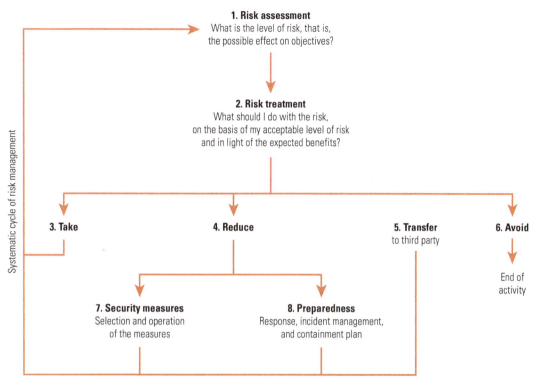

Source: Adapted from OECD 2015.

- *Support to advanced digital skills.* In the United Kingdom, for instance, the Government Digital Services supports a range of programs, such as the Tech Partnership[22] (a network of employers focused on developing digital skills) and Doteveryone[23] (an independent think tank focused on the digital society).

- *Programs aimed specifically at women and girls, who are often underrepresented in the ICT sector.* Examples include the Intel-backed She Will Connect initiative in Nigeria, Kenya, and South Africa,[24] and Mozilla Learning's partnership with UN Women to support a network of web literacy clubs in Kenya and South Africa specifically aimed at upskilling girls and women through face-to-face peer learning (Dhalla 2016).

- *Mentoring and peer learning based programs.* Such programs include Reboot UK (Good Things Foundation 2017), the Swedish IT guide program (which pairs immigrants with elderly Swedes),[25] and the "CompiSternli" program in Switzerland (which pairs children with the elderly).[26]

- The incorporation of *coding into school curricula.* This is done in the e-school program in Estonia[27] and similar programs in Denmark, the United Kingdom, and the United States.

Some lessons and policy recommendations for governments to consider from these various digital skills initiatives include ensuring data literacy programs are multistakeholder (including participants from the government, private sector, and civil society); building on existing programs, where possible, rather than starting from zero; blending traditional nondigital education with data and digital literacy; bridging formal and nonformal sources of education, such as using mobile phones as a learning tool in developing countries, especially for refugees (UNESCO 2018); and developing societal teaching capacity and mentorship programs.

Data innovation

Companies with huge amounts of data at their disposal and the technical capacity and skilled employees to analyze the data will gain competitive advantage (OECD 2015).

In the digital revolution, access to large and diverse data sets is a prerequisite for innovation. Policies geared toward unlocking the reuse potential of data can boost the data economy so that businesses and governments are not left behind, but put forward at the frontier of innovation.

Public and publicly funded data can be at the service of data-driven innovation. Access and reuse of public and publicly funded data can constitute a cornerstone for a data economy. Policies aiming at making more data available and making data more reusable include policies to lower market entry barriers, particularly for SMEs, by reducing charges for the reuse of public sector information.

The nature of data-driven innovation also raises new challenges, including how to safeguard competition and to avoid using data as a barrier to the next generation of entrants and innovators. Given the value of controlling large amounts of data, there can be winner-take-most dynamics of companies benefiting from network effects (that is, where the more people that use a platform or service, the better the experience of everyone else using it). Although it is beyond the scope of this report to discuss competition policies, the treatment of data-sharing policies and the handling of data within intellectual property rights protections will increasingly be central parts of them. Another way that governments can address the risk of excessive first-mover advantage is ensuring that its own data-sharing arrangements do not result in few re-users able to exploit the data in practice. Increased transparency of public data reuse can allow any company, regardless of size, to be aware of the data available and promote a broader spectrum of re-users exploiting the social and economic value of data.

The EU estimates that, in 2016, some 254,850 data companies existed across the union, and that the figure could grow to some 360,000 by 2020 under a high-growth scenario.[28]

- *Government innovation.* Government laboratories such as fab labs, data labs, and urban labs have emerged across regions. In 2016, the government of Mexico launched its Datalab for data analysis to improve Mexico's public policy formulation and management. Among cities, Barcelona's CityLab and Mexico City's Laboratorio para la Ciudad are examples of municipal level interventions for urban innovation using data.

- *Private sector innovation.* Policies are needed to build awareness, capacity, and adoption; and to promote cross-cutting uptake for market analysis, financial inclusion, value chain integration, and know your customer across sectors. As discussed in chapter 5, to ensure these policies reach a majority requires attention to SMEs and to the underlying layer that can connect firms to customers, vendors, associations, governments, and so on.

- *Citizen-driven innovation.* Innovation policy traditionally supports the "supply" side by funding research and development in areas deemed to yield scientific market results. Demand-driven innovation policies, in which processes are driven by the end beneficiaries rather than researchers, aim to ensure instead greater relevance and uptake. This is the case of data policies that consider that social innovation can promote citizen engagement and creative thinking about alternative ways to provide services and address problems. An example of this approach in Tanzania, Data Zetu,[29] is part of the Data Collaboratives for Local Impact program, and aims to empower communities in Tanzania to make better, more evidence-based decisions to improve lives. Data Zetu works with stakeholders to build skills and develop digital and offline tools that make information accessible to everyone. Civic tech, crowdsourced programming, and open innovation processes to tackle development challenges can bring together the skills and technology needed to make a difference in the lives of those who need them most.

- *Development innovation.* Data is also shaping the traditional paths of development. The UN-coined "data revolution" has triggered novel development approaches that help analyze the context, measure impact, and coordinate project efforts on the ground, among others. Data is a cross-cutting tool for achieving the Sustainable Development Goals. Development is about knowledge, and data amplifies the power of development assistance as the building block of knowledge.

- *Data entrepreneurship.* Governments should ensure that other sources of innovation investment, ICT industry stimulation, and start-up incubation are playing their part in supporting the growth of innovative uses of data and of the supporting ecosystem of ICT and other services. In 2015, as noted, the Open Data Incubator for

Europe was launched to support the next generation of digital businesses and fast-track the development of their products. Within the six-month incubation program, companies receive up to €100,000 (US$116,000) in equity-free funding, mentoring, business and data training, high-quality media, visibility at international events, and introductions to investors.

Policies for data-driven development

In examining data policies for the digital economy, it is easy to focus on the dark side—combating cybercrime, threats to data security, loss of privacy, and similar matters. But the data economy is not only about policies to mitigate risks; it is also about policies to maximize value. The true value of data is largely in its use. A strong demand-side "pull" of data is important. It creates and maintains pressure on expanding ubiquity. And it ensures that the wider data ecosystem develops and that data is turned into economic or social value with positive impacts for citizens. As shown throughout this report, the "pull" can come from governments, civil society organizations, the private sector, academia, journalists, international organizations, and donors, as well as from individual citizens. Data-driven development involves all of us.

Notes

1. The Open Data Initiative provides more details at https://theodi.org/topic/data-infrastructure/.

2. Quote attributed to Justice Louis D. Brandeis, available at https://www.brandeis.edu/legacyfund/bio.html.

3. See, for instance, Lindstedt and Naurin 2005 (2), which notes: "Taken one at a time transparency and free and fair elections will not help much to reduce corruption. Taken together, on the other hand, they can be a powerful team."

4. See Directive 95/46/EC on the protection of personal data at https://eur-lex.europa.eu/legal-content/EN/TXT/?uri=CELEX:31995L0046.

5. For more information, see Council of Europe 1985.

6. See https://rankingdigitalrights.org.

7. For information, see http://www.redipd.es.

8. Children's Online Privacy Protection Act of 1998, 15 USC 6501–5.

9. Health Insurance Portability and Accountability Act of 1996 (HIPAA), Pub.L. 104–191, 110 Stat. 1936, enacted August 21, 1996.

10. Emp Media Inc. (MyEx.com), FTC File No. 162-3052 (2018), https://www.ftc.gov/enforcement/casesproceedings/162–3052/emp-media-inc-myexcom.

11. The *Safe Harbor* Agreement was later revoked, following the Schrems case in the ECJ, C-362/14—EUR-Lex—Europa EU.

12. See https://www.privacyshield.gov/welcome.

13. Section 5, FTC Act, 15 USC 41–58, as amended.

14. See Uber Tech., Inc., FTC File No. 152-3054 (2017), https://www.ftc.gov/enforcement/cases-proceedings/152-3054/uber-technologies-inc; Lenovo, Inc., FTC File No. 152–3134 (2017), https://www.ftc.gov/enforcement/casesproceedings/152–3134/lenovo-inc; VTech Elecs. Ltd., FTC File No. 162–3032 (2018), https://www.ftc.gov/enforcement/cases-proceedings/162–3032/vtech-electronics-limited; PayPal, Inc., FTC File No. 162–3102 (2018), https://www.ftc.gov/enforcement/cases-proceedings/162–3102/paypal-inc-matter.

15. https://www.livemint.com/Opinion/MUPJK28VMeoICzl1whSBrJ/Clearing-the-air-on-Aadhaar-data-breach.html.

16. See https://www.gao.gov/assets/670/669810.pdf.

17. See https://dtr.thalesesecurity.com/2017/pdf/2017-thales-data-threat-report-brazil-edition-pr.pdf.

18. See http://www.privacyconference2009.org/media/notas_prensa/common/pdfs/061109_estandares_internacionales_en.pdf.

19. For the definition of data and information security versus the definition of cybersecurity, see ttp://nvlpubs.nist.gov/nistpubs/ir/2013/NIST.IR.7298r2.pdf.

20. For instance, see https://ccdcoe.org/multimedia/national-cyber-security-strategy-guidelines.html and https://apec.org/Groups/SOM-Steering-Committee-on-Economic-and-Technical-Cooperation/Working-Groups/Telecommunications-and-Information.

21. See https://www.kompetansenorge.no/English/Basic-skills/Competenceplus/.

22. See https://www.thetechpartnership.com/.

23. See https://doteveryone.org.uk/.

24. See https://www.intel.com/content/www/us/en/corporate-responsibility/social-impact-and-educational-initiatives/she-will-connect.html.

25. See http://aginghorizons.com/2015/01/program-young-immigrants-team-up-with-older-swedes/.

26. See https://www.compisternli.ch/.

27. See https://e-estonia.com/solutions/education/e-school/.

28. An organization whose main activity is producing data-related products, services, and technologies.

29. See https://datazetu.or.tz/.

References

Agrawal, Ravi. 2017. "India Supreme Court Rules Privacy a 'Fundamental Right' in Landmark Case." CNN.com, August 24. https://www.cnn.com/2017/08/24/asia/indian-court-right-to-privacy/index.html.

APEC (Asia-Pacific Economic Cooperation). 2015. *The APEC Privacy Framework.* Singapore: APEC.

BBC (British Broadcasting Corporation). 2018. "Eric Schneiderman, New York Attorney General, Quits Amid Assault Reports." BBC.com, May 8. https://www.bbc.com/news/world-us-canada-44035718.

Burns, Thaddeus. 2017. "Regulating Machine Data: Less Is More for Global Growth." *WIPO: Magazine*, December. http://www.wipo.int/wipo_magazine/en/2017/06/article_0005.html.

Chander, Anupam, and Uyen Lê. 2015. "Data Nationalism." *Emory Law Journal* 64 (3): 677–739. http://law.emory.edu/elj/content/volume-64/issue-3/articles/data-nationalism.html.

Chang, Lulu. 2016. "The Latest Data Breach Involves the Voting Records of 93.4 Million Mexican Citizens." *Digital Trends*, April 23. https://www.digitaltrends.com/computing/mexico-voting-breach/.

Cisco. 2015. "Mitigating the Cybersecurity Skills Shortage: Top Insights and Actions from Cisco Security Advisory Services." https://www.cisco.com/c/dam/en/us/products/collateral/security/cybersecurity-talent.pdf.

Council of Europe. 1985. "Convention for the Protection of Individuals with Regard to Automatic Processing of Personal Data." Council of Europe, Strasbourg. https://www.coe.int/en/web/conventions/full-list/-/conventions/treaty/108.

Dhalla, Amira. 2016. "New Partnership with UN Women to Teach Key Digital Skills to Women." Mozilla Learning. https://learning.mozilla.org/blog/new-partnership-with-un-women-to-teach-key-digital-skills-to-women.

European Commission. 2018. "New Measures to Boost Key Competences and Digital Skills, as Well as the European Dimension of Education." Press release, January 17. http://europa.eu/rapid/press-release_IP-18-102_en.htm.

European Union. 2012. "Charter of Fundamental Rights of the European Union." 2012/C 326/02. http://eur-lex.europa.eu/legal-content/EN/TXT/?uri=CELEX:12012P/TXT.

———. 2018. "Communication from the Commission to the European Parliament, the Council, the European Economic and Social Committee and the Committee of the Regions 'Towards A Common European Data Space.'" European Commission, Brussels.

Facebook. 2017. "Global Government Request Report." April 27. https://transparency.facebook.com/.

Fell, Gregory, and Mike Barlow. 2016. "Not All Data Is Created Equal." O'Reilly, April 25. https://www.oreilly.com/learning/not-all-data-is-created-equal.

Good Things Foundation. 2017. "Project: Reboot UK." https://www.goodthingsfoundation.org/projects/reboot-uk.

Government of New Zealand. 2011. "New Zealand Data and Information Management Principles." Wellington. https://www.ict.govt.nz/guidance-and-resources/open-government/new-zealand-data-and-information-management-principles/.

Hesseldahl, Arik. 2015. "Why the Federal Government Sucks at Cyber Security." *Recode*, June 23. https://www.recode.net/2015/6/23/11563798/why-the-federal-government-sucks-at-cybersecurity.

ITIF (Information Technology and Innovation Foundation). 2017. "Cross-Border Data Flows: Where Are the Barriers, and What Do They Cost?" May 1. https://itif.org/publications/2017/05/01/cross-border-data-flows-where-are-barriers-and-what-do-they-cost.

Kaminski, Piotr, Chris Rezek, Wolf Richter, and Marc Sorel. 2017. "Protecting Your Critical Digital Assets: Not All Systems and Data Are Created Equal." McKinsey and Company. https://www.mckinsey.com/business-functions/risk/our-insights/protecting-your-critical-digital-assets-not-all-systems-and-data-are-created-equal.

Lindstedt, Catharina, and Daniel Naurin. 2005. "Transparency and Corruption: The Conditional Significance of a Free Press." Quality of Government Institute Working Paper 2005:5, University of Gothenburg, Sweden. https://www.qog.pol.gu.se/digitalAssets/1350/1350633_2005_5-lindstedt_naurin.pdf.

McKinsey Global Institute. 2016. *The Age of Analytics: Competing in a Data-Driven World.* London: McKinsey Global Institute. https://www.mckinsey.com/business-functions/mckinsey-analytics/our-insights/the-age-of-analytics-competing-in-a-data-driven-world.

Noack, Rick. 2018. "European Union's New Privacy Law Made Some Websites Go Dark Today; Here's What Else Has Changed." *Los Angeles Times*, May 25. http://www.latimes.com/business/technology/la-fi-tn-gdpr-europe-privacy-20180525-story.html.

OECD (Organisation for Economic Co-operation and Development). 1980. "Rev. 2013 Guidelines on the Protection of Privacy and Transborder Flows of Personal Data." Paris. http://www.oecd.org/sti/ieconomy/privacy.htm.

———. 2015. *Digital Security Risk Management for Economic and Social Prosperity: OECD Recommendation and Companion Document.* Paris: OECD Publishing. https://doi.org/10.1787/9789264245471-en.

Ohlhausen, Maureen K. 2017. "Remarks at the FTC Informational Injury Workshop." December 12. https://www.ftc.gov/public-statements/2017/12/remarks-ftc-informational-injury-workshop.

Pfeifle, Sam. 2017. "Is the GDPR a Data Localization Law?" International Association of Privacy Professionals, Portsmouth, NH. https://iapp.org/news/a/is-the-gdpr-a-data-localization-law/.

Qatar Ministry of Information and Communications Technology. 2015. "Data Management Policy." http://www.motc.gov.qa /sites/default/files/data_management_policy.pdf.

Reuters. 2017. "Rwanda Regulator Fines MTN Rwanda $8.5 Mln over External IT Hub." May 17. https://www.reuters.com /article/rwanda-telecoms/rwanda-regulator-fines-mtn-rwand a-8-5-mln-over-external-it-hub-idUSL8N1IJ2IJ.

UNCTAD (United Nations Conference on Trade and Development). 2016. "Data Protection Regulations and International Data Flows: Implications for Trade and Development." UNCTAD, Geneva and New York. http://unctad.org/en /PublicationsLibrary/dtlstict2016d1_en.pdf.

———. 2018. "Data Protection and Privacy Legislation Worldwide." Geneva and New York. http://unctad.org/en/Pages/DTL/STI_and _ICTs/ICT4D-Legislation/eCom-Data-Protection-Laws.aspx.

UNESCO (United Nations Educational, Scientific, and Cultural Organization). 2018. *A Lifeline to Learning: Leveraging Technology to Support Education for Refugees.* Paris: UNESCO. http://unesdoc.unesco.org/images/0026/002612/261278e.pdf.

USA Today. 2017. "Rebel Wilson Wins Defamation Case against Publisher." June 15. https://www.usatoday.com/story/life /people/2017/06/15/rebel-wilson-wins-defamation-case -against-publisher/102877120/.

Virtu. 2015. "5 Data Security Challenges Faced by Government Agencies, and What They Can Do about It." September 23. https://www.virtru.com/blog/data-security/.

Warren, Samuel D., and Louis D. Brandeis. 1890. "The Right to Privacy." *Harvard Law Review* 4 (5): 193.

World Bank. 2008. "P106589: Mexico Information Technology (IT) Industry Development Project." Washington, DC. http:// projects.worldbank.org/P106589/information-technology -development?lang=en.

———. 2014. "Open Data for Economic Growth." Washington, DC. http://www.worldbank.org/content/dam/Worldbank /document/Open-Data-for-Economic-Growth.pdf.

World Bank and CGAP (Consultative Group to Assist the Poor). 2018. "Data Protection and Privacy for Alternative Data." Draft GPFI-FCPL Sub-Group Discussion Paper. Group of Twenty (G20). https://www.g20.org/sites/default/files/documentos _producidos/data_protection_and_privacy_for_alternative _data_wbg_0.pdf.

Wright, Morgan. 2018. "A Ransomware Attack Brought Atlanta to Its Knees—And No One Seems to Care." *The Hill*, April 4. http://thehill.com/opinion/cybersecurity/381594-a -ransomware-attack-brought-atlanta-to-its-knees-and-no -one-seems-to.

Data Notes

Data for Development Indicators

This appendix presents a series of statistics related to different data categories. They measure data accessibility, affordability, usage, protection, infrastructure, and availability of public sector data. The data generally refers to 2016 or the latest available data. The coverage and nomenclature shown for economy names comes from the World Bank.[1]

Availability and users

These indicators refer to the technical availability of the potential to use data (mobile broadband coverage) and actual use (internet use). The proportion of the population covered by a mobile network is the sole indicator related to information and communication technology that is tracked for the Sustainable Development Goals. The indicator used is the percentage of the population living within the signal range of a third-generation (3G) mobile network and is sourced from the United Nations.[2] For actual usage, the proportion of the population using the internet is shown, sourced from the World Bank DataBank.[3]

Affordability and usage

Price of 1 gigabyte (GB) of data refers to the lowest price for at least 1 GB per month of mobile data usage (table DN.1). Data are sourced from the Association for Affordable Internet,[4] the Organisation for Economic Co-operation and Development (OECD),[5] Research ICT Africa (RIA),[6] the Internet Society,[7] and ictDATA.[8]

Data are shown in U.S. dollars and as a proportion of gross domestic product (GDP) per capita. Data generally refer to the largest operator by subscriber market share. Note that the OECD data also includes 300 voice calls and is generally postpaid, whereas data from other sources is data only and generally prepaid. Note that many operators provide more than 1 GB for the prices shown. Data usage is shown for two metrics: GB per mobile data user and per all mobile subscriptions regardless of whether data is used. The figures are for monthly consumption. Data come from various sources, including the OECD,[9] national agencies, and mobile operator groups.

Table DN.1 Data and affordability

	Availability and users		Affordability and usage			
Economy	Proportion of population covered by a 3G mobile network, 2015	Individuals using the internet (% of population), 2016	Price of 1 gigabyte (GB) of data (US dollars per month), 2016	Price of 1 GB of data (% of GDP per capita per month), 2016	GB per data user, 2016	GB per mobile subscription, 2016
Afghanistan	40	10.6	4.41	9.4	0.323	0.75
Albania	99	66.4	4.20	1.2		
Algeria	46	43.0	9.72	3.0	0.447	
Angola	100	13.0	19.99	7.7		
Antigua and Barbuda	98	73.0	25.92	2.2		
Argentina	90	71.0	15.78	1.5		0.51
Armenia	100	67.0	4.14	1.4		
Australia	99	88.2	22.82	0.5	1.543	
Austria	98	84.3	13.35	0.4	6.278	
Azerbaijan	97	78.2	2.91	0.9		
Bahamas, The	98	80.0	20.00	1.0		
Bahrain	98	98.0	15.79	0.8		
Bangladesh	71	18.3	2.94	2.6	0.322	0.14
Barbados	98	79.6	13.50	1.0		
Belarus	96	71.1	2.27	0.5		
Belgium	100	86.5	18.33	0.5	0.863	
Belize		44.6	15.00	3.7		
Benin	45	12.0	11.28	17.2	0.339	0.07
Bhutan	80	41.8	3.06	1.3		
Bolivia	27	39.7	7.42	2.9		
Bosnia and Herzegovina	96	54.7	6.72	1.7		
Botswana	92	39.4	28.15	5.0		
Brazil	94	60.9	10.35	1.4	0.63	0.43
Brunei Darussalam	91	90.0	14.49	0.6		
Bulgaria	100	59.8	5.74	0.9		
Burkina Faso	10	14.0	8.05	14.9		
Burundi	0	5.2	5.45	22.9		
Cabo Verde	87	50.3	4.80	1.9		
Cambodia	70	32.4	2.00	1.9		3.00
Cameroon	50	25.0	6.43	7.5	0.249	0.08
Canada	99	89.8	41.35	1.2	1.57	1.225
Central African Republic	23	4.0	6.58	20.7		
Chad	13	5.0	16.45	29.7		
Chile	90	66.0	28.14	2.5		1.2
China	95	53.2	19.92	2.9		
Colombia	100	58.1	10.66	2.2		0.12
Comoros		7.9	8.68	13.4		
Congo, Dem. Rep.	20	6.2	13.00	34.7		

(continued next page)

Table DN.1 *(continued)*

Economy	Availability and users		Affordability and usage			
	Proportion of population covered by a 3G mobile network, 2015	Individuals using the internet (% of population), 2016	Price of 1 gigabyte (GB) of data (US dollars per month), 2016	Price of 1 GB of data (% of GDP per capita per month), 2016	GB per data user, 2016	GB per mobile subscription, 2016
Congo, Rep.	50	8.1	16.45	12.9	0.192	0.06
Costa Rica	99	66.0	16.71	1.7		
Côte d'Ivoire	46	26.5	8.05	6.3	1.065	0.21
Croatia	99	72.7	7.55	0.7		
Cuba	0	38.8				
Cyprus	90	75.9	11.30	0.6	2.827	1.47
Czech Republic	99	76.5	31.74	2.1	0.983	
Denmark	100	97.0	23.14	0.5	4.373	
Djibouti	0	13.1	45.01			
Dominica	60	67.0	17.41	2.9		
Dominican Republic	99	61.3	8.68	1.6		
Ecuador	92	54.1	20.00	4.0		
Egypt, Arab Rep.	98	41.3	1.36	0.5		0.31
El Salvador	73	29.0	5.00	1.4		
Equatorial Guinea		23.8				
Eritrea	92	1.2				
Estonia	100	87.2	10.88	0.7	4.127	
Ethiopia	71	15.4	7.44	12.6		
Fiji	68	46.5	11.92	2.8		
Finland	100	87.7	22.80	0.6	10.948	
France	99	85.6	17.20	0.6	1.618	
Gabon	97	48.1	8.79	1.5		
Gambia, The	86	18.5	6.55	16.6		
Georgia	99	58.0	1.99	0.6		
Germany	96	89.7	28.95	0.8	1.212	
Ghana	80	34.7	4.73	3.8	0.282	0.15
Greece	99	69.1	59.69	4.0	0.718	
Grenada	75	55.9	16.67	2.1		
Guatemala	92	34.5	13.26	3.8		
Guinea	39	9.8	3.30	7.8	0.157	0.07
Guinea-Bissau		3.8	58.29	112.8	0.054	0.02
Guyana	0	35.7	9.69	2.6		
Haiti	50	12.2	3.84	6.2		
Honduras	83	30.0	17.47	8.9		
Hong Kong SAR, China	99	87.5	6.16	0.2	1.477	1.602
Hungary	99	79.3	44.77	4.2	1.423	
Iceland	99	98.2	24.47	0.5	3.921	
India	74	29.6	3.77	2.7		0.88

(continued next page)

Table DN.1 *(continued)*

Economy	Availability and users		Affordability and usage			
	Proportion of population covered by a 3G mobile network, 2015	Individuals using the internet (% of population), 2016	Price of 1 gigabyte (GB) of data (US dollars per month), 2016	Price of 1 GB of data (% of GDP per capita per month), 2016	GB per data user, 2016	GB per mobile subscription, 2016
Indonesia	60	25.4	4.10	1.4		
Iran, Islamic Rep.	60	53.2	3.91	0.9	1.112	0.6
Iraq	55	21.2	12.67	3.3		
Ireland	95	85.0	34.36	0.7	3.1	
Israel	99	79.7	21.85	0.7		
Italy	100	61.3	28.70	1.1	1.672	
Jamaica	90	45.0	15.31	3.8		
Japan	100	93.2	70.72	2.2	2.121	
Jordan	99	62.3	7.08	2.1		
Kazakhstan	73	74.6	4.48	0.7		
Kenya	69	26.0	4.98	4.1		
Kiribati	63	13.7	37.56	31.1		
Korea, Rep.	99	92.8	17.69	0.8	3.833	
Kosovo	91	82.9	5.65	1.8		
Kuwait	97	78.4	16.67	0.7		
Kyrgyz Republic	59	34.5	1.74	1.9		
Lao PDR	65	21.9	5.99	3.1		
Latvia	95	79.8	10.30	0.9	8.21	
Lebanon	97	76.1	19.00	2.9		
Lesotho	96	27.4	7.19	8.6		
Liberia	50	7.3	5.00	13.2	0.178	0.06
Libya	50	20.3	10.80			
Lithuania	100	74.4	4.52	0.4	2.51	1.37
Luxembourg	99	98.1	22.91	0.3	2.912	
Macao SAR, China	100	81.6	12.00	0.2		
Macedonia, FYR	98	72.2	3.64	0.8		
Madagascar	61	4.7	4.67	14.0		
Malawi	32	9.6	5.36	21.4		
Malaysia	92	78.8	6.73	0.8	3.1	1.92
Maldives	100	59.1	12.95	1.8		
Mali	10	11.1	12.08	18.6	0.179	0.038
Malta	100	77.3	13.56	0.6		
Marshall Islands		29.8				
Mauritania	30	18.0	11.71	13.0		
Mauritius	93	52.2	8.62	1.1		
Mexico	89	59.5	11.59	1.7		0.27
Micronesia, Fed. Sts.		33.4	30.00	11.7		
Moldova	99	71.0	2.70	1.7		

(continued next page)

Table DN.1 (continued)

Economy	Availability and users		Affordability and usage			
	Proportion of population covered by a 3G mobile network, 2015	Individuals using the internet (% of population), 2016	Price of 1 gigabyte (GB) of data (US dollars per month), 2016	Price of 1 GB of data (% of GDP per capita per month), 2016	GB per data user, 2016	GB per mobile subscription, 2016
Mongolia	95	22.3	6.76	2.2		
Montenegro	97	69.9	22.93	4.1		
Morocco	80	58.3	4.99	2.1		
Mozambique	50	17.5	2.74	8.6		
Myanmar	79	25.1	2.14	2.0		
Namibia	37	31.0	13.42	3.9		
Nauru	98		22.30	3.4		
Nepal	50	19.7	2.80	4.6	0.177	0.07
Netherlands	99	90.4	30.58	0.8	1.024	
New Zealand	98	88.5	28.49	0.9	1.057	
Nicaragua	75	24.6	13.87	7.7		
Niger	10	4.3	6.58	21.7		
Nigeria	67	25.7	3.21	1.8	0.164	0.08
Norway	99	97.3	25.12	0.4	2.594	
Oman	95	69.9	13.16	1.1		
Pakistan	46	15.5	1.54	1.3	0.464	
Palau	88		49.90	4.4		
Panama	79	54.0	15.00	1.3		
Papua New Guinea	60	9.6	21.70	10.4		
Paraguay	66	51.4	13.35	3.9		
Peru	91	45.5	17.87	3.6		0.42
Philippines	78	55.5	6.02	2.4		
Poland	100	73.3	10.52	1.0	3.548	
Portugal	99	70.4	34.93	2.1	1.521	
Qatar	98	94.3	16.48	0.3		
Romania	100	59.5	4.48	0.6		0.81
Russian Federation	73	73.1	6.86	0.9	2.315	1.43
Rwanda	88	20.0	4.91	8.4	0.271	0.12
Samoa	86	29.4	9.36	2.8		
São Tomé and Príncipe	2	28.0	8.84	6.0		
Saudi Arabia	97	73.8	29.33	1.8		
Senegal	40	25.7	3.06	3.8	0.709	0.198
Serbia	97	67.1	3.67	0.8		
Seychelles	90	56.5	18.33	1.5		
Sierra Leone	20	11.8	17.87	43.2		
Singapore	100	81.0	7.24	0.2		
Slovak Republic	93	80.5	32.41	2.4	0.66	
Slovenia	100	75.5	19.84	1.1	1.419	

(continued next page)

Table DN.1 *(continued)*

Economy	Availability and users		Affordability and usage			
	Proportion of population covered by a 3G mobile network, 2015	Individuals using the internet (% of population), 2016	Price of 1 gigabyte (GB) of data (US dollars per month), 2016	Price of 1 GB of data (% of GDP per capita per month), 2016	GB per data user, 2016	GB per mobile subscription, 2016
Solomon Islands	12	11.0	25.16	15.1		
Somalia	30	1.9				
South Africa	98	54.0	10.75	2.5	0.44	0.26
South Sudan	20	6.7	133.70		0.084	0.02
Spain	99	80.6	38.75	1.8		
Sri Lanka	83	32.1	1.36	0.4	2.1	0.55
St. Kitts and Nevis	100	76.8	17.03	1.2		
St. Lucia	65	46.7	14.81	2.3		
St. Vincent and the Grenadines	100	55.6	14.81	2.5		
Sudan	46	28.0	4.64	2.3	0.361	0.19
Suriname	100	45.4	19.77	3.7		
Swaziland	21	28.6	32.70	14.1	0.16	0.09
Sweden	100	89.7	18.05	0.4	4.383	
Switzerland	100	89.1	31.40	0.5	2.712	
Syrian Arab Republic	70	31.9	8.12		0.165	0.06
Taiwan, China	100	86.3	6.55	0.3	7.4	
Tajikistan	60	20.5	1.52	2.3		
Tanzania	85	13.0	4.68	6.4		
Thailand	97	47.5	5.57	1.1	3.9	
Timor-Leste	96	25.3	15.00	12.8		
Togo	50	11.3	8.23	17.1		
Tonga	70	40.0	10.83	3.5		
Trinidad and Tobago	75	73.3	22.34	1.7		
Tunisia	94	49.6	4.35	1.4		
Turkey	95	58.4	6.65	0.7	2.22	
Turkmenistan	60	18.0	14.29	2.7		
Tuvalu		46.0				
Uganda	60	21.9	8.43	16.4	0.144	0.05
Ukraine	35	52.5	2.82	1.5		
United Arab Emirates	100	90.6	27.25	0.9		
United Kingdom	100	94.8	21.91	0.7	1.839	
United States	100	76.2	46.62	1.0	2.665	
Uruguay	90	66.4	5.23	0.4		0.79
Uzbekistan	32	46.8	4.94	2.8		
Vanuatu	51	24.0	9.22	3.9	0.379	0.104
Venezuela, RB	90	60.0	1.05			0.35
Vietnam	70	46.5	1.78	1.0		

(continued next page)

Table DN.1 (continued)

Economy	Availability and users		Affordability and usage			
	Proportion of population covered by a 3G mobile network, 2015	Individuals using the internet (% of population), 2016	Price of 1 gigabyte (GB) of data (US dollars per month), 2016	Price of 1 GB of data (% of GDP per capita per month), 2016	GB per data user, 2016	GB per mobile subscription, 2016
West Bank and Gaza	0	61.2				
Yemen, Rep.	80	24.6	11.61	14.1	0.103	0.02
Zambia	53	25.5	13.27	13.5	0.217	0.08
Zimbabwe	55	23.1	35.00	41.6		
East Asia and Pacific	82	51.6	16.34	4.2	2.8	1.7
Europe and Central Asia	92	75.2	16.18	1.3	2.9	1.3
Latin America and the Caribbean	81	56.2	14.30	2.8	0.6	0.5
Middle East and North Africa	77	58.0	14.64	2.2	0.5	0.2
North America	99	88.0	43.99	1.1	2.1	1.2
South Asia	68	28.3	4.10	3.0	0.7	0.5
Sub-Saharan Africa	52	20.1	14.05	14.9	0.3	0.1
Low income	43	11.2	14.59	20.7	0.24	0.13
Lower middle income	65	33.6	9.46	5.4	0.44	0.38
Upper middle income	82	53.0	11.50	2.2	1.77	0.65
High income	96	82.5	23.63	1.1	2.91	1.28
World	77	51.7	14.98	5.5	1.82	0.51

Note: Data for groups is compiled using averages. Blank cells indicate that no information is available for the indicator.

Government

These indicators refer to aspects of government involvement with data. Data are provided on the number of open data sets in the economy and the existence of a data protection and privacy law, as well as for the authority responsible for data protection (table DN.2). The number of open data sets is sourced from OpenDataSoft (Mercier 2015). No definitive list of data protection authorities exists. Data have been sourced from the International Conference of Data Protection and Privacy Commissioners.[10] The data should therefore be treated with caution, as there may be cases in which a data protection authority exists in an economy but is not a member of the International Conference of Data Protection and Privacy Commissioners. Data protection and privacy laws have been sourced from the United Nations Conference on Trade and Development.[11] In cases in which economies have reported multiple laws, the one specifically referring to data privacy or protection is listed. Note that, in some

instances, no specific law exists on data privacy and protection and instead the principles are presumably encapsulated in other laws, such as a constitution or electronic transaction act. It is to be noted that, in some instances, the listed statutes refer to draft legislation.

Infrastructure

These indicators refer to the potential for domestic data exchange and the volume of international internet bandwidth to provide an indication of the quality of data transmission. Data are provided on the number of internet exchange points and international internet bandwidth. The number of internet exchange points is sourced from Packet Clearing House.[12] Data on international internet bandwidth is sourced from the International Telecommunications Union (ITU 2017).

Table DN.2 Government data infrastructure and open data

Economy	Government				Data infrastructure	
	Data protection authority	Data privacy and protection legislation	Number of open data sets, 2018	Open data sets per million people	Number of internet exchange points, 2018	International internet bandwidth (bits/s per internet user), 2016
Afghanistan			3	0.09	0	11,967
Albania	Commissioner for Personal Data Protection	Law No. 9887 on the Protection of Personal Data	3	1.04	1	56,964
Algeria			5	0.12	0	40,015
American Samoa						
Andorra	Data Protection Agency	Loi qualifiée 15/2003, du 18 décembre, sur la protection des données personnelles	2	25.99	0	106,390
Angola		Lei No. 22/11 da Protecção de Dados Pessoais de 17 de Junho (in Portuguese)	2	0.07	2	8,796
Antigua and Barbuda		Data Protection Act 2013	1	9.90	0	88,622
Argentina	National Direction for Personal Data Protection	Ley 25.326 de Protección de los Datos Personales	23	0.52	27	41,130
Armenia	Personal Data Protection Agency	Law of the Republic of Armenia on the Protection of Personal Data	3	1.03	1	59,860
Aruba			0	0.00	0	
Australia	Office of the Australian Information Commissioner	Privacy Act 1988	68	2.82	19	88,304
Austria	Austrian Data Protection Authority	Datenschutzgesetz 2000	20	2.29	4	149,988
Azerbaijan		Law on Personal Data 2010	3	0.31	0	34,255
Bahamas, The		Data Protection (Privacy of Personal Information) Act 2003	1	2.56	0	198,447
Bahrain			3	2.11	1	112,770
Bangladesh			4	0.02	1	9,154
Barbados		Data Protection Bill 2005	1	3.51	0	284,571
Belarus		Law of the Republic of Belarus on Information, Informatization and Protection of Information—Law no. 8517	4	0.42	0	168,518
Belgium	Privacy Commission	Law on Privacy Protection in relation to the Processing of Personal Data	28	2.47	1	189,254
Belize			3	8.18	1	44,633

(continued next page)

Table DN.2 *(continued)*

Economy	Data protection authority	Data privacy and protection legislation	Government — Number of open data sets, 2018	Government — Open data sets per million people	Data infrastructure — Number of internet exchange points, 2018	Data infrastructure — International internet bandwidth (bits/s per internet user), 2016
Benin	National Commission for Technology and Freedoms	Loi n°2009-09 du 22 mai 2009 portant organisation de la protection des données à caractère personnel	4	0.37	1	1,656
Bermuda			3	45.92		
Bhutan		Bhutan Information Communications and Media Act 2006	0	0.00	0	18,077
Bolivia		Ley General de Telecomunicaciones, Tecnologías de Información y Comunicación—Ley 167 de 08 agosto de 2011	30	2.76	2	36,347
Bosnia and Herzegovina	Personal Data Protection Agency in Bosnia and Herzegovina	Law on the Protection of Personal Data	4	1.14	0	98,452
Botswana			2	0.89	1	7,880
Brazil		Protection of Personal Data Bill 2011	23	0.11	27	66,181
British Virgin Islands			0		0	
Brunei Darussalam			2	4.73	0	76,226
Bulgaria	Commission for Personal Data Protection	Law for Protection of Personal Data	6	0.84	5	175,869
Burkina Faso	Data Processing and Liberties Commission	Loi n° 010-2004/AN Portant Protection des Données à Caractère Personnel	6	0.32	1	2,810
Burundi			3	0.29	1	6,083
Cabo Verde	National Commission of Data Protection	Lei n° 133/V/2001 of 22 January 2001	4	7.41	0	23,357
Cambodia			2	0.13	2	23,573
Cameroon			7	0.30	0	2,549
Canada	Privacy Commissioner of Canada (Commissariat à la protection de la vie privée du Canada)	Personal Information Protection and Electronic Documents Act	159	4.38	13	141,885
Cayman Islands			1	16.46		
Central African Republic			4	0.87	0	1,695
Chad		Law 007/PR/2015 on the Protection of Personal Data	1	0.07	0	3,762
Channel Islands			0	0.00		

(continued next page)

Economy	Data protection authority	Data privacy and protection legislation	Government		Data infrastructure	
			Number of open data sets, 2018	Open data sets per million people	Number of internet exchange points, 2018	International internet bandwidth (bits/s per internet user), 2016
Chile		Law 19.628 of 1999	14	0.78	6	175,556
China		The Decision of the Standing Committee of the National People's Congress on Strengthening the Network Information Protection (2012)	16	0.01	8	14,699
Colombia	Superintendence of Industry and Commerce of Colombia	Law 1266 of 2008- Habeas Data Act	38	0.78	1	150,871
Comoros			1	1.26	0	12,729
Congo, Dem. Rep.			5	0.08	1	770
Congo, Rep.			6	1.17	1	
Costa Rica	Agency for the Protection of Personal Data of Inhabitants	Ley de Protección de la Persona frente al tratamiento de sus datos personales, N° 8968	13	2.68	1	68,449
Côte d'Ivoire	Telecommunications/ICT Regulatory Body (ARTCI)	Loi n° 2013-450 du 19 juin 2013 relative à la protection des données à caractère personnel	5	0.21	1	6,825
Croatia	Data Protection Agency	Act on Personal Data Protection	9	2.16	1	118,953
Cuba			3	0.26	1	1,152
Curaçao			0	0	1	
Cyprus	Personal Data Protection Commissioner	The Processing of Personal Data (Protection of the Individual) Law	4	3.42	1	188,904
Czech Republic	Office for Personal Data Protection	Law on Personal Data Protection	21	1.99	3	180,697
Denmark	Data Protection Agency	Act on Processing of Personal Data	18	3.14	3	239,874
Djibouti			2	2.12	1	15,228
Dominica		Privacy and Data Protection Bill 2007	1	13.60	1	176,449
Dominican Republic		Ley No. 172-13, sobre Protección de Datos de Carácter Personal del 13 de diciembre de 2013	4	0.38	1	22,061
Ecuador		Protection of Privacy and Personal Data Bill 2016	4	0.24	4	43,677
Egypt, Arab Rep.			8	0.08	2	17,194
El Salvador		Ley de Comercio Electronico y Comunicaciones	6	0.95	0	63,622

(continued next page)

Table DN.2 *(continued)*

Economy	Government				Data infrastructure	
	Data protection authority	Data privacy and protection legislation	Number of open data sets, 2018	Open data sets per million people	Number of internet exchange points, 2018	International internet bandwidth (bits/s per internet user), 2016
Equatorial Guinea		Law 1/2016 (Data protection law)	3	2.46	0	2,397
Eritrea			1	0.19	0	3,601
Estonia	Data Protection Inspectorate	Data Protection Act	5	3.80	3	210,798
Ethiopia			4	0.04	0	2,242
Faroe Islands			0	0.00		
Fiji			2	2.23	0	23,726
Finland	Data Protection Ombudsman	Personal Data Act	26	4.73	4	216,391
France	National Commission of Computing and Freedoms (CNIL)	Law relating to the protection of individuals against the processing of personal data	155	2.32	16	97,653
French Polynesia			0	0.00		
Gabon		Loi n°001/2011 relative à la protection des données à caractère personnel	5	2.53	1	4,844
Gambia, The		Information and Communications Act No. 2 of 2009	2	0.98	1	13,297
Georgia	Office of the Personal Data Protection Inspector of Georgia	Law of Georgia on Personal Data Protection	3	0.81	1	92,145
Germany	Federal Data Protection Commissioner	Federal Data Protection Act	57	0.69	19	107,489
Ghana	Data Protection Commission (GDPC)	Data Protection Act (Act No. 843) 2012—DPA	4	0.14	1	9,851
Gibraltar	Data Protection Commissioner		0	0		
Greece	Hellenic Data Protection Authority	Law on the Protection of individuals with regard to the processing of personal data	5	0.47	1	68,698
Greenland			0	0.00	0	
Grenada			0	0.00	1	229,948
Guam			0	0.00		
Guatemala			4	0.24	0	24,022
Guinea			3	0.24	0	589
Guinea-Bissau			2	1.10	0	4,707
Guyana			3	3.88	0	34,675
Haiti			3	0.28	1	2,337

(continued next page)

Economy	Data protection authority	Data privacy and protection legislation	Government		Data infrastructure	
			Number of open data sets, 2018	Open data sets per million people	Number of internet exchange points, 2018	International internet bandwidth (bits/s per internet user), 2016
Honduras		Anteproyecto de Ley de Protección de Datos Personales y Acción de Hábeas Data de Honduras	1	0.11	1	33,443
Hong Kong SAR, China	Privacy Commissioner for Personal Data		0	0.00		4,906,023
Hungary	National Authority for Data Protection and Freedom of Information	Act on Informational Self-Determination and Freedom of Information	4	0.41	1	154,765
Iceland	Data Protection Authority	Law on the Protection and Processing of Personal Data 1989	8	23.93	1	997,830
India		Information Technology Act 2000	6	0.00	13	15,956
Indonesia		Law of the Republic of Indonesia Number 11 of 2008 Concerning Electronic Information and Transactions	8	0.03	7	24,947
Iran, Islamic Rep.		Law on Electronic Commerce	3	0.04	4	15,238
Iraq		Draft Data Protection and Privacy Law	0	0.00	0	
Ireland	Data Protection Commissioner	Data Protection Act, 1988	15	3.14	3	183,943
Isle of Man	Data Protection Registrar		0	0		
Israel	The Israeli Law, Information and Technology Authority	Privacy Protection Act 1981	8	0.94	1	158,696
Italy	Data Protection Commission	Decreto Legislativo 30 giugno 2003, n. 196— Codice in materia di protezione dei dati personali	56	0.92	8	82,335
Jamaica		Data Protection Bill 2012	5	1.74	1	47,949
Japan	Personal Information Protection Commission	Act on the Protection of Personal Information	20	0.16	16	83,010
Jordan		Data Protection Bill	6	0.63	0	8,229
Kazakhstan		Law on personal data and their protection, 21 May 2013	0	0.00	0	87,235
Kenya		Data Protection Bill 2012	9	0.19	2	69,014
Kiribati			0	0.00	0	4,426
Korea, Dem. People's Rep.			0	0.00	0	

(continued next page)

Table DN.2 (continued)

Economy	Government				Data infrastructure	
	Data protection authority	Data privacy and protection legislation	Number of open data sets, 2018	Open data sets per million people	Number of internet exchange points, 2018	International internet bandwidth (bits/s per internet user), 2016
Korea, Rep.	Personal Information Protection Commission	Korea's Personal Information Protection Act was promulgated in 2011 as amended	10	0.20	3	54,252
Kosovo	National Agency for Personal Data Protection, AMDP		2	1.10	1	
Kuwait		Law No. 20 of 2014	8	1.97	0	69,516
Kyrgyz Republic		Law on Personal Data 2008	2	0.33	1	65,377
Lao PDR			3	0.44	1	17,487
Latvia	State Data Inspectorate	Law on Protection of Personal Data of Natural Persons	3	1.53	2	246,666
Lebanon			1	0.17	2	55,086
Lesotho		Data Protection Act 2012	4	1.82	1	4,484
Liberia			1	0.22	1	
Libya			2	0.32	0	5,286
Liechtenstein	Data Protection Commissioner	Gesetz über die Abänderung des Datenschutzgesetzes, 2002	0	0.00	1	
Lithuania	State Data Inspectorate	Law on Legal Protection of Personal Data	10	3.48	3	198,564
Luxembourg	National Data Protection Commission	Data Protection Law	3	5.15	1	8,397,884
Macao SAR, China			0	0.00		252,868
Macedonia, FYR	Directorate of Personal Data Protection	Law on Personal Data Protection	3	1.44	0	109,004
Madagascar		Loi No. 2014-38	3	0.12	1	14,258
Malawi		Electronic Transactions and Cybersecurity Act 2016	5	0.28	1	4,201
Malaysia		Personal Data Protection Act 2010	4	0.13	1	42,627
Maldives			2	4.79	0	59,669
Mali	Personal Data Protection Authority (Autorité de Protection de Données à Caractère Personnel)	Loi n° 2013-015 du 21 mai 2013	5	0.28	1	598
Malta	Data Protection Commissioner	Data Protection Act 2001	3	6.87	1	1,596,254
Marshall Islands			0	0.00	0	
Mauritania			2	0.47	0	4,477
Mauritius	Data Protection Office of Mauritius	Data Protection Act 2004	3	2.37	1	63,491

(continued next page)

Economy	Data protection authority	Data privacy and protection legislation	Government		Data infrastructure	
			Number of open data sets, 2018	Open data sets per million people	Number of internet exchange points, 2018	International internet bandwidth (bits/s per internet user), 2016
Mexico	National Institute for Transparency, Access to Information and Personal Data Protection	Ley Federal de Protección de Datos Personales en Posesión de los Particulares 2010	23	0.18	1	37,598
Micronesia, Fed. Sts.			2	19.06	0	
Moldova	National Center for Personal Data Protection	Law on Personal Data Protection 2007	5	1.41	0	144,087
Monaco	Supervisory Commission for Personal Information	Act controlling personal data processing 1993	1	25.97	0	95,232
Mongolia			2	0.66	1	166,056
Montenegro	Agency for Personal Data Protection and Free Access to Information	Law on Personal Data Protection 2008	3	4.82	1	202,876
Morocco	National Commission for the Control and the Protection of Personal Data	Law No. 09-08/2009 on the protection of people toward data protection of a personal nature	4	0.11	0	25,702
Mozambique			3	0.10	1	1,115
Myanmar			5	0.09	1	6,426
Namibia			4	1.61	1	15,915
Nauru			1	76.63	0	
Nepal		Right to Information Act, 2064 (2007)	8	0.28	1	3,886
Netherlands	Dutch Data Protection Authority	Personal Data Protection Act 1998	53	3.11	8	196,105
New Caledonia			3	10.79	0	
New Zealand	Privacy Commissioner (Te Mana Matapono Matatapu)	Privacy Act 1993	19	4.05	7	109,601
Nicaragua		Ley No. 787 Ley de Protección de Datos Personales	2	0.33	1	29,161
Niger		Projet de loi sur la protection des données à caractère personnel	3	0.15	0	
Nigeria		Data Protection Bill 2011	4	0.02	2	11,257
Northern Mariana Islands			0	0.00		
Norway	Data Inspectorate	Personal Data Act 2000	6	1.15	5	268,953
Oman		Royal Decree no. 69 of 2008—Electronic Transactions Law	2	0.45	0	66,071
Pakistan		Electronic Data Protection Act 2005—Draft	6	0.03	1	16,636

(continued next page)

Table DN.2 *(continued)*

Economy	Data protection authority	Data privacy and protection legislation	Government		Data infrastructure	
			Number of open data sets, 2018	Open data sets per million people	Number of internet exchange points, 2018	International internet bandwidth (bits/s per internet user), 2016
Palau			1	46.51	0	
Panama		Personal Data Protection Bill 2016	4	0.99	1	55,072
Papua New Guinea			2	0.25	1	
Paraguay		Ley 1682/2001 Reglamenta la Informacion de Caracter Privado	4	0.59	1	21,015
Peru	National Authority for Data Protection	Ley N° 29733—Ley de Protección de Datos Personales	19	0.60	1	33,315
Philippines	National Privacy Commission	Data Privacy Act of 2012	5	0.05	1	43,440
Poland	Inspector General for Personal Data Protection	Act on the Protection of Personal Data 1997	6	0.16	10	83,299
Portugal	National Data Protection Commission	Lei da proteçao de dados pessoais 1991	6	0.58	1	177,808
Puerto Rico			0	0.00	1	
Qatar		Law No. 13 of 2016 Concerning Privacy and Protection of Personal Data	2	0.78	1	86,950
Romania	National Supervisory Authority for Personal Data Protection	Law on the protection of individuals with regard to the processing of personal data etc. (2001)	6	0.30	3	155,516
Russian Federation		Federal Law Regarding Personal Data 2006	8	0.06	27	51,888
Rwanda			4	0.34	1	7,455
Samoa			3	15.37	0	13,159
San Marino		Law regulating the Computerized Collection of Personal Data 1983	1	30.12	0	
São Tomé and Príncipe		Data Protection Law 2016	2	10.00	0	37,317
Saudi Arabia			10	0.31	0	78,163
Senegal	Commission of Personal Data Protection, CDP	Loi n° 2008-12 du 25 janvier 2008 sur la protection des données à caractère personnel	3	0.19	1	4,977
Serbia	Commissioner for Information of Public Importance and Personal Data Protection	Law on Personal Data Protection 2008	4	0.57	1	26,292
Seychelles		Data Protection Act 2003	4	42.25	0	52,433

(continued next page)

Economy	Government				Data infrastructure	
	Data protection authority	Data privacy and protection legislation	Number of open data sets, 2018	Open data sets per million people	Number of internet exchange points, 2018	International internet bandwidth (bits/s per internet user), 2016
Sierra Leone			3	0.41	0	
Singapore	Personal Data Protection Commission	Personal Data Protection Act 2012	4	0.71	5	982,923
Sint Maarten (Dutch part)					1	
Slovak Republic	Inspection Unit for the Protection of Personal Data	Act on the Protection of Personal Data 1992	6	1.11	3	52,351
Slovenia	Information Commissioner of the Republic of Slovenia	Personal Data Protection Act 1990	8	3.87	1	239,168
Solomon Islands			2	3.34	0	11,971
Somalia			3	0.21	0	
South Africa	Information Regulator	Protection of Personal Information Act 4 of 2013	12	0.21	6	263,030
South Sudan			2	0.16	0	
Spain	Data Protection Agency	Organic Law 15/1999 on Personal Data Protection	72	1.55	5	112,997
Sri Lanka			2	0.09	1	22,038
St. Kitts and Nevis		Privacy and Data Protection Bill 2012	0	0.00	0	165,372
St. Lucia		Data Protection Act 2011	1	5.62	1	7,558
St. Martin (French part)						
St. Vincent and the Grenadines		Privacy Act 2003	0	0.00	0	188,740
Sudan			4	0.10	1	2,035
Suriname		The Constitution of the Republic of Suriname, Article 17	3	5.37	0	66,533
Swaziland		Data Protection Bill	3	2.23	0	
Sweden	Data Inspection Board	Personal Data Act 1998	33	3.33	9	505,650
Switzerland	Federal Data Protection Commissioner	Federal Act on Data Protection, 1992	16	1.91	3	269,222
Syrian Arab Republic			0	0.00	0	12,813
Taiwan, China		Personal Data Protection Law	11	0.47	3	97,652
Tajikistan		Law on Protection of Information (December 2, 2002, № 71)	2	0.23	0	
Tanzania		Data Protection Bill 2013	7	0.13	3	1,741
Thailand		Personal Data Protection Bill 2011	16	0.23	2	49,244
Timor-Leste			3	2.36	1	1,888

(continued next page)

Table DN.2 *(continued)*

Economy	Government				Data infrastructure	
	Data protection authority	Data privacy and protection legislation	Number of open data sets, 2018	Open data sets per million people	Number of internet exchange points, 2018	International internet bandwidth (bits/s per internet user), 2016
Togo			2	0.26	1	4,490
Tonga			2	18.67	0	33,947
Trinidad and Tobago		Data Protection Act 2011	2	1.47	2	182,808
Tunisia	National Personal Data Authority	Law 63/2004	10	0.88	2	31,167
Turkey	Personal Data Protection Authority	Data Protection Law 2016	4	0.05	2	68,058
Turkmenistan			1	0.18	0	
Tuvalu			2	180.23	0	
Uganda		The Data Protection and Privacy Bill, 2015	7	0.17	1	5,510
Ukraine	Ukrainian Parliament Commissioner for Human Rights	Law on Personal Data Protection 2011	8	0.18	6	79,885
United Arab Emirates		Dubai International Financial Centre (DIFC) Data Protection Law	3	0.32	2	133,749
United Kingdom	Information Commissioner's Office	Data Protection Act 1998	154	2.35	9	449,137
United States	Federal Trade Commission	Privacy Act of 1974	993	3.07	89	126,545
Uruguay	Regulatory and Control Unit of Personal Data	La Ley 18331 Protección de Datos Personales y Acción de Habeas Data"del 11 agosto del año 2008 y el Decreto reglamentario 414/2009	7	2.03	0	96,707
Uzbekistan			2	0.06	1	5,683
Vanuatu			2	7.40	1	21,921
Venezuela, RB			3	0.10	0	18,937
Vietnam		Law on Protection of Consumers' Rights 2010	4	0.04	3	91,252
Virgin Islands (U.S.)					0	
West Bank and Gaza			5	1.10	1	0
Yemen, Rep.		Law of the Right of Access to Information 2012	2	0.07	0	
Zambia		The Electronic Communications and Transactions Act, Act Number 21 of 2009—the Electronic Communications Act	2	0.12	1	3,925
Zimbabwe		Draft Data Protection Bill 2016	2	0.12	1	9,119

Note: Blank cells indicate that no information is available for this country on this indicator.

Digital Adoption Index

The Digital Adoption Index is a global index that measures countries' digital adoption across three dimensions of the economy: people, government, and business. The index covers 180 countries on a 0–1 scale and emphasizes the "supply side" of digital adoption to maximize coverage and simplify theoretical linkages (map DN.1). The overall index is the simple average of three subindexes. Each subindex comprises technologies necessary for the respective agent to promote development in the digital era: increasing productivity and accelerating broad-based growth for *business*, expanding opportunities and improving welfare for *people*, and increasing the efficiency and accountability of service delivery for *government*. Although data and theoretical constraints prohibit any index from providing a comprehensive view of an economy, the Digital Adoption Index (DAI) provides a useful framing mechanism for digital adoption across economic agents and countries. By measuring the relative adoption of digital technologies, the index can assist policy makers in designing a digital strategy with tailored policies to promote digital adoption across different user groups.[13]

The DAI is intended to reflect actual adoption of digital technologies across the economy, not perceptions of adoption. Accordingly, indicators comprising the index represent subscriptions, access, or adoption and eschew public or elite opinion surveys. Most data come from the International Telecommunication Union or the World Bank. Other sources include Eurostat, GSMA, and Netcraft (table DN.3). Data were collected for two time periods: 2014 and 2016. The *business* subindex measures the quality of digital infrastructure needed for e-commerce and other business functions, comprising the number of secure servers and international internet bandwidth, as well as the percentage of businesses with websites as a proxy for their more general online business activities. The *people* subindex measures the extent and quality of individuals' connections to the digital world, comprising access to mobile-cellular phones, basic internet, and mobile and fixed broadband. And the *government* subindex measures the adoption of core administrative systems to automate and streamline government activities and digital identification systems and online public services that allow the government to better serve the public.

Map DN.1 Digital Adoption Index score, by country

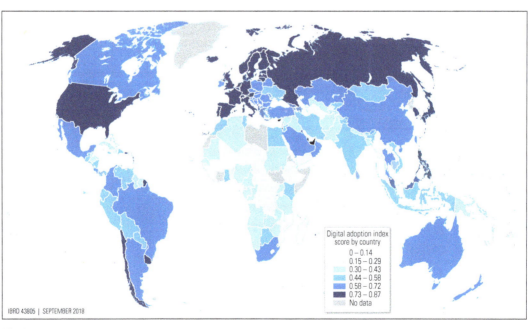

Source: World Bank 2018.
Note: The Digital Adoption Index measures digital adoption for 180 countries.

Table DN.3 Data sources for the Digital Adoption Index

Subindex	Indicator	Source
Business	Internet bandwidth	ITU
	Business websites	Eurostat and World Bank
	Secure servers	Netcraft
People	Mobile-cellular subscriptions	ITU
	Mobile broadband	GSMA
	Internet use	ITU
	Fixed broadband	ITU
Government	Core administrative systems	World Bank
	Digital identification	World Bank
	Online public services	UNDESA

Source: World Bank 2018.
Note: ITU = International Telecommunication Union; UNDESA = United Nations Department of Economic and Social Affairs.

Missing values are estimated and indicators normalized to create a complete and balanced data set. A few indicators—particularly the percentage of businesses with websites—are missing observations for many countries. Instead of dropping the countries, missing values are imputed using data on per capita income, internet use, and geographical region. Data are normalized on a 0–1 scale so that each indicator has equal weight within a subindex. In all but one case, indicators are normalized across both years, not within each individual year. Observed changes can therefore be considered absolute changes in value for particular countries, not merely a reordering based on relative trajectories between countries.[14] For example, the DAI score for India increased from 0.44 to 0.51 over the period 2014–16. This means that India made progress over the period, increasing digital adoption. If scores were normalized within years (not across years), it would not be possible to determine if an increase in India's score meant India made progress or other countries regressed.

Normalized data is averaged so that the DAI's constituent indicators have equal weight at each level. For example, the government indicator of core administrative systems is composed of four categorical variables collected by the World Bank. After the scores are normalized, the simple average is calculated. The resulting average represents the country's score for core administrative systems. The core administrative systems score is then averaged with the scores for digital identification and online public services, which are generated using a similar process. And the resulting average at that level represents the government subindex score. The business and people subindexes follow the same process. The overall DAI varies on a 0–1 scale because its source indicators are normalized to that scale. As with the subindexes, 0 is the lowest possible score on the DAI, representing no adoption of digital technologies, and 1 is the highest possible score, representing full adoption of digital technologies. Theoretically, a country can score a perfect 1 if it has the best score on all the indicators comprising the DAI or a perfect 0 if it has the worst score on all the indicators. But in practice, DAI scores ranged 0.14–0.87 in 2014 and 0.15–0.87 in 2016 (table DN.4).

Table DN.4 Digital Adoption Index and subindexes, by country and year

Country	Digital Adoption Index		Business subindex		People subindex		Government subindex	
	2014	2016	2014	2016	2014	2016	2014	2016
Afghanistan	0.30	0.34	0.30	0.34	0.09	0.12	0.52	0.56
Albania	0.54	0.61	0.55	0.62	0.39	0.46	0.69	0.74
Algeria	0.37	0.43	0.45	0.50	0.28	0.42	0.38	0.38
Andorra	0.59	0.64	0.78	0.83	0.67	0.74	0.33	0.35
Angola	0.32	0.33	0.38	0.41	0.12	0.13	0.45	0.46
Antigua and Barbuda	0.46	0.48	0.60	0.61	0.45	0.57	0.33	0.25
Argentina	0.64	0.69	0.68	0.69	0.56	0.63	0.68	0.73

(continued next page)

Table DN.4 *(continued)*

Country	Digital Adoption Index		Business subindex		People subindex		Government subindex	
	2014	2016	2014	2016	2014	2016	2014	2016
Armenia	0.61	0.62	0.68	0.71	0.41	0.48	0.73	0.67
Australia	0.69	0.71	0.76	0.77	0.72	0.78	0.57	0.59
Austria	0.81	0.86	0.84	0.88	0.82	0.87	0.79	0.85
Azerbaijan	0.55	0.59	0.47	0.51	0.51	0.52	0.67	0.75
Bahamas, The	0.48	0.53	0.68	0.74	0.43	0.50	0.32	0.35
Bahrain	0.76	0.79	0.70	0.75	0.77	0.84	0.81	0.77
Bangladesh	0.31	0.37	0.30	0.36	0.15	0.19	0.48	0.57
Barbados	0.57	0.65	0.78	0.83	0.53	0.63	0.40	0.48
Belarus	0.53	0.59	0.70	0.74	0.56	0.65	0.33	0.39
Belgium	0.76	0.78	0.84	0.85	0.68	0.73	0.75	0.76
Belize	0.38	0.40	0.56	0.58	0.21	0.29	0.36	0.34
Benin	0.21	0.22	0.33	0.33	0.12	0.15	0.18	0.20
Bhutan	0.38	0.44	0.43	0.47	0.24	0.37	0.47	0.50
Bolivia	0.44	0.48	0.49	0.55	0.27	0.30	0.56	0.59
Bosnia and Herzegovina	0.55	0.60	0.64	0.68	0.42	0.47	0.59	0.64
Botswana	0.46	0.47	0.48	0.48	0.43	0.47	0.48	0.47
Brazil	0.65	0.68	0.65	0.68	0.55	0.55	0.77	0.82
Brunei Darussalam	0.57	0.63	0.66	0.69	0.45	0.53	0.61	0.66
Bulgaria	0.57	0.63	0.67	0.69	0.57	0.62	0.46	0.57
Burkina Faso	0.22	0.24	0.26	0.28	0.11	0.15	0.31	0.27
Burundi	0.23	0.26	0.30	0.31	0.02	0.06	0.37	0.42
Cabo Verde	0.37	0.43	0.45	0.49	0.39	0.43	0.28	0.38
Cambodia	0.36	0.40	0.35	0.41	0.30	0.39	0.43	0.39
Cameroon	0.27	0.30	0.23	0.28	0.13	0.15	0.45	0.46
Canada	0.67	0.69	0.78	0.79	0.64	0.69	0.58	0.60
Central African Republic	0.14	0.15	0.28	0.32	0.01	0.01	0.12	0.11
Chad	0.18	0.23	0.19	0.29	0.03	0.05	0.31	0.34
Chile	0.72	0.76	0.77	0.82	0.50	0.56	0.91	0.89
China	0.50	0.59	0.47	0.55	0.40	0.52	0.63	0.69
Colombia	0.61	0.64	0.64	0.67	0.42	0.48	0.76	0.76
Comoros	0.22	0.25	0.30	0.36	0.06	0.08	0.30	0.32
Congo, Dem. Rep.	0.19	0.21	0.14	0.17	0.06	0.05	0.38	0.40
Congo, Rep.	0.29	0.31	0.34	0.36	0.18	0.22	0.37	0.35
Costa Rica	0.61	0.66	0.65	0.68	0.54	0.68	0.62	0.63
Croatia	0.58	0.65	0.70	0.75	0.54	0.58	0.51	0.61
Cuba	0.21	0.24	0.24	0.29	0.07	0.12	0.31	0.30
Cyprus	0.62	0.68	0.76	0.82	0.68	0.77	0.42	0.44
Czech Republic	0.69	0.72	0.82	0.86	0.64	0.66	0.61	0.65
Denmark	0.78	0.79	0.93	0.92	0.88	0.90	0.52	0.56
Djibouti	0.28	0.30	0.45	0.47	0.06	0.09	0.34	0.33

(continued next page)

Table DN.4 *(continued)*

Country	Digital Adoption Index		Business subindex		People subindex		Government subindex	
	2014	2016	2014	2016	2014	2016	2014	2016
Dominica	0.45	0.50	0.54	0.55	0.37	0.47	0.44	0.48
Dominican Republic	0.46	0.50	0.51	0.52	0.30	0.37	0.56	0.60
Ecuador	0.52	0.57	0.66	0.68	0.33	0.39	0.58	0.63
Egypt, Arab Rep.	0.51	0.53	0.45	0.49	0.32	0.38	0.75	0.71
El Salvador	0.48	0.50	0.54	0.56	0.34	0.40	0.57	0.55
Equatorial Guinea	0.17	0.19	0.36	0.38	0.12	0.13	0.02	0.04
Estonia	0.77	0.83	0.76	0.85	0.73	0.80	0.81	0.85
Ethiopia	0.23	0.27	0.24	0.26	0.07	0.15	0.37	0.40
Fiji	0.43	0.46	0.52	0.54	0.30	0.38	0.47	0.47
Finland	0.79	0.81	0.92	0.92	0.84	0.83	0.61	0.67
France	0.74	0.75	0.76	0.77	0.69	0.73	0.78	0.76
Gabon	0.35	0.36	0.42	0.42	0.35	0.35	0.29	0.31
Gambia, The	0.33	0.36	0.38	0.40	0.22	0.29	0.39	0.39
Georgia	0.56	0.60	0.62	0.64	0.41	0.48	0.66	0.67
Germany	0.80	0.84	0.85	0.87	0.74	0.78	0.81	0.87
Ghana	0.38	0.45	0.35	0.42	0.27	0.39	0.51	0.55
Greece	0.58	0.61	0.69	0.71	0.61	0.68	0.43	0.42
Grenada	0.51	0.53	0.64	0.65	0.38	0.42	0.52	0.53
Guatemala	0.44	0.52	0.56	0.57	0.25	0.33	0.50	0.67
Guinea	0.21	0.21	0.20	0.13	0.10	0.15	0.31	0.34
Guinea-Bissau	0.23	0.26	0.26	0.30	0.07	0.10	0.35	0.38
Guyana	0.32	0.36	0.49	0.57	0.19	0.21	0.28	0.29
Haiti	0.25	0.25	0.34	0.31	0.11	0.12	0.30	0.32
Honduras	0.41	0.43	0.48	0.51	0.21	0.27	0.53	0.50
Hungary	0.64	0.69	0.67	0.77	0.61	0.65	0.63	0.65
Iceland	0.70	0.74	0.94	0.97	0.76	0.82	0.42	0.42
India	0.44	0.51	0.43	0.50	0.16	0.23	0.74	0.80
Indonesia	0.39	0.46	0.34	0.42	0.30	0.41	0.54	0.54
Iran, Islamic Rep.	0.42	0.51	0.42	0.53	0.26	0.44	0.56	0.55
Iraq	0.26	0.30	0.28	0.33	0.17	0.20	0.33	0.38
Ireland	0.64	0.66	0.81	0.83	0.62	0.65	0.49	0.50
Israel	0.75	0.79	0.73	0.77	0.67	0.74	0.85	0.85
Italy	0.73	0.77	0.73	0.75	0.64	0.68	0.83	0.87
Jamaica	0.44	0.50	0.52	0.58	0.33	0.42	0.48	0.49
Japan	0.82	0.83	0.73	0.76	0.79	0.84	0.93	0.91
Jordan	0.52	0.55	0.52	0.50	0.45	0.57	0.60	0.58
Kazakhstan	0.63	0.67	0.54	0.60	0.53	0.57	0.83	0.84
Kenya	0.40	0.45	0.51	0.57	0.15	0.20	0.55	0.59
Kiribati	0.20	0.21	0.41	0.40	0.04	0.09	0.15	0.15
Korea, Rep.	0.84	0.86	0.74	0.75	0.80	0.84	0.99	0.98

(continued next page)

Country	Digital Adoption Index		Business subindex		People subindex		Government subindex	
	2014	2016	2014	2016	2014	2016	2014	2016
Kuwait	0.63	0.63	0.71	0.73	0.71	0.67	0.48	0.50
Kyrgyz Republic	0.43	0.50	0.49	0.61	0.31	0.35	0.49	0.54
Lao PDR	0.20	0.26	0.24	0.34	0.14	0.17	0.22	0.27
Latvia	0.69	0.73	0.70	0.77	0.63	0.71	0.74	0.71
Lebanon	0.52	0.57	0.62	0.67	0.50	0.56	0.44	0.49
Lesotho	0.26	0.29	0.25	0.30	0.21	0.25	0.33	0.32
Liberia	0.21	0.24	0.27	0.29	0.10	0.13	0.24	0.29
Lithuania	0.75	0.79	0.77	0.80	0.67	0.75	0.80	0.83
Luxembourg	0.84	0.86	0.93	0.94	0.85	0.87	0.74	0.77
Macedonia, FYR	0.50	0.57	0.61	0.66	0.48	0.51	0.43	0.55
Madagascar	0.23	0.25	0.34	0.38	0.05	0.06	0.32	0.31
Malawi	0.24	0.26	0.36	0.39	0.04	0.07	0.30	0.32
Malaysia	0.65	0.69	0.52	0.55	0.59	0.64	0.85	0.87
Maldives	0.48	0.51	0.63	0.64	0.47	0.58	0.35	0.31
Mali	0.31	0.29	0.31	0.28	0.25	0.22	0.39	0.37
Malta	0.78	0.86	0.92	0.94	0.72	0.79	0.71	0.84
Marshall Islands	0.19	0.22	0.44	0.52	0.07	0.09	0.07	0.04
Mauritania	0.30	0.34	0.32	0.38	0.20	0.24	0.38	0.39
Mauritius	0.54	0.62	0.58	0.63	0.47	0.57	0.58	0.65
Mexico	0.54	0.60	0.59	0.63	0.35	0.44	0.68	0.74
Moldova	0.56	0.60	0.68	0.70	0.44	0.55	0.54	0.57
Mongolia	0.52	0.54	0.63	0.65	0.29	0.35	0.65	0.61
Montenegro	0.54	0.62	0.55	0.62	0.59	0.68	0.49	0.55
Morocco	0.52	0.56	0.54	0.60	0.40	0.42	0.63	0.64
Mozambique	0.28	0.25	0.33	0.26	0.13	0.17	0.37	0.33
Myanmar	0.17	0.26	0.22	0.28	0.11	0.27	0.18	0.23
Namibia	0.37	0.38	0.52	0.50	0.26	0.34	0.33	0.31
Nepal	0.30	0.37	0.32	0.35	0.16	0.25	0.42	0.50
Netherlands	0.83	0.84	0.92	0.91	0.75	0.80	0.81	0.81
New Zealand	0.67	0.71	0.76	0.77	0.72	0.79	0.53	0.56
Nicaragua	0.38	0.46	0.47	0.50	0.26	0.37	0.40	0.50
Niger	0.16	0.16	0.23	0.24	0.04	0.05	0.20	0.18
Nigeria	0.37	0.42	0.29	0.36	0.17	0.21	0.65	0.68
Norway	0.78	0.80	0.86	0.88	0.78	0.81	0.70	0.72
Oman	0.64	0.65	0.65	0.68	0.60	0.65	0.68	0.63
Pakistan	0.37	0.40	0.40	0.47	0.13	0.16	0.57	0.57
Panama	0.55	0.57	0.62	0.62	0.45	0.55	0.56	0.55
Papua New Guinea	0.31	0.34	0.53	0.55	0.06	0.09	0.32	0.38
Paraguay	0.46	0.54	0.58	0.62	0.30	0.37	0.51	0.64
Peru	0.52	0.55	0.59	0.61	0.34	0.43	0.62	0.62

(continued next page)

Table DN.4 *(continued)*

Country	Digital Adoption Index		Business subindex		People subindex		Government subindex	
	2014	2016	2014	2016	2014	2016	2014	2016
Philippines	0.44	0.49	0.53	0.57	0.38	0.44	0.41	0.47
Poland	0.65	0.69	0.73	0.76	0.64	0.68	0.58	0.63
Portugal	0.74	0.79	0.72	0.76	0.66	0.73	0.83	0.87
Qatar	0.68	0.71	0.74	0.76	0.70	0.76	0.60	0.60
Romania	0.62	0.64	0.64	0.65	0.51	0.57	0.71	0.72
Russian Federation	0.69	0.74	0.65	0.71	0.60	0.70	0.82	0.82
Rwanda	0.41	0.43	0.41	0.42	0.13	0.19	0.69	0.67
Samoa	0.31	0.36	0.46	0.51	0.17	0.25	0.30	0.33
Saudi Arabia	0.66	0.67	0.66	0.68	0.69	0.72	0.64	0.60
Senegal	0.33	0.35	0.39	0.39	0.19	0.23	0.41	0.43
Serbia	0.60	0.69	0.63	0.67	0.50	0.57	0.68	0.82
Seychelles	0.56	0.60	0.65	0.68	0.51	0.58	0.51	0.53
Sierra Leone	0.24	0.27	0.19	0.19	0.13	0.20	0.40	0.42
Singapore	0.87	0.87	0.84	0.85	0.80	0.80	0.96	0.96
Slovak Republic	0.65	0.69	0.69	0.75	0.59	0.67	0.66	0.64
Slovenia	0.64	0.71	0.83	0.86	0.59	0.63	0.51	0.65
Solomon Islands	0.21	0.27	0.32	0.42	0.12	0.15	0.20	0.24
South Africa	0.59	0.64	0.65	0.69	0.45	0.50	0.67	0.73
Spain	0.74	0.77	0.76	0.78	0.62	0.67	0.85	0.84
Sri Lanka	0.43	0.48	0.40	0.44	0.28	0.38	0.61	0.61
St. Kitts and Nevis	0.47	0.53	0.72	0.71	0.50	0.61	0.20	0.25
St. Lucia	0.43	0.40	0.55	0.44	0.35	0.35	0.40	0.41
St. Vincent and the Grenadines	0.46	0.50	0.65	0.66	0.33	0.40	0.38	0.43
Sudan	0.29	0.30	0.30	0.37	0.19	0.20	0.37	0.32
Suriname	0.43	0.49	0.48	0.52	0.55	0.62	0.27	0.32
Swaziland	0.28	0.32	0.44	0.46	0.17	0.20	0.24	0.28
Sweden	0.80	0.83	0.92	0.94	0.85	0.85	0.64	0.70
Switzerland	0.79	0.82	0.89	0.89	0.84	0.89	0.66	0.69
Syrian Arab Republic	0.27	0.32	0.44	0.51	0.18	0.22	0.17	0.22
Tajikistan	0.29	0.32	0.38	0.42	0.20	0.24	0.28	0.32
Tanzania	0.30	0.34	0.29	0.28	0.11	0.17	0.48	0.57
Thailand	0.57	0.62	0.55	0.57	0.57	0.68	0.58	0.62
Timor-Leste	0.26	0.29	0.23	0.27	0.26	0.29	0.30	0.31
Togo	0.21	0.25	0.37	0.37	0.09	0.14	0.17	0.24
Tonga	0.29	0.33	0.39	0.45	0.17	0.22	0.31	0.31
Trinidad and Tobago	0.51	0.59	0.57	0.64	0.49	0.57	0.48	0.55
Tunisia	0.53	0.56	0.60	0.61	0.41	0.46	0.56	0.60
Turkey	0.60	0.63	0.64	0.68	0.38	0.43	0.77	0.79
Turkmenistan	0.24	0.27	0.41	0.44	0.23	0.29	0.08	0.08
Tuvalu	0.25	0.29	0.50	0.53	0.17	0.26	0.07	0.07

(continued next page)

Table DN.4 *(continued)*

Country	Digital Adoption Index		Business subindex		People subindex		Government subindex	
	2014	2016	2014	2016	2014	2016	2014	2016
Uganda	0.28	0.34	0.28	0.32	0.10	0.14	0.45	0.56
Ukraine	0.45	0.54	0.61	0.67	0.38	0.47	0.37	0.47
United Arab Emirates	0.80	0.82	0.75	0.78	0.76	0.80	0.88	0.89
United Kingdom	0.74	0.76	0.88	0.90	0.77	0.80	0.55	0.59
United States	0.72	0.75	0.76	0.78	0.66	0.73	0.74	0.73
Uruguay	0.73	0.76	0.65	0.68	0.64	0.71	0.91	0.88
Uzbekistan	0.31	0.40	0.26	0.36	0.22	0.31	0.45	0.53
Vanuatu	0.27	0.32	0.43	0.51	0.14	0.20	0.23	0.26
Venezuela, RB	0.50	0.49	0.53	0.55	0.40	0.40	0.56	0.52
Vietnam	0.47	0.52	0.51	0.59	0.41	0.43	0.49	0.54
Yemen, Rep.	0.27	0.26	0.25	0.25	0.15	0.16	0.41	0.36
Zambia	0.29	0.34	0.30	0.33	0.14	0.18	0.44	0.52
Zimbabwe	0.30	0.33	0.38	0.43	0.17	0.21	0.36	0.35

All but a handful of countries increased their DAI scores in the period 2014–16, with most countries maintaining their relative positions. Overall, DAI was highly correlated with per capita income in 2014 and 2016, and there was improvement across the income spectrum (figure DN.1). The positive correlation between income and digital adoption is again apparent at the aggregate level. All of the top 10 countries in 2016 were high income, with eight of them scoring in the top 10 in both years for which data is available: Austria, Germany, Japan, the Republic of Korea, Luxembourg, Netherlands, Singapore, and Sweden (figure DN.2, panel a). All of the largest improvements came from middle-income countries, which as a group grew more than high-income countries. On the other hand, low-income countries grew most slowly as a group, indicating a failure to converge with the rest of the world (figure DN.2, panel b).

Figure DN.1 Changes in Digital Adoption Index scores and per capita income, 2014–16

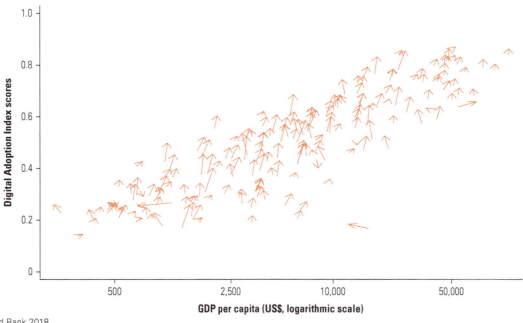

Source: World Bank 2018.

Figure DN.2 Top Digital Adoption Index scores, 2016, and largest improvements, 2014–16

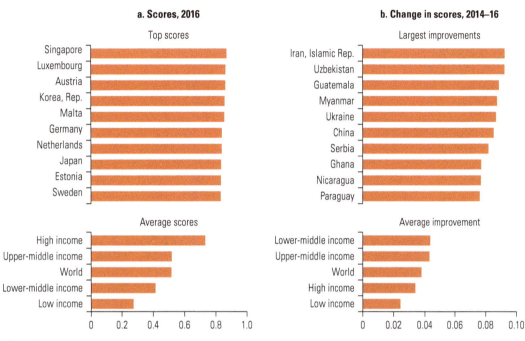

a. Scores, 2016

b. Change in scores, 2014–16

Source: World Bank 2018.

Notes

1. See "World Bank Country and Lending Groups" at https:// datahelpdesk.worldbank.org/knowledgebase/articles/906519 -world-bank-country-and-lending-groups.

2. SDG Indicators Global Database at https://unstats.un.org /sdgs/indicators/database/?indicator=9.c.1.

3. https://data.worldbank.org/indicator/it.net.user.zs.

4. http://a4ai.org/broadband-pricing-data-2017/.

5. See "Broadband Portal" at http://www.oecd.org/sti/broadband /broadband-statistics/.

6. https://researchictafrica.net/ramp_indices_portal/.

7. https://www.internetsociety.org/resources/doc/2017/sidsreport/.

8. http://www.ictdata.org.

9. See "Broadband Portal" at http://www.oecd.org/sti/broadband /broadband-statistics/.

10. https://icdppc.org/participation-in-the-conference/list-of -accredited-members/.

11. http://unctad.org/en/Pages/DTL/STI_and_ICTs/ICT4D -Legislation/eCom-Data-Protection-Laws.aspx.

12. Internet exchange point directory reports (http://wwww.pch .net/ixpdir/summary).

13. For the complete methodology of the DAI, see "Digital Adoption Index" at http://www.worldbank.org/en/publication /wdr2016/Digital-Adoption-Index.

14. The only indicator that is normalized within years is the Online Service Index calculated by the UN Department of Economic and Social Affairs for each of its biennial reports. The latter does not make available source data that would allow for normalizing the Online Service Index across years.

References

ITU (International Telecommunications Union). 2017. *Measuring the Internet Society Report 2017.* Vol. 2: ICT Country Profiles. Geneva: ITU. https://www.itu.int/en/ITU-D/Statistics/Pages /publications/mis2017.aspx.

Mercier, Rémi. 2015. "How We Put Together a List of 2600+ Open Data Portals around the World for the Open Data Community." OpenDataSoft Blog, November 2. https://www.opendatasoft .com/2015/11/02/how-we-put-together-a-list-of-1600-open-data -portals-around-the-world-to-help-open-data-community/.

World Bank. 2018. *Digital Adoption Index.* 2018 update. http:// www.worldbank.org/en/publication/wdr2016/Digital -Adoption-Index.

Bibliography

3GPP. 2017. "Industry Support for 3GPP NR Announcement." Press release, December 21. http://www.3gpp.org/news-events /3gpp-news/1931-industry_pr_5g.

Abazorius, Abby. 2016. "How Data Can Help Change the World." *MIT News*, Cambridge, MA, September 26. http://news.mit .edu/2016/IDSS-celebration-big-data-change-world-0926.

Abdelkafi, Nizar, Sergiy Makhotin, and Thorsten Posselt. 2013. "Business Model Innovations for Electric Mobility: What Can Be Learned from Existing Business Model Patterns?" *International Journal of Innovation Management* 17 (1). https://doi.org/10.1142/S1363919613400033.

Accenture. 2015. "Guarding and Growing Personal Data Value." https://www.accenture.com/t20150821T065218__w__/us-en /_acnmedia/Accenture/Conversion-Assets/DotCom/Docu ments/Global/PDF/Dualpub_15/Accenture-Guarding-and -Growing-Personal-Data-Value-Narrative-Repo.

Agrawal, Ravi. 2017. "India Supreme Court Rules Privacy a 'Fundamental Right' in Landmark Case." CNN.com, August 24. https://www.cnn.com/2017/08/24/asia/indian -court-right-to-privacy/index.html.

Akamai. 2016. *Q1 2016: State of the Internet.* https://www .akamai.com/us/en/our-thinking/state-of-the-internet-re port/index.jsp.

Aker, Jenny C. 2010. "Information from Markets Near and Far: Mobile Phones and Agricultural Markets in Niger." *American Economic Journal: Applied Economics* 2 (3): 46–59. https:// www.aeaweb.org/articles?id=10.1257/app.2.3.46.

Alliance for Affordable Internet. 2016. "The Impacts of Emerging Mobile Data Services in Developing Countries." Research Brief No. 2. http://1e8q3q16vyc81g8l3h3md6q5f5e.wpengine .netdna-cdn.com/wp-content/uploads/2016/05/Measur ingImpactsofMobileDataServices_ResearchBrief2.pdf.

Andrews, D., C. Criscuolo, and P. N. Gal. 2016. "The Best versus the Rest: The Global Productivity Slowdown, Divergence across Firms and the Role of Public Policy." Productivity Working Paper 5, OECD Publishing, Paris. https://www.oecd .org/global-forum-productivity/library/OECD%20Produc tivity%20Working%20Paper%20N%C2%B05.pdf.

Anthony, Sebastian. 2012. "$1.5 Billion: The Cost of Cutting London-Tokyo Latency by 60ms." *ExtremeTech*, March 20. https://www.extremetech.com/extreme/122989-1-5-billion -the-cost-of-cutting-london-toyko-latency-by-60ms.

APEC (Asia-Pacific Economic Cooperation). 2015. *The APEC Privacy Framework.* Singapore: APEC.

Armstrong, Mark. 2006. "Competition in Two-Sided Markets." *RAND Journal of Economics* 17 (3): 688–91.

Badran, Mona Farid. 2014. "Access and Use of ICTs in Female-Owned SMEs in Selected Arab Countries and Brazil: A Comparative Study." Working Paper 2014/12, Maastricht School of Management. https://www.msm.nl/resources /uploads/2014/05/MSM-WP2014-12.pdf.

Bain and Company. 2013. "Big Data: The Organizational Challenge." https://www.bain.com/insights/big_data_the_organizational _challenge/.

Bakhshi, Hasan, Albert Bravo-Biosca, and Juan Mateos-Garcia. 2014. "The Analytical Firm: Estimating the Effect of Data and Online Analytics on Firm Performance." Working Paper 14/05. https://www.nesta.org.uk/report/the-analytical-firm -estimating-the-effect-of-data-and-online-analytics-on-firm -performance/.

———. 2014. "Inside the Datavores: Technical Report." Nesta. https://www.nesta.org.uk/report/inside-the-datavores-technical-report/.

Barnett, Jr., Thomas. 2016. "The Zettabyte Era Officially Begins (How Much Is That?)." SP360: Service Provider, September 9. https://blogs.cisco.com/sp/the-zettabyte-era-officially-begins-how-much-is-that.

BBC (British Broadcasting Corporation). 2017. "Google Apologises after Ads Appear Next to Extremist Content." March 20. https://www.bbc.com/news/business-39325916.

———. 2018. "Eric Schneiderman, New York Attorney General, Quits Amid Assault Reports." BBC.com, May 8. https://www.bbc.com/news/world-us-canada-44035718.

Bean, Charles. 2016. "Independent Review of UK Economic Statistics." Final Report of the Independent Review of UK Economic Statistics (to the Government of the United Kingdom), led by Professor Sir Charles Bean of the London School of Economics. https://www.gov.uk/government/publications/independent-review-of-uk-economic-statistics-final-report.

Bell, M. 2015. "BMW, Audi, Daimler Buy Nokia's Mapping Unit: An Autonomous Future Is Nigh." Car, December 8. www.carmagazine.co.uk/car-news/industry-news/mercedes-benz/bmw-audi-and-daimler-purchase-nokias-here-system-an-autonomous-future-is-nigh/.

Bergvinson, David. 2017. "Digital Agriculture Empowers Farmers." Business Today, January 15. https://www.businesstoday.in/magazine/features/digital-agriculture-empowers-farmers/story/242966.html.

Bershidsky, Leonard. 2017. "Google and Facebook Too Can Be Disrupted." Bloomberg, December 8. https://www.bloomberg.com/view/articles/2017-12-08/google-and-facebook-too-can-be-disrupted.

Beye, Birago Diene Moctar. 2015. "The Impact of OTT on Telecommunication Services Provided by Operators in Senegal." Presentation at SAWAS 2015, Marrakesh, Morocco. https://financedocbox.com/Tax_Planning/72673602-The-impact-of-ott-on-telecommunication-services-provided-by-operators-in-senegal.html.

Boateng, Richard, Joseph Budu, Alfred Sekyere Mbrokoh, Eric Ansong, Sheena Lovia Boateng, and Augustus Barnnet Anderson. 2017. "Digital Enterprises in Africa: A Synthesis of Current Evidence." http://believeoverhope.org/pearlrichards/index.php/2017/08/20/digital-enterprises-in-africa-a-synthesis-of-current-evidence/.

Boffey, Daniel. 2017. "Google Fined Record €2.4bn by EU over Search Engine Results." The Guardian, June 27. https://www.theguardian.com/business/2017/jun/27/google-braces-for-record-breaking-1bn-fine-from-eu.

Bohannon, John. 2016. "Satellite Images Can Map Poverty." Science, August 18. http://www.sciencemag.org/news/2016/08/satellite-images-can-map-poverty.

Booth, Gregory D. 2017. "A Long Tail in the Digital Age: Music Commerce and the Mobile Platform in India." Asia Music 48 (1): 85–113.

Bort, Julie. 2016. "Now Facebook Plans to Eat the $500 Billion Telecom Equipment Market." Business Insider, November 1. http://www.businessinsider.com/facebook-voyager-optical-switch-telecom-infra-project-2016-11.

Bosco, Claudio, Victor Alegana, Tom Bird, Carla Pezzulo, Graeme Hornby, Alessandro Sorichetta, Jessica Steele, Cori Ruktanonchai, Nick Ruktanonchai, Erik Wetter, Linus Bengtsson, and Andrew J. Tatem. 2017. Mapping Indicators of Female Welfare at High Spatial Resolution. WorldPop Project and Flowminder Foundation. http://www.data2x.org/wp-content/uploads/2017/02/Mapping-Indicators-of-Female-Welfare-at-High-Spatial-Resolution.pdf.

Brahm, Chris, Aaron Cheris, and Lori Sherer. 2016. "What Big Data Means for Customer Loyalty." Brief, Bain and Company, August 7. http://www.bain.com/publications/articles/what-big-data-means-for-customer-loyalty.aspx.

Brandom, Russell. 2017. "Apple's New Anti-tracking System Will Make Google and Facebook Even More Powerful." The Verge, June 6. https://www.theverge.com/2017/6/6/15747300/apple-safari-ad-tracking-cookie-blocker-google-facebook-privacy.

Broadband Commision Working Group on Education. 2017. "Digital Skills for Life and Work." http://unesdoc.unesco.org/images/0025/002590/259013e.pdf.

Brynjolfsson, Erik, Lorin M. Hitt, and Heekyung Hellen Kim. 2011. "Strength in Numbers: How Does Data-Driven Decision Making Affect Firm Performance?" Unpublished. https://papers.ssrn.com/sol3/papers.cfm?abstract_id=1819486.

BSA The Software Alliance. 2016. "Seizing Opportunity through License Compliance." http://globalstudy.bsa.org/2016/index.html.

Burns, Thaddeus. 2017. "Regulating Machine Data: Less Is More for Global Growth." WIPO: Magazine, December. http://www.wipo.int/wipo_magazine/en/2017/06/article_0005.html.

Burson, Forrest. 2016. "6 Ways Amazon Is Changing Supply Chain Management in 2016." Software Advice. https://www.softwareadvice.com/resources/amazon-supply-chain-management/.

BusinessTech. 2018. "A First Look at Amazon's New Offices in Cape Town." https://businesstech.co.za/news/business/227745/a-first-look-at-amazons-new-offices-in-cape-town/.

Caldwelladr, Carole, and Emma Graham-Harrison. 2018. "Revealed: 50 Million Facebook Profiles Harvested for Cambridge Analytica in Major Data Breach." The Guardian, March 17. https://www.theguardian.com/news/2018/mar/17/cambridge-analytica-facebook-influence-us-election.

Campolo, Alex, Madelyn Sanfilippo, Meredith Whittaker, and Kate Crawford. 2017. "AI Now 2017 Report." https://assets.content

ful.com/8wprhhvnpfc0/1A9c3ZTCZa2KEYM64Ws
c2a/8636557c5fb14f2b74b2be64c3ce0c78/_AI_Now
_Institute_2017_Report_.pdf.

Cannataci, Joseph. 2016. "A More In-Depth Look at Open Data and Big Data." Annex 11 in *Report of the Special Rapporteur on the Right to Privacy*. A/HRC/31/64. Geneva: Office of the High Commissioner for Human Rights.

———. 2017. "Report of the Special Rapporteur on the Right to Privacy." Doc. A/72/43103. Office of the High Commissioner for Human Rights, Geneva.

Capgemini Consulting. 2018. "Open Data Maturity in Europe, 2017." https://www.capgemini.com/wp-content/uploads/2017/11/rep ort-open-data-maturity-in-europe-2017.pdf.

Carey, Bjorn. 2016. "Smartphone Speech Recognition Can Write Text Messages Three Times Faster than Human Typing." *Stanford News Services*, August 24. https://news.stanford .edu/2016/08/24/stanford-study-speech-recognition-fast er-texting/.

Casselman, Ben. 2017. "A Start-Up Slump Is a Drag on the Economy; Big Business May Be to Blame." *New York Times*, September 20. https://www.nytimes.com/2017/09/20/busi ness/economy/startup-business.html.

Caughill, P. 2017. "Skype Can Now Translate Your Voice Calls into 10 Different Languages in Real-Time." *Futurism*, April 10. https://futurism.com/skype-can-now-translate-your-voice -calls-into-10-different-languages-in-real-time/.

Cavoukian, Ann. 2017. "Ethical Standards in Artificial Intelligence: AI Ethics by Design." Presentation to UN Global Pulse, December 13.

CGAP (Consultative Group to Assist the Poor). 2015. "Mobile Money and APIs." World Bank, Washington, DC. http://www .cgap.org/blog/series/mobile-money-and-apis.

Chander, Anupam, and Uyen Lê. 2015. "Data Nationalism." *Emory Law Journal* 64 (3): 677–739. http://law.emory.edu/elj /content/volume-64/issue-3/articles/data-nationalism.html.

Chang, Lulu. 2016. "The Latest Data Breach Involves the Voting Records of 93.4 Million Mexican Citizens." *Digital Trends*, April 23. https://www.digitaltrends.com/computing/mexico -voting-breach/.

Change Dyslexia. 2018. "The Best Tool to Detect and Improve Dyslexia Related Skills" (in Spanish). https://www.changedys lexia.org/.

Cheng, Steve, Matthias Daub, Axel Domeyer, and Martin Lundqvist. 2017. "Using Blockchain to Improve Data Management in the Public Sector." McKinsey and Company. https://www.mckinsey.com/business-functions/digital-mc kinsey/our-insights/using-blockchain-to-improve-data -management-in-the-public-sector.

Chevalier, Judith, and Dina Mayzlin. 2006. "The Effect of Word of Mouth on Sales: Online Book Reviews." *Journal of Marketing Research* 43 (3): 345–54. https://msbfile03.usc.edu/digital measures/mayzlin/intellcont/chevalier_mayzlin06-1.pdf.

CIGI (Centre for International Governance Innovation). 2017. "2017 CIGI-Ipsos Global Survey on Internet Security and Trust." https://www.cigionline.org/internet-survey-2017.

Cisco. 2017. "Cisco Visual Networking Index: Forecast and Methodology, 2016–2021." https://www.cisco.com/c/en/us /solutions/collateral/service-provider/visual-networking-in dex-vni/complete-white-paper-c11-481360.pdf.

CNNIC (China Internet Network Information Center). 2016. "Statistical Report on Internet Development in China." https://cnnic.com.cn/IDR/ReportDownloads/.

Confessore, Nicholas, Gabriel J. X. Dance, Richard Harris, and Mark Hansen. 2018. "The Follower Factory." *New York Times*, January 27. https://www.nytimes.com/interactive/2018/01/27 /technology/social-media-bots.html.

Constantinou, Ioanna, Attila Marton, and Virpi Kristiina Tuunainen. 2017. "Four Models of Sharing Economy Platforms." *MIS Quarterly Executive* 16 (4): 231–51. http:// misqe.org/ojs2/index.php/misqe/article/viewFile/798/474.

Constine, Josh. 2016. "Facebook Has Connected 40m People with Internet.org." *Tech Crunch*, November 2. https://techcrunch .com/2016/11/02/omnipresent/.

Council of Europe. 1985. "Convention for the Protection of Individuals with Regard to Automatic Processing of Personal Data." Council of Europe, Strasbourg. https://www.coe.int/en /web/conventions/full-list/-/conventions/treaty/108.

Cutler, Ben, Spencer Fowers, Jeffrey Kramer, and Eric Peterson. 2017. "Want an Energy-Efficient Data Center? Build It Underwater." *IEEE Spectrum: Technology, Engineering, and Science News*, February 21. http://spectrum.ieee.org/computing/hardware /want-an-energyefficient-data-center-build-it-underwater.

da Silva, Issa Sikiti. 2014. "Mali Digital Plan 2020 to Reorganise Economy." *Biztech Africa*, December 9. http://www.biztechaf rica.com/article/mali-digital-plan-2020-reorganiseecon omy/9327/.

Dallas, George. 2014. "Making Sense of Internet Platforms: Network Effects and Two Sided Markets." https://georgemdal las.wordpress.com/2014/06/05/making-sense-of-internet -platforms-network-effects-and-two-sided-markets/.

Data for Climate Action. 2017. "Grand Prize Winner: Electro-Mobility: Cleaning Mexico City's Air with Transformational Climate Policies through Big Data Pattern Analysis in Traffic and Social Mobility." http://www.dataforclimateaction.org /meet-the-winners/.

Data Privacy Project. 2018. "Code of Conduct: Data Science Code of Professional Conduct." http://www.datascienceassn.org /code-of-conduct.html.

Dave, Paresh. 2017. "Credit Giant Equifax Says Social Security Numbers, Birth Dates of 143 Million Consumers May Have

Been Exposed." *Los Angeles Times*, September 7. http://www.latimes.com/business/technology/la-fi-tn-equifax-data-breach-20170907-story.html.

Davenport, Thomas H., Don Cohen, and Al Jacobson. 2005. "Competing on Analytics." Babson Executive Education: Knowledge Research Center. http://www.babsonknowledge.org/analytics.pdf.

Deloitte Review. 2013. "Data as the New Currency: Government's Role in Facilitating the Exchange." *Deloitte Review* 13. https://deloitte.wsj.com/riskandcompliance/files/2013/11/DataCurrency_report.pdf.

Dewey, Catherine. 2016. "98 Personal Data Points That Facebook Uses to Target Ads to You." *Washington Post*, August 18. https://www.washingtonpost.com/news/the-intersect/wp/2016/08/19/98-personal-data-points-that-facebook-uses-to-target-ads-to-you/?utm_term=.8e8b6b4fb92b.

Dhalla, Amira. 2016. "New Partnership with UN Women to Teach Key Digital Skills to Women." Mozilla Learning. https://learning.mozilla.org/blog/new-partnership-with-un-women-to-teach-key-digital-skills-to-women.

DLA Piper. 2018. "Data Privacy Scorebook." https://www.dlapiperdataprotection.com/scorebox/index.html.

Dutch Data Center Association. 2017. "The Economic Impact of Multi-tenant Data Centers in the Netherlands." https://www.vijfhart.nl/wp-content/uploads/2017/02/report_-_2017_-_economic_impact_dutch_data_centers.pdf.

Earth Institute of Colombia University and Ericsson. 2016. *How Information and Communications Technology can Accelerate Action on the Sustainable Development Goals.* Ericsson. https://www.ericsson.com/res/docs/2016/ict-sdg.pdf.

Economic Times. 2017. "Railways to Use Artificial Intelligence for Preventing Signal Failures." November 22. https://energy.economictimes.indiatimes.com/news/power/railways-to-use-artificial-intelligence-for-preventing-signal-failures/61747929.

E-Estonia. 2017. "Artificial Intelligence Is the Next Step for E-Governance in Estonia." https://e-estonia.com/artificial-intelligence-is-the-next-step-for-e-governance-state-adviser-reveals/.

Einav, Liran, and Jonathan Levin. 2014. "The Data Revolution and Economic Analysis." *Innovation Policy and the Economy* 14: 1–24.

Eisenmann, Thomas R., Geoffrey Parker, and Marshall Van Alstyne. 2011. "Platform Envelopment." *Strategic Management Journal* 32 (12): 1270–85.

Elahee, K., and S. Jugoo. 2013. "Ocean Thermal Energy for Air-Conditioning: Case Study of a Green Data Center." *Energy Sources, Part A: Recovery, Utilization, and Environmental Effects* 35 (7): 679–84. doi:10.1080/15567036.2010.504941.

Elgan, Mike. 2016. "Artificial Intelligence Needs Your Data, All of It." *ComputerWorld*, February 22. https://www.computerworld.com/article/3035595/emerging-technology/artificial-intelligence-needs-your-data-all-of-it.html.

EMC Corporation. 2014. "Digital Universe Invaded by Sensors." Press release, April 9. https://www.emc.com/about/news/press/2014/20140409-01.htm.

Enders, Albrecht, Harald Hungenberg, Hans-Peter Denker, and Sebastian Mauch. 2008 "The Long Tail of Social Networking: Revenue Models of Social Networking Sites." *European Management Journal* 26 (3): 199–211.

Ericsson. 2016. "Internet of Things to Overtake Mobile Phones by 2018: Ericsson Mobility Report." Press release, June 1. https://www.ericsson.com/en/press-releases/2016/6/internet-of-things-to-overtake-mobile-phones-by-2018-ericsson-mobility-report.

Ernst and Young. 2016. "Digital Supply Chain: It Is All about That Data." https://www.ey.com/Publication/vwLUAssets/Digital_supply_chain_-_its_all_about_the_data/%24FILE/EY-digital-supply-chain-its-all-about-that-data-final.pdf.

Espinet, X., W. Wang, and S. Mehndiratta. 2017. "Low-Budget Techniques for Road Network Mapping and Road Condition Assessment That Are Accessible to Transport Agencies in Developing Countries." *Transportation Research Record: Journal of the Transportation Research Board* no. 2634: 1–7.

Etherington, Darrell. 2017. "Otonomo Raises $25m to Help Automakers Make Money from Connected Cars." *TechCrunch*, April 7. https://techcrunch.com/2017/04/07/otonomo-raises-25m-to-help-automakers-make-money-from-connected-cars/.

EU Digital SME Alliance. 2017. "European Cybersecurity Strategy: Fostering the SME Ecosystem." https://www.cyberwatching.eu/news-events/news/european-cybersecurity-strategy-fostering-sme-ecosystem.

European Commission. 2011. "Data Is the New Gold." Opening Remarks, Press Conference on Open Data Strategy, December 12. https://ec.europa.eu/digital-single-market/en/news/data-new-gold.

———. 2018. "Communication from the Commission to the European Parliament, the Council, the European Economic and Social Committee and the Committee of the Regions 'Towards A Common European Data Space.'" European Commission, Brussels.

———. 2018. "New Measures to Boost Key Competences and Digital Skills, as Well as the European Dimension of Education." Press release, January 17. http://europa.eu/rapid/press-release_IP-18-102_en.htm.

European Parliament. 2016. "Towards a Thriving Data-Driven Economy." http://www.europarl.europa.eu/sides/getDoc.do?pubRef=-//EP//TEXT+TA+P8-TA-2016-0089+0+DOC+XML+V0//EN.

European Union. 2012. "Charter of Fundamental Rights of the European Union." 2012/C 326/02. http://eur-lex.europa.eu/legal-content/EN/TXT/?uri=CELEX:12012P/TXT.

———. 2018. "The EU General Data Protection Regulation (GDPR)." https://www.eugdpr.org.

———. n.d. "Data Protection Factsheet." http://ec.europa.eu /justice/data-protection/files/factsheets/factsheet_data _protection_en.pdf.

———. n.d. "Data Protection: Rules for the Protection of Personal Data Inside and outside the EU." https://ec.europa.eu/info /law/law-topic/data-protection_en.

Evans, David S. 2013. "Economics of Vertical Restraints for Multi-sided Platforms." Working Paper, Coase-Sandor Institute for Law and Economics, Chicago. https://chicagounbound.uchi cago.edu/cgi/viewcontent.cgi?article=1187&context=law _and_economics.

———. 2013. "Some Empirical Aspects of Multi-sided Platform Industries." *Review of Network Economics* 2 (3): 191–209.

Evans, David S., and Richard Schmalansee. 2016. *Matchmakers: The New Economics of Multisided Platforms.* Boston: Harvard Business Review Press.

Facebook. 2017. "Global Government Request Report." April 27. https://transparency.facebook.com/.

Facebook: Internet.org. 2015. "One Year In: Internet.org Free Basic Services." Blog, July 27. https://info.internet.org/en/blog/2015 /07/27/one-year-in-internet-org-free-basic-services/.

Facebook: Internet.org. n.d. "Where We've Launched." https://info .internet.org/en/story/where-weve-launched/.

Fell, Gregory, and Mike Barlow. 2016. "Not All Data Is Created Equal." O'Reilly, April 25. https://www.oreilly.com/learning /not-all-data-is-created-equal.

Fernandez, Liliana, and Richard Heeks. 2016. "Measuring the Barriers to Big Data for Development: Design-Reality Gap Analysis in Colombia's Public Sector." Working Paper, University of Manchester, Manchester, UK.

Fiegerman, Seth. 2018. "More than 20 States Sue to Stop FCC's Net Neutrality Repeal." CNN, January 16. http://money.cnn .com/2018/01/16/technology/net-neutrality-lawsuit/index .html.

Field, Matthew. 2018. "DuckDuckGo: The Private Search Engine Standing Up to Google." *Technology Intelligence*, April 23. https://www.telegraph.co.uk/technology/2018/04/23/duck duckgo-tiny-private-search-engine-standing-google/.

FlashGlobal. 2018. "Walmart: 3 Keys to Successful Supply Chain Management Any Business Can Follow." April 12. https:// flashglobal.com/blog/supply-chain-management-walmart/.

Flexenclosure. 2017. "Flexenclosure to Deploy Two eCentre Cable Landing Stations for SSCC in Samoa." Press release, February 27. http://www.flexenclosure.com/flexenclosure-de ploys-two-ecentre-cable-landing-stations-for-sscc-in -samoa/.

Floridi, Luciano, and Mariarosaria Taddeo. 2016. "What Is Data Ethics?" *Philosophical Transactions of the Royal Society A*

374 (2083): 20160360. http://rsta.royalsocietypublishing.org /content/roypta/374/2083/20160360.full.pdf.

Ford. 2016. "From Autonomy to Snowtonomy: How Ford Fusion Hybrid Autonomous Research Vehicle Can Navigate in Winter." https://media.ford.com/content/fordmedia/fna/us /en/news/2016/03/10/how-fusion-hybrid-autonomous -vehicle-can-navigate-in-winter.html.

———. 2016. "Ford Tripling Autonomous Vehicle Development Fleet, Accelerating On-Road Testing of Sensors and Software." https://media.ford.com/content/fordmedia/fna/us/en /news/2016/01/05/ford-tripling-autonomous-vehicle-de velopment-fleet--accelerating.html.

Frieden, Rob. 2017. "The Internet of Platforms and Two-Sided Markets: Legal and Regulatory Implications for Competition and Consumers." Working paper, College of Communications, Pennsylvania State University, State College, PA. https://ssrn .com/abstract=3051766.

Gaba, K. M., and B. Sánchez-Andrade Nuño. 2016. "Eyes in the Sky Help Track Rural Electrification." World Bank blog, January 21. http://blogs.worldbank.org/energy/eyes-sky-help-track -rural-electrification.

Garrahan, Matthew. 2016. "Advertising: Facebook and Google Build a Duopoly." *Financial Times*, June 23. https://www.ft .com/content/6c6b74a4-3920-11e6-9a05-82a9b15a8ee7.

Garret, R. Kelly. 2016. "Facebook's Problem Is More Complicated Than Fake News." *Scientific American*, November 17. https:// www.scientificamerican.com/article/facebook-s-problem-is -more-complicated-than-fake-news/.

Gartner. 2015. "Gartner Says Australian Organizations to Spend A$2.5 Billion on Data Center Systems in 2015." Press release, May 17. http://www.gartner.com/newsroom/id/3054918.

GfK. 2017. "Willingness to Share Personal Data in Exchange for Benefits or Rewards." https://www.gfk.com/fileadmin/user _upload/country_one_pager/NL/images/Global-GfK _onderzoek_-_delen_van_persoonlijke_data.pdf.

Global Fishing Watch. 2018. "Vessel Monitoring Data: Indonesia." http://globalfishingwatch.org/indonesia-vms.

Goldstein, Phil. 2013. "Report: Skype Makes Up One-Third of All International Phone Traffic." *FierceWireless*, February 15. https://www.fiercewireless.com/wireless/report-skype-makes -up-one-third-all-international-phone-traffic.

Good Things Foundation. 2017. "Project: Reboot UK." https:// www.goodthingsfoundation.org/projects/reboot-uk.

Government of Canada. 2017. "Policy on Information Management." http://www.tbs-sct.gc.ca/pol/doc-eng.aspx?id =12742.

Government of Colombia. 2018. "Emprende con Datos Finalizó con Más 60 Equipos Apoyados" [Start with Data Finished with More Than 60 Teams Supported]. Ministry of ICT. http://www.mintic.gov.co/portal/604/w3-article-73884.html.

Government of New Zealand. 2011. "New Zealand Data and Information Management Principles." Wellington. https://www.ict.govt.nz/guidance-and-resources/open-government/new-zealand-data-and-information-management-principles/.

Government of the United Kingdom. 2013. "Shakespeare Review: An Independent Review of Public-Sector Information." May 15. https://www.gov.uk/government/publications/shakespeare-review-of-public-sector-information.

———. 2016. "Review of Information Security at HM Revenue and Customs." http://webarchive.nationalarchives.gov.uk/20100407163917/http://www.hm-treasury.gov.uk/d/poynter_review250608.pdf.

———. 2017. "Digital Economy Act."

———. n.d. "Data Sharing in Government." Blog. http://datasharing.org.uk/index.html.

Graef, Inge, Sih Yuliana Wahyuningtyas, and Peggy Valcke. 2015. "Assessing Data Access Issues in Online Platforms." *Telecommunications Policy* 39 (5): 375–87.

Green, Andy. 2018. "Canada's PIPEDA Breach Notification Regulations Are Finalized!" *Varonis*, May 3. https://blog.varonis.com/canadas-pipeda-breach-notification-regulations-finalized/.

Greengard, Samuel. 2010. "Cloud Computing and Developing Nations." *Communications of the ACM* 53 (5): 18–20. https://cacm.acm.org/magazines/2010/5/87255-cloud-computing-and-developing-nations/fulltext.

GSMA. 2017. *Embracing the Digital Revolution Policies for Building the Digital Economy*. Digital Transformation Report 2017. GSMA. https://www.gsma.com/publicpolicy/wp-content/uploads/2017/02/GSMA_DigitalTransformationReport2017_Web.pdf.

Gunawan, Imana. 2017. "App Helps Indonesian Capital Get 'Smart' to Improve Public Services." *Humanosphere*, January 6. http://www.humanosphere.org/social-business/2017/01/app-helps-indonesian-capital-get-smart-to-improve-public-services/.

Haddad, Ryan, Tim Kelly, Teemu Leinonen, and Vesa Saarinen. 2014. *Using Location Data from Mobile Phones to Enhance the Science of Delivery*. Washington, DC: World Bank. https://openknowledge.worldbank.org/handle/10986/19316.

Harari, Y. N. 2017. *Homo Deus: A Brief History of Tomorrow*. New York: Harper.

Harwell, Drew. 2018. "Companies Race to Gather a Newly Prized Currency: Our Body Measurements." *Washington Post*, January 16. https://www.washingtonpost.com/business/economy/companies-race-to-gather-a-newly-prized-currency-our-body-measurements/2018/01/16/5af28d98-f6e8-11e7-beb6-c8d48830c54d_story.html?noredirect=on&utm_term=.4eb7f0e18af4.

Heeks, Richard. 2017. "Development Informatics." Working paper, Global Development Institute, University of Manchester, Manchester, UK.

Heeks, Richard, and Jaco Renken. 2016. "Data Justice for Development: What Would It Mean?" Working paper, University of Manchester, Manchester, UK.

Hellemans, Alexander. 2015. "Why IoT Needs 5G." *IEEE Spectrum*, May 20. http://spectrum.ieee.org/tech-talk/computing/networks/5g-taking-stock.

Henten, Anders, and Iwona Windekilde. 2016. "Transaction Costs and the Sharing Economy." *Info* 18 (1): 1–15.

Hesseldahl, Arik. 2015. "Why the Federal Government Sucks at Cyber Security." *Recode*, June 23. https://www.recode.net/2015/6/23/11563798/why-the-federal-government-sucks-at-cybersecurity.

Hsu, Tiffany. 2018. "For Many Facebook Users, a 'Last Straw' That Led Them to Quit." *New York Times*, March 21. https://www.nytimes.com/2018/03/21/technology/users-abandon-facebook.html.

Hungenberg, Harald, Hans-Peter Denker, and Sebastian Mauch. 2008. "The Long Tail of Social Networking: Revenue Models of Social Networking Sites." *European Management Journal* 26 (3): 199–211.

IBM (International Business Machines Corporation). 2013. *Harness the Power of Big Data: The IBM Big Data Platform*. New York: McGraw-Hill.

———. 2016. "IBM: 10 Key Marketing Trends for 2017 and Ideas for Exceeding Customer Expectations." https://www-01.ibm.com/common/ssi/cgi-bin/ssialias?htmlfid=WRL12345USEN.

———. 2016. "What Is Big Data?" https://www.ibm.com/big-data/us/en/.

———. 2018. "IBM Watson for Genomics Helps Doctors Give Patients New Hope." https://www.ibm.com/watson/health/oncology-and-genomics/genomics/.

IDC (International Data Corporation). 2017. "Impact Assessment of Odine Program: Open Data Incubator Europe." https://opendataincubator.eu/.

IEEE (Institute of Electrical and Electronics Engineers). 2016. "The IEEE Global Initiative on Ethics of Autonomous and Intelligent Systems: Ethically Aligned Design; A Vision for Prioritizing Wellbeing with Artificial Intelligence and Autonomous Systems V.1." The IEEE Global Initiative on Ethics of Autonomous and Intelligent Systems. http://standards.ieee.org/develop/indconn/ec/autonomous_systems.html.

Iimi, Atsushi, A. K. Farhad Ahmed, Edward Charles Anderson, Adam Stone Diehl, Laban Mayo, Tatiana Peralta Quiros, and Kulwinder Singh Rao. 2016. "New Rural Access Index: Main Determinants and Correlation to Poverty." Policy Research Working Paper 7876, World Bank, Washington, DC.

Ingram, Matthew. 2017. "Facebook and Google Need to Be Regulated, Says British News Industry." *Fortune*, March 9. http://fortune.com/2017/03/09/facebook-google-regulated/.

Intel. 2013. "Intel: She Will Connect Initiative." https://www.intel .com/content/www/us/en/corporate-responsibility/social-im pact-and-educational-initiatives/she-will-connect.html.

Internet Society. 2017. "A Case Study in Local Content Hosting: Speed, Visits, and Cost of Access." https://www.internetsoci ety.org/doc/case-study-local-content-rwanda.

IOM (International Organization for Migration). 2017. *Fatal Journeys: Improving Data on Missing Migrants.* Part 1, vol. 3. Geneva: IOM. https://publications.iom.int/system/files/pdf /fatal_journeys_volume_3_part_1.pdf.

ITIF (Information Technology and Innovation Foundation). 2017. "Cross-Border Data Flows: Where Are the Barriers, and What Do They Cost?" May 1. https://itif.org/publications/2017/05 /01/cross-border-data-flows-where-are-barriers-and-what -do-they-cost.

ITU (International Telecommunication Union). 2015. "Interoperability in the Digital Ecosystem." GSR Discussion Paper, ITU, Geneva. https://www.itu.int/en/ITU-D /Conferences/GSR/Documents/GSR2015/Discussion_papers _and_Presentations/Discussionpaper_interoperability.pdf.

———. 2017. "AI for Good Global Summit 2017." https://www .itu.int/en/ITU-T/AI/Pages/201706-default.aspx

———. 2017. "ICT Facts and Figures." https://www.itu.int/en /ITU-D/Statistics/Pages/facts/default.aspx.

———. 2017. *Measuring the Internet Society Report 2017.* Vol. 2: ICT Country Profiles. Geneva: ITU. https://www.itu.int/en /ITU-D/Statistics/Pages/publications/mis2017.aspx.

Jean, Neal, Marshall Burke, Michael W. Xie, Matthew Davis, David B. Lobell, and Stegano Ermon. n.d. "Sustainability and Artificial Intelligence Lab: Combining Satellite Imagery and Machine Learning to Predict Poverty." Stanford University. http://sustain.stanford.edu/predicting-poverty.

Juniper Research. 2016. "Understanding the Personal Data Economy: The Emergence of a New Data Value-Exchange." https://mobileecosystemforum.com/personal-data-econ omy-whitepaper/.

Kalia, Amul. 2017. "Here's How to Protect Your Privacy from Your Internet Service Provider." Electronic Frontier Foundation, April 3. https://www.eff.org/deeplinks/2017/04/heres-how -protect-your-privacy-your-internet-service-provider.

Kaminski, Piotr, Chris Rezek, Wolf Richter, and Marc Sorel. 2017. "Protecting Your Critical Digital Assets: Not All Systems and Data Are Created Equal." McKinsey and Company. https:// www.mckinsey.com/business-functions/risk/our-insights /protecting-your-critical-digital-assets-not-all-systems-and -data-are-created-equal.

Kapoor, S. 2017. "Artificial Intelligence: Re-imagining Big Data's Applicability." CXOtoday.com, July 17. www.cxotoday.com /story/artificial-intelligence-re-imagining-big-datas-applic ability/.

Kastrenakes, Jacob. 2017. "The FCC Just Killed Net Neutrality." *The Verge,* December 14. https://www.theverge.com/2017/12/14 /16776154/fcc-net-neutrality-vote-results-rules-repealed.

Katz, Raul, and P. Koutroumpis. 2012. "The Economic Impact of Telecommunications in Senegal." *Communications and Strategies* 2 (86): 21–42. https://www8.gsb.columbia.edu/citi /sites/citi/files/files/Senegal_Telecoms_Report_version%20 finale%5B1%5D.pdf.

Kelly, Heather, and Scott McLean. 2017. "Your Browser History Is for Sale, Here's What You Need to Know." *CNNMoney,* April 6. http://money.cnn.com/2017/04/05/technology/online -privacy-faq/.

Kelly, Michael, and David Satola. 2017. "The Right to Be Forgotten." *University of Illinois Law Review* 1. https://papers.ssrn.com /sol3/papers.cfm?abstract_id=2965685.

Kelly, Tim, and Carlo Maria Rossotto. 2012. *Broadband Strategies Handbook.* Washington, DC: World Bank. https://openknow ledge.worldbank.org/handle/10986/6009.

Kenney, M., and J. Zysman. 2016. "The Rise of the Platform Economy." *Issues in Science and Technology* 32 (3): 61–69.

Kharpal, Arjun. 2016. "5 Reasons Why Uber Sold Its China Business to Didi Chuxing." CNBC, August 1. https://www .cnbc.com/2016/08/01/5-reasons-why-uber-sold-its-china -business-to-didi-chuxing.html.

Kitchin, Rob. 2014. *The Data Revolution: Big Data, Open Data, Data Infrastructures and Their Consequences.* London: Sage.

Koçoğlu, İpek, Salih Zeki İmamoğlu, Hüseyin İnce, and Halit Keskin. 2011. "The Effect of Supply Chain Integration on Information Sharing: Enhancing the Supply Chain Performance." *Procedia—Social and Behavioral Sciences* 24: 1630–49. https://www.sciencedirect.com/science/article/pii /S1877042811015448.

Krambeck, H., and L. Qu. 2015. "Toward an Open Transit Service Data Standard in Developing Asian Countries." *Transportation Research Record: Journal of the Transportation Research Board* no. 2538: 30–36.

Lal Das, Prasanna, Stephan Beisswenger, Srikanth Mangalam, and Rasit Yuce. 2017. "Internet of Things: The New Government to Business Platform—A Review of Opportunities, Practices, and Challenges." World Bank, Washington, DC. http://docu ments.worldbank.org/curated/en/610081509689089303/Inter net-of-things-the-new-government-to-business-platform-a -review-of-opportunities-practices-and-challenges.

Le Bras, Tom. 2015. "Online Overload—It's Worse Than You Thought." Infographic, Dash Lane Blog, July 21. https://blog .dashlane.com/infographic-online-overload-its-worse-than -you-thought/.

Leavitt, Neal. 2010. "Network-Usage Changes Push Internet Traffic to the Edge." *Computer* [IEEE] 43 (10): 13–15. http://ieeex plore.ieee.org/document/5604156.

Leber, Jessica. 2013. "In a Data Deluge, Companies Seek to Fill a New Role." *MIT Technology Review*, May 22. https://www.technologyreview.com/s/513866/in-a-data-deluge-companies-seek-to-fill-a-new-role/.

Lee, T. B. 2017. "Bitcoin's Insane Energy Consumption, Explained." https://arstechnica.com/tech-policy/2017/12/bitcoins-insane-energy-consumption-explained/.

Lehtiniemi, Tuukka. 2017. "Personal Data Spaces: An Intervention in Surveillance Capitalism?" *Surveillance and Society* 15 (5). https://ojs.library.queensu.ca/index.php/surveillance-and-society/article/view/6424.

Lewis, Paul. 2017. "'Our Minds Can Be Hijacked': The Tech Insiders Who Fear a Smartphone Dystopia." *The Guardian*, October 6. https://www.theguardian.com/technology/2017/oct/05/smartphone-addiction-silicon-valley-dystopia.

Li, A. 2016. "Google Translate Adds 13 New Languages Bringing Total to 103." https://9to5google.com/2016/02/17/google-translate-13-languages.

Lindstedt, Catharina, and Daniel Naurin. 2005. "Transparency and Corruption: The Conditional Significance of a Free Press." Quality of Government Institute Working Paper 2005:5, University of Gothenburg, Sweden. https://www.qog.pol.gu.se/digitalAssets/1350/1350633_2005_5-lindstedt_naurin.pdf.

LinkedIn. 2017. "Brilent, the Intelligent Candidate Recommendation Engine." https://www.linkedin.com/pulse/brilent-intelligent-candidate-recommendation-engine-edouard-murat/.

Lomas, Natasha. 2017. "Form an Orderly Queue! Google Wants Your Blood (and Other Bodily Fluids). Oh and Your Medical Records." TechCrunch. https://techcrunch.com/2017/04/21/form-an-orderly-queue-google-wants-your-blood-and-other-bodily-fluids-oh-.

Luleå University of Technology. 2014. "National Agenda for the Internet of Things: Summary of the Project IoT Sweden." https://iotsverige.se/wp-content/uploads/2014/12/Agendan-eng-29-sep-2014-korr4.pdf.

Lyons, Elizabeth, Zakkoyya Lewis, Brian Mayrsohn, and Jennifer Rowland. 2014. "Behavior Change Techniques Implemented in Electronic Lifestyle Activity Monitors: A Systematic Content Analysis." *Journal of Medical Internet Research* 16 (8). http://doi.org/10.2196/jmir.3469.

Maaroof, Abbas. 2015. "Big Data and the 2030 Agenda for Sustainable Development." Report for UN-ESCAP. http://www.unescap.org/sites/default/files/Final%20Draft_%20stock-taking%20report_For%20Comment_301115.pdf.

Madrigal, Alexis C. 2012. "I'm Being Followed: How Google—and 104 Other Companies—Are Tracking Me on the Web." *The Atlantic,* February 29. https://www.theatlantic.com/technology/archive/2012/02/im-being-followed-how-google-151-and-104-other-companies-151-are-tracking-me-on-the-web/253758/.

Magna Global. 2017. "Advertising Forecasts: Winter Update (Dec 4, 2017)." https://www.magnaglobal.com/wp-content/uploads/2017/12/MAGNA-Global-Forecast_Winter-Update_Final.pdf.

Marshall, Aarian. 2017. "The Secret Uber Data That Could Fix Your Daily Commute." *Wired*, February 3. https://www.wired.com/2017/02/ubers-coughing-data-nyc-fix-commute/

Mastercard. 2012. "Nigerians Enjoy the Convenience, Pricing and Choice of Online Shopping—MasterCard Survey." Press release, May 1. https://www1.mastercard.com/content/intelligence/en/research/press-release/2012/Nigerians-enjoy-the-convenience-pricing-and-choice-of-online-shopping.html.

Matheson, Rob. 2016. "Optimizing Parking in the Busiest Places." *MIT News*, October 25. http://news.mit.edu/2016/smarking-data-analytics-optimizing-parking-1012.

Matthee, Marianne, and André Heymans. 2013. "How South African SMEs Can Become Better Candidates for Export Finance." *Managing Global Transitions* 11 (4): 391–407.

Matthey, James. 2018. "There's Something Unusual about Simona Halep's Australian Open Dress." News.com.au, January 26. https://www.news.com.au/sport/tennis/australian-open/theres-something-unusual-about-simona-haleps-australian-open-dress/news-story/28d7ce2da03fb00a9ad2bd5a79093156.

Mbiti, Isaac M., and David N. Weil. 2011. "Mobile Banking: The Impact of M-Pesa in Kenya." Working Paper 17129, National Bureau of Economic Research, Cambridge, MA. https://ssrn.com/abstract=1866089.

McGoogan, Cara. 2017. "Yahoo Hack Warning: What Happened and Should You Be Worried?" *The Telegraph*, February 16. https://www.telegraph.co.uk/technology/2017/02/16/yahoo-hack-warning-happened-should-worried/.

McGregor, Lorna. 2017. "Ethical Development of AI." Statement at the ITU AI for Good Summit, June.

McKinsey Global Institute. 2011. *Big Data: The Next Frontier for Innovation, Competition, and Productivity*. https://www.mckinsey.com/~/media/McKinsey/Business%20Functions/McKinsey%20Digital/Our%20Insights/Big%20data%20The%20next%20frontier%20for%20innovation/MGI_big_data_full_report.ashx.

———. 2016. *The Age of Analytics: Competing in a Data-Driven World*. London: McKinsey Global Institute. https://www.mckinsey.com/business-functions/mckinsey-analytics/our-insights/the-age-of-analytics-competing-in-a-data-driven-world.

———. 2016. "Digital Globalization: The New Era of Global Flows." New York. https://www.mckinsey.com/business-functions/digital-mckinsey/our-insights/digital-globalization-the-new-era-of-global-flows.

———. 2017. "Digital Transformation: Raising Supply-Chain Performance to New Levels." https://www.mckinsey.com/business-functions/operations/our-insights/digital-transformation-raising-supply-chain-performance-to-new-levels.

———. 2017. "Jobs Lost, Jobs Gained: Workforce Transitions in a Time of Automation." https://www.mckinsey.com/~/media /McKinsey/Global%20Themes/Future%20of%20 Organizations/What%20the%20future%20of%20work%20 will%20mean%20for%20jobs%20skills%20and%20wages /MGI-Jobs-Lost-Jobs-Gained-Report-December-6-2017.ashx.

———. 2018. "Digital Reinvention: Unlocking the 'How.'" https:// www.mckinsey.com/~/media/McKinsey/Business%20 Functions/McKinsey%20Digital/Our%20Insights /Digital%20Reinvention%20Unlocking%20the%20how /Digital-Reinvention_Unlocking-the-how.ashx.

Meeker, Mary. 2016. *Internet Trends 2016: Code Conference.* Menlo Park, CA: Kleiner, Perkins, Caufield, Byers (KPCB).

———. 2017. *Internet Trends 2017: Code Conference.* Annual Report. Menlo Park, CA: Kleiner, Perkins, Caufield, Byers (KPCB). https://www.kleinerperkins.com/perspectives/internet -trends-report-2017

Mercier, Rémi. 2015. "How We Put Together a List of 2600+ Open Data Portals around the World for the Open Data Community." OpenDataSoft Blog, November 2. https://www.opendatasoft .com/2015/11/02/how-we-put-together-a-list-of-1600-open -data-portals-around-the-world-to-help-open-data -community/.

Microsoft Translator. n.d. "What Is Neural Network Based Translation?" https://microsofttranslator.uservoice.com /knowledgebase/articles/1099027-what-is-neural-network -based-translation

Millicom. 2016. "Tigo Business Paraguay's Data Center Awarded 'Best Modular Implementation' by Prestigious International Sector Magazine." Press release, September 28. http://www .millicom.com/media/6762386/Data-Center-Award_-Eng.pdf.

———. n.d. "Investing in State-of-the-Art Data Centers." News feature. http://www.millicom.com/media/millicom-news -features/data-centers.

Mineo, Liz. 2017. "On Internet Privacy, Be Very Afraid." *Harvard Gazette*, August 24. https://news.harvard.edu/gazette /story/2017/08/when-it-comes-to-internet-privacy-be-very -afraid-analyst-suggests/.

MIT (Massachusetts Institute of Technology). "MIT Institute for Data, Systems, and Society." https://idss.mit.edu/.

MIT (Massachusetts Institute of Technology) Technology Review. 2014. "Researchers Test Personal Data Market to Find Out How Much Your Information Is Worth." July 9. https://www .technologyreview.com/s/528866/researchers-test-personal-data -market-to-find-out-how-much-your-information-is-worth/.

Morey, Timothy, Theodore Forbath, and Allison Schoop. 2015. "Customer Data: Designing for Transparency and Trust." *Harvard Business Review*, May.

Moss, Sebastian. 2017. "The Kingdom of Bhutan Opens First Government Data Center." *Data Centre Dynamics,* March 27. http://www.datacenterdynamics.com/content-tracks/colo -cloud/the-kingdom-of-bhutan-opens-first-government -data-center/98052.fullarticle.

Mozilla. 2018. "The Internet Health Report." https://internet healthreport.org/.

Munster, Brett. 2017. "Could Blockchain Disrupt Facebook and Google's Business Model?" *Medium.* https://medium.com /road-less-ventured/could-blockchain-disrupt-facebook -and-googles-business-model-fda614de492d.

Murdock, Jason. 2018. "Mark Zuckerberg Says 'Delete Facebook' Protest Had No Meaningful Impact on His Business." *Newsweek*, April 5. http://www.newsweek.com/zuckerberg -says-deleting-facebook-has-no-meaningful-impact-his -business-872876.

Naone, Erica. 2011. "How Useful Is Personalized Search?" *MIT Technology Review*, April 11. https://www.technologyreview .com/s/423596/how-useful-is-personalized-search/.

Neal, Dave. 2016. "Swedish Deseat Software Will Help You Delete Yourself from the Internet." *The Inquirer*, November 25. https://www.theinquirer.net/inquirer/news/2478419/swedish -deseat-software-will-help-you-delete-yourself-from-the -internet.

Nelson, P. 2016. "Just One Autonomous Car Will Use 4,000 GB of Data/Day." *Networkworld*, December 7. https://www.network world.com/article/3147892/internet/one-autonomous-car -will-use-4000-gb-of-dataday.html.

Netcraft. 2017. "February 2017 Web Server Survey." https://news .netcraft.com/archives/2017/02/27/february-2017-web-serv er-survey.html.

Noack, Rick. 2018. "European Union's New Privacy Law Made Some Websites Go Dark Today; Here's What Else Has Changed." *Los Angeles Times*, May 25. http://www.latimes .com/business/technology/la-fi-tn-gdpr-europe-privacy -20180525-story.html.

Nugraha, Y., Kautsarina, and A. S. Sastrosubroto. 2015. "Towards Data Sovereignty in Cyberspace." Working paper presented at the Third International Conference on Information and Communication Technology. https://www.cs.ox.ac.uk/files /7463/Towards%20Data%20Sovereignty%20in%20 Cyberspace_Nugraha.pdf.

NUSDeltares. 2014. "Neptune OMS for Singapore Coastal Quality." http://www.nusdeltares.org/projects/neptune/.

O'Brien, Sarah Ashley. 2016. "Why Facebook Was Launching a Satellite into Space." CNN.com, September 1. http://money .cnn.com/2016/09/01/technology/facebook-satellite-explo sion/.

O'Conner, M. C. 2017. "Dumpster Diving Robots: Using AI for Smart Recycling." *IQ*, July 5. https://iq.intel.com/dumpster -diving-robots-using-ai-for-smart-recycling/.

ODIHQ (Open Data Institute). 2015. "The Economic Impact of Open Data: What Do We Already Know?" Medium, November 2.

https://medium.com/@ODIHQ/the-economic-impact-of -open-data-what-do-we-already-know-1a119c1958a0.

OECD (Organisation for Economic Co-operation and Development). 1980 (2013). "Guidelines on the Protection of Privacy and Transborder Flows of Personal Data." Paris. http://www.oecd.org/sti/ieconomy/privacy.htm.

———. 2013. "The OECD Privacy Framework." OECD, Paris. http://www.oecd.org/internet/ieconomy/oecd_privacy _framework.pdf.

———. 2015. "Data-Driven Innovation for Growth and Well-Being: What Implications for Governments and Businesses." STI Policy Note, OECD, Paris. https://www.oecd.org/sti /ieconomy/PolicyNote-DDI.pdf.

———. 2015. *Digital Security Risk Management for Economic and Social Prosperity: OECD Recommendation and Companion Document.* Paris: OECD Publishing. https://doi.org/10.1787 /9789264245471-en.

———. 2017. "Key Issues for Digital Transformation in the G20." G20 Germany Presidency and OECD Conference, January 12. https://www.oecd.org/g20/key-issues-for-digital-transforma tion-in-the-g20.pdf.

Ofcom. 2016. "Adults' Media Use and Attitudes." https://www .ofcom.org.uk/__data/assets/pdf_file/0026/80828/2016 -adults-media-use-and-attitudes.pdf.

———. 2018. "Ofcom Kicks Off Auction to Improve Mobile Broadband and Prepare for 5G." https://www.ofcom.org.uk /about-ofcom/latest/media/media-releases/2018/start-spec trum-auction.

Ohlhausen, Maureen K. 2017. "Remarks at the FTC Informational Injury Workshop." December 12. https://www.ftc.gov/public -statements/2017/12/remarks-ftc-informational-injury -workshop.

Open Data Institute. n.d. "Data Infrastructure." https://theodi.org /topic/data-infrastructure/.

Open Government Working Group. n.d. "Open Government Data." http://opengovernmentdata.org/.

Open Knowledge International. n.d. *Open Data Handbook.* http:// opendatahandbook.org.

———. n.d. *The Open Definition.* http://opendefinition.org/.

Packet Clearing house. n.d. "Internet Exchange Point Directory Reports." http://wwww.pch.net/ixpdir/summary.

Palmer, N. 2014. "Cracking Patterns in Big Data Saves Colombian Rice Farmers Huge Losses." Research Program on Climate Change, Agriculture, and Food Security (CCAFS), Montpellier, France. https://ccafs.cgiar.org/research/annual-report/2014 /cracking-patterns-in-big-data-saves-colombian-rice-farmers -huge-losses.

PARIS21 (Secretariat of the Partnership in Statistics for Development in the 21st Century). 2015. *A Road Map for A Country-Led Data Revolution.* Paris: OECD Publishing.

http://www.oecd-ilibrary.org/development/a-road-map-for -a-country-led-data-revolution_9789264234703-en.

Partnership on AI. 2018. "Partners." https://www.partnershiponai .org/partners/.

Pentland, Alex. 2015. *Social Physics: How Social Networks Can Make Us Smarter.* Reissue ed. New York: Penguin.

Peterson, Tim. 2015. "Facebook Users Are Posting 75% More Videos Than Last Year." *AdAge*, January 7. http://adage.com /article/digital/facebook-users-posting-75-videos -year/296482/.

Pfeifle, Sam. 2017. "Is the GDPR a Data Localization Law?" International Association of Privacy Professionals, Portsmouth, NH. https://iapp.org/news/a/is-the-gdpr-a-data -localization-law/.

Piwek, Lukasz, David A. Ellis, Sally Andrews, and Adam Johnson. 2016. "The Rise of Consumer Health Wearables: Promises and Barriers." *PLOS*, February 2. http://journals.plos.org/plos medicine/article?id=10.1371/journal.pmed.1001953.

Poppe, Krijn J., Sjaak Wolfert, Cor Verdouw, and Tim Verwaart. 2013. *Information and Communications Technologies as a Driver for Change in Agri-Food Chains.* https://s3.amazonaws .com/academia.edu.documents/40043142/542e8ba40cf277 d58e8ebffd.pdf20151115-68247-1ccjezq.pdf?AWSAccess KeyId=AKIAIWOWYYGZ2Y53UL3A&Expires=1537343545 &Signature=ZMUDN6eXwMB17wLKmsIDXAZ zfR4%3D&response-content-disposition=inline%3B%20 filename%3DInformation_and_Communication _Technology.pdf.

Price, R. 2017. "Mapping Apps Are Reportedly Directing People Fleeing the Southern California Wildfires to Areas That Are on Fire." *Business Insider*, December 7. http://www.businessin sider.com/la-fires-gps-apps-directing-people-areas-fire-lapd -2017-12.

Priyadarshinee, Pragati, Rakesh Raut, Manoj Jha, and Bhaskar B. Gardas. 2017. "Understanding and Predicting the Determinants of Cloud Computing Adoption: A Two Staged Hybrid SEM-Neural Networks Approach." *Computers in Human Behavior* 76: 341–62.

Qatar Ministry of Information and Communications Technology. 2015. "Data Management Policy." http://www.motc.gov.qa /sites/default/files/data_management_policy.pdf.

Ragoobar, Tricia, Jason Whalley, and David Harle. 2011. "Public and Private Intervention for Next-Generation Access Deployment: Possibilities for Three European Countries." *Telecommunications Policy* 35 (9): 827–41.

Rango, M., and M. Vespe. 2017. "Big Data and Alternative Data Sources on Migration: From Case Studies to Policy Support." Summary Report, European Commission. https://bluehub .jrc.ec.europa.eu/bigdata4migration/uploads/attachments /cjdelbdgo00hnqazv3u7xi6pd-big-data-workshop-draft-sum mary-report.pdf.

Reinsdorf, Marshall, and Gabriel Quiros. 2018. *Measuring the Digital Economy.* Washington, DC: International Monetary Fund.

Reuters. 2017. "Rwanda Regulator Fines MTN Rwanda $8.5 Mln over External IT Hub." May 17. https://www.reuters.com /article/rwanda-telecoms/rwanda-regulator-fines-mtn-rwan da-8-5-mln-over-external-it-hub-idUSL8N1IJ2IJ.

Reuters Market Light. 2015. "Addressing Farmers Problems through Digital India Initiative." https://www.mygov.in /sites/default/files/user_comments/Digital%20India -Agriculture.pdf.

Richter, Wolf. 2018. "Online Ad Revenues Are Surging, but 2 Companies Are Getting Most of the Spoils." *Business Insider*, April 27. http://www.businessinsider.com/online-ads-rev enues-going-to-google-and-facebook-the-most-2017-4.

RICTA. 2015. "Growing the Rwandan Internet Content Hosted in Rwanda." https://ricta.org.rw/sites/default/files/resources /1kwebsites_project_finalversion_0.pdf.

Robertson, A. 2017. "What Makes YouTube's Surreal Kids' Videos So Creepy?" *The Verge*, November 21. https://www.theverge .com/culture/2017/11/21/16685874/kids-youtube-video -elsagate-creepiness-psychology.

Rochet, Jean-Charles, and Jean Tirole. 2003. "Platform Competition in Two-Sided Markets." *European Economic Association* 1 (4): 990–1029.

Rohlfs, J. 1974. "Theory of Interdependent Demand for a Communications Service." *Bell Journal of Economics and Management Science* 5 (1): 16–37.

Romano, Aja. 2018. "How Facebook Made It Impossible to Delete Facebook." *VOX*, March 22. https://www.vox.com/culture /2018/3/22/17146776/delete-facebook-difficult.

Roosendaal, Arnold, Marc van Lieshout, and Anne Fleur van Veenstra. 2014. "Personal Data Markets." TNO Innovation for Life. http://publications.tno.nl/publication/34612412/riZsP9 /TNO-2014-R11390.pdf.

Rosenwald, Michael. 2015. "The Digital Media Industry Needs to React to Ad Blockers . . . or Else." *Colombia Journalism Review*, September/October. https://www.cjr.org/business_of_news /will_ad_blockers_kill_the_digital_media_industry.php.

Russell, Stuart, and University of California at Berkeley. 2017. "Statement at the ITU AI for Global Good Summit." Geneva, June. https://www.youtube.com/watch?v=FsSfB8aKTuI.

Ruutu, Sampsa, Thomas Casey, and Ville Kotivirta. 2017. "Development and Competition of Digital Service Platforms: A System Dynamics Approach." *Technological Forecasting and Social Change* 117: 119–30.

Salem, Fadi. 2017. *The Arab World Online: Digital Transformations and Societal Trends in the Age of the 4th Industrial Revolution.* Vol. 3. Dubai: Mohammed Bin Rashid School of Government. https://img0bm.b8cdn.com/images/uploads/article_docs /arab_world_online_2017_4ir_d_fadi_salem_34792_EN.pdf.

Sandvine. 2015. "Global Internet Phenomena: Latin America & North America." https://www.sandvine.com/hubfs/down loads/archive/2015-global-internet-phenomena-report-latin -america-and-north-america.pdf.

SAS Institute. n.d. "Big Data Analytics." https://www.sas.com/en _us/insights/analytics/big-data-analytics.html.

Schwab, Klaus. 2017. *The Fourth Industrial Revolution.* New York: Crown Business.

Scott, Mark, and Mike Isaacs. 2016. "Facebook Restores Iconic Vietnam War Photo It Censored for Nudity." *New York Times*, September 9. https://www.nytimes.com/2016/09/10/technol ogy/facebook-vietnam-war-photo-nudity.html?_r=0.

Seller, Marianne, and Paul Gray. 1999. "A Survey of Database Marketing." Center for Research on Information Technology and Organizations, University of California at Irvine. https:// escholarship.org/uc/item/36z642kj.

Sengupta, Anirban, and Steven N. Wiggins. 2014. "Airline Pricing, Price Dispersion, and Ticket Characteristics On and Off the Internet." *American Economic Journal: Economic Policy* 6 (1): 272–307.

Sengupta, Ritam, Richard Heeks, Chattapadhyay Sumandro, and Christopher Foster. 2017. "Exploring Big Data for Development: An Electricity Sector Case Study from India." Working paper, University of Manchester, Manchester, UK.

Seybert, Heidi, and Petronela Reineckle. n.d. "Internet and Cloud Services: Statistics on Use by Individuals." EuroStat. http:// ec.europa.eu/eurostat/statistics-explained/index.php /Internet_and_cloud_services_-_statistics_on_the_use_by _individuals.

Shehabi, A., S. J. Smith, N. Horner, I. Azevedo, R. Brown, J. Koomey, E. Masanet, D. Sartor, M. Herrlin, and W. Lintner. 2016. "United States Data Center Energy Usage Report." Lawrence Berkeley National Laboratory, Berkeley, CA. https:// pubarchive.lbl.gov/islandora/object/ir%3A1005775 /datastream/PDF/view.

Sherman, Alex. 2018. "Uber Is Preparing to Sell Southeast Asia Unit to Grab in Exchange for Stake in Company: Sources." CNBC News, February 16. https://www.cnbc.com /2018/02/16/uber-preparing-to-sell-southeast-asia-unit-to -grab.html.

Shu, Catherine. 2018. "Waze Signs Data-Sharing Deal with AI-Based Traffic Management Startup Waycare." *Tech Crunch*, April 26. https://techcrunch.com/2018/04/26/waze-signs -data-sharing-deal-with-ai-based-traffic-management-star tup-waycare/.

Simonite, Tim. 2014. "Sell Your Personal Data for $8 a Month." *MIT Technology Review*, February 12. https://www.technol ogyreview.com/s/524621/sell-your-personal-data-for-8-a -month/.

Simons, Gary F., and Charles D. Fenning, eds. 2018. "English." *Ethnologue: Languages of the World.* 21st ed. English.

Dallas, TX: SIL International. https://www.ethnologue.com/language/eng.

Singer, Natasha. 2012. "Mapping, and Sharing, the Consumer Genome." *New York Times*, June 17. https://www.nytimes.com/2012/06/17/technology/acxiom-the-quiet-giant-of-consumer-database-marketing.html.

Sloane, Garett. 2018. "What Facebook Crisis? Ad Sales Skyrocket to $11.8 Billion, Users Don't #delete." *AdAge*, April 25. http://adage.com/article/digital/privacy-concerns-facebook-ad-sales-hits-11-8-billion/3s13271/.

Smith, Eve. 2018. "A Memo to Big Tech: The Techlash against Amazon, Facebook and Google—And What They Can Do." *The Economist*, January 20. https://www.economist.com/briefing/2018/01/20/the-techlash-against-amazon-facebook-and-google-and-what-they-can-do.

Statistics New Zealand. 2016. "Statistics New Zealand's Strategic Intentions for the Period 2016/17–19/20 Annual Report for the Year Ended 30 June 2016." Wellington. https://www.stats.govt.nz/about-us/corporate-publications/.

Still, Kaisa, Marko Seppänen, Heidi Korhonen, Katri Valkokari, Arho Suominen, and Miika Kumpulainen. 2017. "Business Model Innovation of Startups Developing Multisided Digital Platforms." In *2017 IEEE 19th Conference on Business Informatics (CBI 2017)*, Vol. 2, 70–75. http://ieeexplore.ieee.org/stamp/stamp.jsp?tp=&arnumber=8012942&isnumber=8012382.

Stuart, Elizabeth, Emma Samman, William Avis, and Tom Berliner. 2015. *The Data Revolution: Finding the Missing Millions.* Research Report Series, Overseas Development Institute. London: Development Progress. https://www.odi.org/sites/odi.org.uk/files/odi-assets/publications-opinion-files/9604.pdf.

Suominen, Kati. 2017. "Accelerating Digital Trade in Latin America and the Caribbean." Working paper, Inter-American Development Bank, Washington, DC. https://publications.iadb.org/bitstream/handle/11319/8166/Accelerating-Digital-Trade-in-Latin-America-and-the-Caribbean.PDF.

Surowiecki, James. 2016. "Why Startups Are Struggling." *Technology Review*, June 15. https://www.technologyreview.com/s/601497/why-startups-are-struggling/.

Swanson, Alexandra, Margaret Kosmala, Chris Lintott, Robert Simpson, Arfon Smith, and Craig Packer. 2015. "Snapshot Serengeti, High-Frequency Annotated Camera Trap Images of 40 Mammalian Species in an African Savanna." *Nature*. Scientific Data. https://www.nature.com/articles/sdata201526.

Syntonic. 2017. "Syntonic Expands to Latin America and Lending Mobile Carriers." January 21. https://syntonic.com/2017/01/syntonic-expands-to-latin-america-with-leading-mobile-carriers/.

Tan, Barney, Shan Ling Pan, Ziangua Lu, and Lihua Huang. 2015. "The Role of IS Capabilities in the Development of Multi-sided Platforms: The Digital Ecosystem Strategy of Alibaba.com." *Journal of the Association for Information Systems* 16 (4): 248–80.

Täuscher, Karl. n.d. "Business Models in the Digital Economy: An Empirical Study of Digital Markets." Working paper, Fraunhofer MOEZ, Fraunhofer Center for International Management and Knowledge Economy, Leipzig. https://www.imw.fraunhofer.de/content/dam/moez/de/documents/Working_Paper/Working_Paper_Digital_Marketplaces_final.pdf.

Täuscher, Karl, and Sven M. Laudien. 2017. "Uncovering the Nature of Platform-Based Business Models: An Empirical Taxonomy." Paper presented at the 50th Hawaii International Conference on System Sciences (HICSS), Manoa, HI. https://scholarspace.manoa.hawaii.edu/bitstream/10125/41802/1/paper0653.pdf.

———. 2018. "Understanding Platform Business Models: A Mixed Methods Study of Marketplaces." *European Management Journal* 36 (3): 319–29.

TechMoran. 2017. "Jumia Launches Offline Experiential Centers in Kenya." September 14. https://techmoran.com/jumia-launches-offline-experiential-centers-in-kenya/.

Telecom Regulatory Authority of India. 2016. "TRAI Releases the Prohibition of Discriminatory Tariffs for Data Services Regulations." http://www.trai.gov.in/notifications/press-release/trai-releases-prohibition-discriminatory-tariffs-data-services.

Thailand National Statistical Office. 2016. "The 2016 Household Survey on the Use of Information and Communication Technology." Ministry of Information and Communication Technology. http://web.nso.go.th/en/survey/ict/ict_house16.htm.

The Economist. 2017. "The World's Most Valuable Resource Is No Longer Oil, but Data." May 6. https://www.economist.com/news/leaders/21721656-data-economy-demands-new-approach-antitrust-rules-worlds-most-valuable-resource.

———. 2018. "A Bold Scheme to Dominate Ride-Hailing." May 10. https://www.economist.com/briefing/2018/05/10/a-bold-scheme-to-dominate-ride-hailing.

———. 2018. "How to Fix What Has Gone Wrong with the Internet." Special Report, June 28. https://www.economist.com/special-report/2018/06/28/how-to-fix-what-has-gone-wrong-with-the-internet.

———. 2018. "The Techlash against Amazon, Facebook and Google—And What They Can Do." January 20. https://www.economist.com/briefing/2018/01/20/the-techlash-against-amazon-facebook-and-google-and-what-they-can-do.

The Green Grid. 2016. "The 'Big Bad Data Police' Will Call If We Don't Get More Efficient." News release, September 5. https://www.thegreengrid.org/en/newsroom/news-releases/green-grid-big-bad-data-police-will-call.

The Guardian. n.d. "The Cambridge Analytica Files." https://www.theguardian.com/news/series/cambridge-analytica-files.

Thornhill, John. 2018. "Social Media Users of the World Unite." *Financial Times*, February 5. https://www.ft.com/content/ea6c3a0c-0843-11e8-9650-9c0ad2d7c5b5.

Toonders, J. 2014. "Data Is the New Oil of the Digital Economy." *Wired*. https://www.wired.com/insights/2014/07/data-new-oil-digital-economy/.

Touger, Glenn Evan. 2018. "What's the Difference between Artificial Learning (AI), Machine Learning, and Deep Learning?" Prowesscorp, August 3. www.prowesscorp.com/whats-the-difference-between-artificial-intelligence-ai-machine-learning-and-deep-learning/.

Tsai, Wen Chun. 2016. "Analyzing the Emergence of Alibaba Group from Business Ecosystem Perspective." *Journal of International Management Studies* 11 (2): 53–64.

Tucker, C. 2017. "Privacy, Algorithms and Artificial Intelligence." Working Paper 14011, National Bureau of Economic Research, Cambridge, MA. http://www.nber.org/chapters/c14011.pdf.

Turovsky, Barak. 2016. "Found in Translation: More Accurate, Fluent Sentences in Google Translate." Google, November 15. https://blog.google/products/translate/found-translation-more-accurate-fluent-sentences-google-translate/.

UN Broadband Commission. 2017. "Working Group on Education: Digital Skills for Life and Work." Report, Broadband Commission for Sustainable Development. http://unesdoc.unesco.org/images/0025/002590/259013e.pdf.

UN Data Revolution Group. 2014. "A World That Counts: Mobilising the Data Revolution for Sustainable Development." http://www.undatarevolution.org/wp-content/uploads/2014/12/A-World-That-Counts2.pdf.

UN Global Pulse. 2014. "Nowcasting Food Prices in Indonesia Using Social Media Signals." Global Pulse Project Series, no. 1. https://www.unglobalpulse.org/projects/nowcasting-food-prices.

———. 2015. *Using Twitter Data to Analyze Public Sentiment on Fuel Subsidy Policy Reform in El Salvador.* Global Pulse Project Series, no. 13. www.unglobalpulse.org/sites/default/files/UNGP_ProjectSeries_ElSalvador_Fuel_2015_0.pdf.

———. 2016. "A Guide to Data Innovation for Development: From Idea to Proof of Concept." http://unglobalpulse.org/sites/default/files/UNGP_BigDataGuide2016_%20Web.pdf.

———. 2016. "Haze Gazer: A Crisis Analysis Tool." Tool Series, no. 2. http://unglobalpulse.org/sites/default/files/2-pager%20Haze%20Gazer%20-%20Feb%202017_0.pdf.

———. 2017. "Inferring Commuting Statistics in the Greater Jakarta Area with Twitter." https://www.unglobalpulse.org/projects/inferring-commuting-statistics-greater-jakarta-area-twitter.

———. 2017. "Social Media and Forced Displacement: Big Data Analytics and Machine-Learning." White paper. http://unglobalpulse.org/sites/default/files/White%20Paper%20Social%20Media%203_0.pdf.

———. 2017. "Using Machine Learning to Analyse Radio Content in Uganda." http://unglobalpulse.org/sites/default/files/Radio%20Analysis%20Report_Preview%20%283%29.pdf.

———. 2018. "Data Innovation Risk Assessment Tool." Data Innovation for Development Guide. http://unglobalpulse.org/sites/default/files/Privacy%20Assessment%20Tool%20.pdf.

UNCTAD (United Nations Conference on Trade and Development). 2015. "Review of E-Commerce Legislation Harmonization in the Economic Community of West African States." UNCTAD, Geneva and New York. http://unctad.org/en/PublicationsLibrary/dtlstict2015d2_en.pdf.

———. 2016. "Data Protection Regulations and International Data Flows: Implications for Trade and Development." UNCTAD, Geneva and New York. http://unctad.org/en/PublicationsLibrary/dtlstict2016d1_en.pdf.

———. 2017. *Information Economy Report 2017: Digitalization, Trade and Development.* Geneva: UNCTAD. http://unctad.org/en/PublicationsLibrary/ier2017_en.pdf.

———. 2018. "Data Protection and Privacy Legislation Worldwide." UNCTAD, Geneva and New York. http://unctad.org/en/Pages/DTL/STI_and_ICTs/ICT4D-Legislation/eCom-Data-Protection-Laws.aspx.

UNDG (United Nations Development Group). 2017. "Data Privacy, Ethics, and Protection: Guidance Note on Big Data and the Achievement of the 2030 Agenda." https://undg.org/wp-content/uploads/2017/11/UNDG_BigData_final_web.pdf.

———. 2017. "Guidance Note on Big Data for Achievement of the 2030 Agenda: Data Privacy, Ethics and Protection." https://undg.org/wp-content/uploads/2017/11/UNDG_BigData_final_web.pdf

UNDP (United Nations Development Programme) and UN Global Pulse. 2016. *A Guide to Data Innovation for Development: From Idea to Proof of Concept.* http://www.undp.org/content/undp/en/home/librarypage/development-impact/a-guide-to-data-innovation-for-development---from-idea-to-proof-.html.

UNESCO (United Nations Educational, Scientific, and Cultural Organization). 2018. *A Lifeline to Learning: Leveraging Technology to Support Education for Refugees.* Paris: UNESCO. http://unesdoc.unesco.org/images/0026/002612/261278e.pdf.

UNICEF. 2015. "Procedure for Ethical Standards in Research, Evaluation, Data Collection and Analysis." CF/PD/DRP/2015-001. April 1. https://www.unicef.org/supply/files/ATTACHMENT_IV-UNICEF_Procedure_for_Ethical_Standards.PDF.

UNICEF and Facebook. n.d. "A Case Study: Data and Social Media Can Lead to Healthier Lives." Infographic. http://neo-assets .s3.amazonaws.com/news/FB-UNICEF-Big.png.

United Nations. 2015. *Transforming Our World: The 2030 Agenda for Sustainable Development.* New York: UN Publishing. https://sustainabledevelopment.un.org/post2015/transfor mingourworld.

Uptime Institute. 2012. "Data Center Site Infrastructure Tier Standard: Topology." http://www.gpxglobal.net/wp-content /uploads/2012/10/TIERSTANDARD_Topology_120801.pdf.

Upwork. 2018. "Upwork Releases Q4 2017 Skills Index, Ranking the 20 Fastest-Growing Skills for Freelancers." Press release, February 7. https://www.upwork.com/press/2018/02/07/q4 -2017-skills-index/.

United States, Executive Office of the President. 2016. *Big Data: A Report on Algorithmic Systems, Opportunity, and Civil Rights.* Washington, DC: White House. https://www.whitehouse.gov /sites/default/files/microsites/ostp/2016_0504_data _discrimination.pdf.

United States, White House, Office of the Press Secretary. 2016. "Fact Sheet: Data by the People, for the People—Eight Years of Progress Opening Government Data to Spur Innovation, Opportunity, and Economic Growth." White House, Washington, DC. September 28. https://www.whitehouse.gov /the-press-office/2016/09/28/fact-sheet-data-people-people -eight-years-progress-opening-government.

USA Today. 2017. "Rebel Wilson Wins Defamation Case against Publisher." June 15. https://www.usatoday.com/story/life /people/2017/06/15/rebel-wilson-wins-defamation-case -against-publisher/102877120/.

Van Alstyne, M. 2016. "Platform Shift: How New Biz Models Are Changing the Shape of Industry." Video. https://www .youtube.com/watch?v=8OFRD66pI0Y.

van Zyl, Gareth. 2014. "MTN Unveils Africa's First Solar Data Centre Cooling System." *ITWeb Africa*, July 10. http://www .itwebafrica.com/cloud/517-south-africa/233194-mtn-un veils-africas-first-solar-data-centre-cooling-system.

Vector. 2017. "Operational Performance for the 9 Months Ended 31 March 2017." Market release, April 26. https://www.vector .co.nz/news/operational-performance-for-the-9-months -ended-31.

Verge, Jason. 2015. "PLDT Building Eighth Philippines Data Center for $29m." Data Center Knowledge, April 28. http:// www.datacenterknowledge.com/archives/2015/04/28/pldt -building-eighth-philippines-data-center-29m.

Verhulst, Stefaan. 2014. "Mapping the Next Frontier of Open Data: Corporate Data Sharing." Blog, United Nations Global Pulse, September 17. http://unglobalpulse.org/mapping-corporate -data-sharing.

Virtu. 2015. "5 Data Security Challenges Faced by Government Agencies, and What They Can Do about It." September 23. https://www.virtru.com/blog/data-security/.

Wang, Teresa, and Malay Gandhi. 2014. "The Future of Biosensing Wearables: A Review of the Current Landscape and Future of Biosensing Wearables." Rock Health. https://rockhealth.com /reports/the-future-of-biosensing-wearables/.

Wang, W., and F. Guo. 2016. "RoadLab: Revamping Road Condition and Road Safety Monitoring by Crowdsourcing with Smartphone App." Paper presented at the 95th Annual Meeting of the Transportation Research Board, Washington, DC, January 10–14.

Warren, Mark. 2016. "The Cure for Cancer Is Data—Mountains of Data." *Wired*, October 19. https://www.wired.com/2016/10 /eric-schadt-biodata-genomics-medical-research/.

Warren, Samuel D., and Louis D. Brandeis. 1890. "The Right to Privacy." *Harvard Law Review* 4 (5): 193.

Wesolowski, A., T. Qureshi, M. F. Boni, P. R. Sundsøy, M. A. Johansson, S. B. Rasheed, K. Engø-Monsen, and C. O. Buckee. 2015. "Impact of Human Mobility on the Emergence of Dengue Epidemics in Pakistan." *National Academy of Sciences* 112 (38): 11887–92.

WFP (World Food Programme). 2015. *WFP Guide to Personal Data Protection and Privacy.* Rome: WFP. https://docs.wfp .org/api/documents/e8d24e70cc11448383495caca154cb97 /download/.

Whitler, Kimberly A. 2016. "The Personal Data Revolution: Why It's Time for Marketers to Care." *Forbes*, September 18. https:// www.forbes.com/sites/kimberlywhitler/2016/09/18/the-per sonal-data-revolution-why-its-time-for-marketers-to -care/#488b46db5681.

Wikipedia. n.d. "DARPA Network Challenge." https://en.wikipedia .org/wiki/DARPA_Network_Challenge.

Williams, Chris, Davide Strusani, David Vincent, and David Kovo. 2016. "The Economic Impact of Next-Generation Mobile Services: How 3G Connections and the Use of Mobile Data Impact GDP Growth." Chapter 1.6 in *The Global Information Technology Report.* Geneva: World Economic Forum. http:// www3.weforum.org/docs/GITR/2013/GITR_Chapter1.6 _2013.pdf.

Wong, Julia Carrie. 2016. "Mark Zuckerberg Accused of Abusing Power after Facebook Deletes 'Napalm Girl' Post." *The Guardian*, September 9. https://www.theguardian.com/tech nology/2016/sep/08/facebook-mark-zuckerberg-napalm-girl -photo-vietnam-war.

World Bank. 2008. "P106589: Mexico Information Technology (IT) Industry Development Project." World Bank, Washington, DC. http://projects.worldbank.org/P106589/information -technology-development?lang=en.

———. 2014. "Open Data for Economic Growth." Transport and ICT Global Practice, Washington, DC. World Bank, Washington, DC. http://www.worldbank.org/content/dam /Worldbank/document/Open-Data-for-Economic-Growth .pdf.

———. 2016. "Philippines: Real-Time Data Can Improve Traffic Management in Major Cities." Press Release, April 5. World Bank, Washington, DC. http://www.worldbank.org/en/news /press-release/2016/04/05/philippines-real-time-data -can-improve-traffic-management-in.

———. 2016. *Big Data: Innovation Challenge: Pioneering Approaches to Data-Driven Development.* Washington, DC: World Bank.

———. 2016. *World Development Report 2016: Digital Dividends.* Washington, DC: World Bank. doi:10.1596/978-1-4648-0671-1.

———. 2017. *Big Data in Action for Government: Big Data Innovation in Public Services, Policy, and Engagement.* Washington, DC: World Bank. http://documents.worldbank .org/curated/en/176511491287380986/Big-data-in-action -for-government-big-data-innovation-in-public-services -policy-and-engagement.

———. 2017. *Doing Business 2017: Equal Opportunity for All.* Washington, DC: World Bank. http://www.doingbusiness.org /reports/global-reports/doing-business-2017.

———. 2017. "Internet of Things: The New Government to Business Platform—A Review of Opportunities, Practices, and Challenges." World Bank, Washington, DC. http://docu ments.worldbank.org/curated/en/610081509689089303 /Internet-of-things-the-new-government-to-business-plat form-a-review-of-opportunities-practices-and-challenges.

———. 2017. "RAM—Rural Accessibility Hub. GitiHub." World Bank, Washington, DC. https://github.com/WorldBank -Transport/ram-backend.

———. 2018. *Digital Adoption Index.* 2018 update. http://www.world bank.org/en/publication/wdr2016/Digital-Adoption-Index.

———. n.d. India Lights Platform. http://india.nightlights.io/.

World Bank and CGAP (Consultative Group to Assist the Poor). 2018. "Data Protection and Privacy for Alternative Data." Draft GPFI-FCPL Sub-Group Discussion Paper. Group of Twenty (G20). https://www.g20.org/sites/default/files/docu mentos_producidos/data_protection_and_privacy_for _alternative_data_wbg_0.pdf.

World Bank Group. 2018. *Africa's Pulse*, no. 17 (April). https:// www.openknowledge.worldbank.org/handle/10986/29667.

World Economic Forum. 2011. "Personal Data: The Emergence of a New Asset Class." World Economic Forum, Geneva. http:// www3.weforum.org/docs/WEF_ITTC_PersonalDataNew Asset_Report_2011.pdf.

———. 2013. "Unlocking the Value of Personal Data: From Collection to Usage." World Economic Forum, Geneva. http:// www3.weforum.org/docs/WEF_IT_UnlockingValuePersonal Data_CollectionUsage_Report_2013.pdf.

Wright, Morgan. 2018. "A Ransomware Attack Brought Atlanta to Its Knees—And No One Seems to Care." *The Hill*, April 4. http://thehill.com/opinion/cybersecurity/381594-a-ransom ware-attack-brought-atlanta-to-its-knees-and-no-one -seems-to.

Zannier, Federico. n.d. "A Bite of Me." https://www.kickstarter .com/projects/1461902402/a-bit-e-of-me/description.

Contributors

Mona Badran (World Bank, Digital Development, consultant)—chapter 4

Associate Professor, Faculty of Economics and Political Science, Cairo University, Egypt

Mona is an economist with a main focus on digital economics, economics of telecommunications, and information and communication technology's role in development. She has extensive consulting experience working for numerous private sector clients and international organizations, such as the World Bank, International Telecommunication Union (ITU), GSMA, United Nations Economic and Social Commission for West Asia, and International Labour Organization. For more than five years, she advised the Egyptian Ministry of Investment, where she led the research department. Numerous times, she was awarded Cairo University's International Publications Award for publishing in Thomson Reuters–indexed journals in the area of Information and Communication Technologies for Development.

Phillippa Biggs (International Telecommunication Union)—chapter 3

Senior Policy Analyst, ITU

Phillippa has been an economist and qualified accountant with the International Telecommunication Union (ITU) since 2005. She holds a Natural Sciences degree from Cambridge University, an accountancy qualification from the Institute of Chartered Accountants in England and Wales, and a master's in Economics for Development from Oxford University. Prior to joining the ITU, Phillippa worked as an Economic Affairs Officer at the United Nations Conference on Trade and Development and as a consultant with the United Nations Industrial Development Organization in Tanzania and Egypt. She is chief author of the *State of Broadband* report, *Confronting the Crisis* reports and *Fast-Forward Progress* report. She analyzes developments in broadband, voice over internet protocol, and 3G markets around the world.

Eva Clemente Miranda (World Bank, Finance Competitiveness and Innovation)—chapters 5 and 6

Eva, a Spanish national, started her journey at the World Bank Group in early 2012 when she joined the Digital Development Unit. As an Information and Communication Technology (ICT) Policy Specialist, she has assisted client countries in their efforts to harness the benefits of ICT-enabled innovation. As data has become an essential ingredient for innovation in today's digital economy, Eva's work has increasingly focused on supporting data policies and data-driven innovation and entrepreneurship in Latin America and Africa at the national and subnational levels. Currently, in the Finance, Competitiveness, and Innovation Global Practice, she promotes the digital economy agenda for Africa.

Elena Gasol Ramos (World Bank, Finance Competitiveness and Innovation)—chapters 5 and 6

Elena, a lawyer by training, is a Senior Private Sector Specialist with the World Bank, based in Washington, DC. She currently leads the Bank's engagement on digital economy, entrepreneurship, and innovation in Kenya and Burundi. She also provides advice to governments on data protection issues. Prior to this her work included a variety of positions within and outside the World Bank Group, in both Europe and the United States. Her areas of expertise include data protection and data security, consumer protection, and ICT policy and regulation. She is a member of both the Salamanca and New York bars and has taught comparative privacy law, with a focus on e-privacy, at the Georgetown University Law Center. She has a master's in European Law from the College of Europe in Bruges, Belgium, and an LLM from Georgetown University Law Center.

Rachel Firestone (Hala Systems—formerly World Bank, Digital Development)—chapter 4

Rachel is the Director of Operations at Hala Systems, a social enterprise that uses advanced technologies to save lives in conflict zones, to combat disinformation, and to bring accountability for war crimes. She specializes in information and communication technology (ICT) and sustainable development for communities in conflict and spent several years with the World Bank working on projects in Somalia and the Horn of Africa. Prior to joining the World Bank staff, she spent four years in India working on self-advocacy and protection programs with communities affected by conflict and natural disaster. Rachel completed her master's at Georgetown University, with a concentration in Global Politics and Security.

Roku Fukui (World Bank, Digital Development, consultant)—Executive Summary and chapter 4

Roku works as a consultant with the World Bank Group's Digital Development Department. He focuses on various aspects of digital development and has worked primarily in Afghanistan and Somalia. His research interests cover information and communication technology for development and mobile innovation. Roku received his MA in International Economics and International Relations from the Johns Hopkins School of Advanced International Studies. He is an above-average cryptocurrency investor.

Christine Howard (World Bank, Digital Development)—Bibliography and Publication

Christine is a Program Assistant with the Digital Development Department at the World Bank. She joined the World Bank staff in 2012 after graduating with her bachelor's in Political Science and Creative Writing earlier that year. Since joining the staff, she has supported and contributed to multiple digital development–related research, programs, and initiatives. She creates original art, short stories, and poems. Her poetry has been published in *The Dulcimer*, a student-led literary and art magazine.

Tim Kelly (World Bank, Digital Development)—Editor, Executive Summary, and chapters 1, 2, and 5

Tim is a Lead Digital Development Specialist based in Nairobi. He is the editor of this report and the overall Information and Communications Technology for Development series. He worked previously at the Organisation for Economic Co-operation and Development and International Telecommunication Union, having joined the World Bank staff in 2008. His other World Bank publications include the policy chapter in the *2016 World Development Report, Maximizing Mobile,* and *ICTs for Post-conflict Reconstruction,* as well as the *Broadband Strategies Handbook* (with Carlo Rossotto). In addition to his analytical work and technical assistance, he is also co–task team leader for digital development investment lending programs in Comoros, Ghana, Malawi, Niger, Tanzania, and Somalia.

Robert Kirkpatrick (UN Global Pulse)—chapter 3

Robert is the Director of UN Global Pulse, a UN initiative driving a big data revolution for global development and resilience. Prior to joining the UN staff, Robert cofounded and led software development for two pioneering private sector humanitarian technology teams, first at Groove Networks, and later as Lead Architect for Microsoft Humanitarian Systems. From 2007 to 2009 he served as Chief Technology Officer of the nonprofit InSTEDD. Robert was a member of the UN Secretary-General's Independent Expert Advisory Group on a Data Revolution for Sustainable Development (2014) and currently sits on InSTEDD's Board of Directors, as well as the World Economic Forum's Global Agenda Council on Data-Driven Development.

Prasanna Lal Das (World Bank, Finance, Competitiveness, and Innovation)—chapters 5 and 6

Prasanna works on entrepreneurship, data/digital strategy, and disruptive technologies in the Finance, Competitiveness and Innovation Global Practice at the World Bank Group. His most recent publication is "Internet of Things—The Next Government to Business Platform." His current work includes projects on technologies such as blockchain, Internet of Things, and machine learning applied to development questions such as financial inclusion, growth of small and medium-sized enterprises, and entrepreneurship ecosystem diagnostics. Prasanna managed the Bank Group's open financial data program and led the development of its open trade and competitiveness data platform. Prasanna holds a master's degree in Modern Indian History. He can be followed on Twitter @prasannalaldas.

Bradley Larson (World Bank, East Asia Pacific, consultant)—Data Notes

Bradley Larson is a consultant with the Macroeconomics, Trade, and Investment Global Practice, working primarily on issues related to the digital economy of East Asia. Previously, he led data analysis and visualization for three World Development Reports: *Learning to Realize Education's Promise* (2018), *Governance and the Law* (2017), and *Digital Dividends* (2016). He has also worked for the World Bank's Public Sector Governance unit, the Special Inspector General for Iraq Reconstruction, and the Center for Strategic and International Studies. He has an MA in International Economics and Strategic Studies from the Johns Hopkins School of Advanced International Studies.

Miguel Luengo-Oroz (UN Global Pulse)—chapter 3

Miguel is the Chief Data Scientist at UN Global Pulse. As the first data scientist at the United Nations, since 2011, Miguel has created and managed teams that have implemented more than 30 innovation projects worldwide with governments and UN agencies. He also advises the government of Spain in regard to its artificial intelligence strategy. He is the founder of MalariaSpot.org at the Universidad Politecnica de Madrid—video games and crowdsourcing for medical diagnosis. Over the last 15 years, he has coauthored more than 40 scientific publications. Prior to joining the United Nations, Miguel worked as an antidisciplinary scientist in French and Spanish institutions in fields like artificial creativity and genetics.

Michael Minges (World Bank, Digital Development, consultant)—chapters 2, 5, and 6 and Data Notes

Michael Minges is the lead consultant at ICTData, where he provides advice and analysis on digital technology issues for a range of clients including governments, the private sector, and international organizations. He previously worked at the International Telecommunication Union and International Monetary Fund. Michael drafted the technology chapter for the World Bank's *Broadband Strategies Toolkit*. Recent assignments include analyzing the impact of broadband in least developed countries, developing an e-commerce strategy for Oman, and evaluating the Taza Koom digital transformation initiative in the Kyrgyz Republic. He holds an MBA from George Washington University.

Tatiana Nadyseva (World Bank, Digital Development, consultant)—chapter 4

Tatiana joined the World Bank as a consultant to work on the "People and Data" chapter for this report. She previously worked in the sphere of advocacy, gender equality, and information and communication technology–enabled employment, but her real passion lies in the sphere of technological evolution. She received her BSc and postgraduate diploma in Economics from Saint Petersburg University of Engineering and Economics and her MSc in Technology (Operations and Innovation Management) from Aalborg University. Apart from being a tech enthusiast, Tatiana is also an environmentalist, vegan, digital nomad, and photographer.

Siddhartha Raja (World Bank, Digital Development)—chapter 4

Siddhartha Raja is a Digital Development Specialist with the World Bank Group. His work focuses on connecting more people to better and cheaper internet and digital technologies. He has assisted governments in designing and implementing policy reform and investment programs that have expanded broadband connectivity, helped people develop their digital skills and find work online, and generated exponential improvements in international connectivity, bringing people closer to information, markets, and public services. He has a bachelor's degree in Telecommunications Engineering from the University of Bombay and a master's degree in Infrastructure Policy Studies from Stanford University, has studied media law and policy at the University of Oxford, and has a doctorate in Telecommunications Policy from the University of Illinois.

Liudmyla (Mila) Romanoff (UN Global Pulse)— chapter 3

Mila is the Legal and Privacy Specialist at the UN Global Pulse, where she leads the data privacy and risk management program and is responsible for establishing legal mechanisms for public-private data partnerships. Mila is the lead drafter of the first UN system–wide framework on data privacy and digital ethics, formally adopted by United Nations Development Group. She currently coordinates the UN Global Pulse Data Privacy Advisory Group and cofacilitates the UN Privacy Policy Group. Previously, she advised two permanent country missions to the UN and worked in the private sector as a commercial contracting and litigation attorney. Mila sits on several legal and privacy associations and privacy advisory boards. She is licensed to practice law in Ukraine and New York.

Carlo Rossotto (World Bank, Digital Development)— chapter 5

Carlo Maria Rossotto is a Lead ICT Specialist at the World Bank and leads the Digital Economy Window of the Digital Development Partnership, the Bank's new Trust Fund Facility bringing together governments and leading technology firms to foster digital development. At the World Bank, he has been responsible for lending and technical assistance operations in Europe, the Middle East, North Africa, and East Asia. Carlo is one of the Bank's leading authorities on broadband and the digital economy. He has advised top-level policy makers on broadband, technology, and development in over 40 engagements, including the Russian Federation, Ukraine, the European Union, the Arab Republic of Egypt, Algeria, Tunisia, Morocco, and Jordan and in West Bank and Gaza, Cambodia, Bosnia and Herzegovina, Libya, and Iraq. He worked previously at the Inter-American Development Bank and in management consulting, advising leading European technology firms on demand analysis, marketing, corporate strategy, and regulatory affairs. He holds postgraduate degrees in Economics and Business Administration from Bocconi University in Milan and in Financial and Commercial Regulation from the London School of Economics.

Felicia Vacarelu (UN Global Pulse)—chapter 3

Felicia leads communications and social media activities for UN Global Pulse, manages media outreach, and helps build and maintain fruitful relationships with partners. Over the past eight years, she has worked with various UN offices and departments, coming to Global Pulse from the Food and Agriculture Organization in Rome. Prior to working for the United Nations, Felicia was Media and Outreach Coordinator for the 2009 Black Sea Energy and Economic Forum in Romania. She also held several editorial and journalistic positions at Mediafax, one of Romania's most prestigious news agencies. To strengthen her knowledge in the field, she is currently pursuing a master's in Media and Public Relations from the University of Leicester in the United Kingdom.

www.ingramcontent.com/pod-product-compliance
Lightning Source LLC
Chambersburg PA
CBHW080416060326
40689CB00019B/4268